Iraq's Oil and Gas Industry

Oil, an integral part of the contemporary global economy, is considered a driving force behind the 2003 invasion of Iraq. Hydrocarbon reserves in Iraq have a significant role to play in global supply, with oil revenue accounting for more than 90% of Iraqi government income.

This book provides a comprehensive insight into the key foundations of Iraq's oil industry and assists in the development of a core area of domestic law to promote economic recovery following years of instability. It addresses the development of oil legislation and the formation of contracts since the US and allied occupation of Iraq in 2003. Legislation is assessed against the framework of the constitution along with the different types of oil agreements and their terms. The book looks at three main aspects of oil legislation, beginning with the validity and interpretation of the constitution as any subsequent legislation governing oil policy will be based upon this. The work then discusses whether the draft oil and gas law of 2007 and any subsequent oil legislation, including the law implemented by the Kurdish Regional Government in 2007, is valid. Finally, the book analyses the legitimacy of oil agreements entered into by the central and regional governments and whether these contain terms beneficial to the state and contracting party.

Providing an in-depth analysis of the origins and development of the legal framework of the oil industry in Iraq, the book acts as both a reference source and a springboard for future research across a range of legal, economic and policy perspectives. It will appeal to practitioners and academics working in energy law and international investment law, as well as policy-makers, legal advisors and those working in governments and energy companies.

Janan Al-Asady, PhD, is a commercial Barrister in London, UK.

Routledge Research in Energy Law and Regulation

Regulation in the European Electricity Sector
Maciej M. Sokolowski

Law and Green Energy Policies
Roy Partain

Nuclear Energy Regulation, Risk and the Environment
Abdullah Al Faruque

Local Content Oil and Gas Law in Africa
Lessons from Nigeria and Beyond
Pereowei Subai

Host Government Agreements and the Law in the Energy Sector
The case of Azerbaijan and Turkey
Hakan Sahin

Iraq's Oil and Gas Industry
The Legal and Contractual Framework
Janan Al-Asady

Iraq's Oil and Gas Industry

The Legal and Contractual Framework

Janan Al-Asady

Routledge
Taylor & Francis Group
LONDON AND NEW YORK

First published 2020
by Routledge
2 Park Square, Milton Park, Abingdon, Oxon OX14 4RN

and by Routledge
52 Vanderbilt Avenue, New York, NY 10017

Routledge is an imprint of the Taylor & Francis Group, an informa business

British Library Cataloguing-in-Publication Data
A catalogue record for this book is available from the British Library

Library of Congress Cataloging-in-Publication Data
Names: Al-Asady, Janan.
Title: Iraq's oil and gas industry: the legal and contractual framework / Janan Al-Asady.
Description: Abingdon, Oxon; New York, NY: Routledge, 2019. |
Series: Routledge research in energy law and regulation |
Based on author's thesis (doctoral – University of London, School of Oriental and African Studies, 2016) issued under title: A legal analysis of Iraq's upstream oil industry. | Includes bibliographical references.
Identifiers: LCCN 2019007292 (print) | LCCN 2019007636 (ebook) |
ISBN 9780429054181 (ebk) | ISBN 9780367149697 (hbk)
Subjects: LCSH: Petroleum law and legislation—Iraq.
Classification: LCC KMJ3366 (ebook) | LCC KMJ3366 .A949 2019 (print) |
DDC 343.56709/395—dc23
LC record available at https://lccn.loc.gov/2019007292

ISBN: 978-0-367-14969-7 (hbk)
ISBN: 978-0-429-05418-1 (ebk)

Typeset in Galliard
by codeMantra

Dedicated to a nation that was once the cradle of civilisation and rich with human knowledge yet continually suffering the worst exploitation by external influences. This book is written in the hope that one day Iraq may eventually overcome its burdens and emerge as a benchmark and global leader not only in the development of natural resources but in a variety of sectors including brokering and promoting peace in the region and further afield.

For my family – past, present and future.

Contents

Foreword

It is a privilege to provide the foreword to this book. I was approached by SOAS to be the external marker on the author's thesis, which is the basis of this book. Accepting the invitation to examine the thesis, I duly received it and proceeded to 'flick through' it, as is my normal practice. Eight hours later, I was still reading the thesis, indicating how engrossing the volume was.

Upon reading the book, two things came to mind – revolutionary and ground-breaking, in both the content and the analysis. It covers the legal issues and contractual framework of the Iraqi oil and gas industry. Part of the analysis addresses the legal concepts surrounding property ownership and sovereignty of Iraqi oil and gas. Such an analysis includes the role of Sharia Law in natural resource ownership, providing an excellent analysis within the Islamic context.

The main section of the book (part II) undertakes an analysis of the historical legal context as well as the current legal framework, including the Kurdish regions. The analysis of the legal aspects of oil and gas extraction in Iraq is high quality, and is clear, concise and accurate. It provides the reader with a deep and complete understanding of the complex legal issues relating to Iraqi oil and gas extraction.

Perhaps the greatest contribution of this book is the author's sensitivity to, and incorporation of, the political issues existing alongside and integral to legal issues concerning oil and gas exploitation. The book considers the internal and external influences on Iraqi society, politics and law. In particular it does not shy away from the role of the United States in Iraq, arising from both US foreign policy (especially the Carter Doctrine) and the unauthorised occupation of the United States since 2003. The book also analyses how all stakeholders can benefit from oil extraction within the existing political, economic and constitutional context.

I recommend this book to all readers. I have been interested in Iraqi oil and gas law and politics for a very long time, particularly the changes after the US occupation. This volume is an extraordinary consideration of the interwoven legal and political issues, and any reader who is interested in oil and gas development in this region should place this on their essential reading list.

Professor Tina Soliman Hunter
Director, Centre for Energy Law,
University of Aberdeen

Acknowledgements

I would like to thank my parents and my sister for their support and encouragement, professor Ballantyne who made the whole endeavour possible, Ian Edge who assisted in shaping the research for this book, Dr. Dawoud El-Alami and Professor Tina Hunter for their support in publishing this work.

Dr. Gunnar Beck and Dr. Jean-Philipe Dequen for their valued friendship, advice and support for my research.

Dr. Mehiyar Kathem for the countless discussions about so many crucial issues on Iraq. Ahmed Jiyad for the informative discussions, research and presentations.

BP Archives – Peter Housego, Bethan Thomas and Joanne Burman all of whom have been incredibly kind, helpful and supportive in addition to showing interest in my research. Iraq Oil Report and Ben Lando for access to resources.

Support staff at SOAS and IALS, BISI, Chatham House. The Hollings Centre, Target Exploration and the Iraq Oil Ministry.

And finally, my husband for his constant interest, encouragement and support in the difficult stages of finalising this book.

Abbreviations and acronyms

APOC	Anglo-Petroleum Oil Company
Basra	The most oil rich region in Iraq located in the south
Bpd	Barrels per day (quantification of oil production)
Bbl/BnB	Billion barrels
BIT	Bilateral Investment Treaty
Boe	Barrel of oil equivalent
Capex	Capital expenditure
CBI	Central Bank of Iraq
CoM	Council of Ministers
Constitution	2005 Iraqi Constitution
Conventional	Oil Hydrocarbons from traditional extractive processes
CoR	Council of Representatives
CPA	Coalition Provisional Authority
Crude Oil	"Crude oil comprises crude oil, natural gas liquids, refinery feedstocks, and additives as well as other hydrocarbons (including emulsified oils, synthetic crude oil, mineral oils extracted from bituminous minerals such as oil shale, bituminous sand, etc., and oils from coal liquefaction). Crude oil is a mineral oil consisting of a mixture of hydrocarbons of natural origin and associated impurities, such as sulphur. It exists in the liquid phase under normal surface temperatures and pressure and its physical characteristics (density, viscosity, etc.) are highly variable. It includes field or lease condensates (separator liquids) which are recovered from associated and non-associated gas where it is commingled with the commercial crude oil stream". [Source: IEA Glossary definition]
DFI	Development Fund for Iraq
Disputed Territories	Nineveh, Erbil, Kirkuk, Diyala governorates
DOGL	Draft Oil and Gas Law (mainly versions of 2007 and 2011)

DP	Delivery Point
DPSC	Development and Production Service Contract
DPTSC	Development and Production Technical Service Contract
E&P	Exploration and Production
EDP	Exploration, development and production
EDPSC	Exploration, Development and Production Service Contract
EIA	Energy Information Administration (US Government)
EITI	Extractive Industries Transparency Initiative
ERP	Enhanced Redevelopment Plan
FDP	Field Development Plan
FOGC	Federal Oil and Gas Council
GC	Governing Council
HC	Host Country
Hydrocarbon Resources	Oil and Gas resources
ICC	International Chamber of Commerce
ICDR	International Centre for Dispute Resolution
IAMB	International Advisory and Monetary Board of Iraq
IEA	International Energy Agency
IMF	International Monetary Fund
INOC	Iraq National Oil Company
IOC	International Oil Company
IPC	Iraq Petroleum Company
IPR	Initial Production Rate
JV	Joint Venture
Kirkuk	An oil rich region of Iraq currently in dispute as to whether it should form part of the Kurdish region or remain within the main territory Iraq.
KRG	Kurdish Regional Government
Kurdish Region	An area of north Iraq that has semi-autonomous status from the central government.
LIBOR	London Inter-Bank Offered Rate
Mbpd	Million barrels per day
Mboe	Million barrels of oil equivalent
MOC	Midlands Oil Company/Maysan Oil Company
MoO	Ministry of Oil
MoOM	Ministry of Oil and Minerals (predecessor to MoO)
MoP	Ministry of Petroleum
MPDC	Ministry of Planning and Development Cooperation
M/T	Million tons
NCS	Norwegian Continental Shelf
NOC	National Oil Company
NIOC	National Iranian Oil Company
NPR	Net Production Rate

OAPEC	Organisation of Arab Petroleum Exporting Countries
ODGPC	Oil Distribution and Gas Processing Company
OEC	Oil Exploration Company
OGA	Oil & Gas Authority
OGL	Oil and Gas Law
OGPCP	Office of Government Public Contract Policy
OPEC	Organisation of the Petroleum Exporting Countries
Pb	Per barrel
PCLD	Petroleum Contracts and Licencing Directorate
PF	Payment Fund
PFTSC	Producing Field Technical Service Contract
PMP	Production Measurement Point
PPT	Plateau Production Target
PSA	Production Sharing Agreement
PCLD	Petroleum Contracts and Licensing Directorate
PSC	Production Sharing Contract
RCC	Revolutionary Command Council
R-factor	$\frac{\text{Cumulative receipts}}{\text{Cumulative costs}}$
ROC	Regional Oil Company
ROR	Rate of Return
R/P	Reserve to production
SC	Service Contract
SCOP	State Company for Oil Production
SOC	South Oil Company
SODOP	State Organisation for Distribution of Oil Products
SOG	State Organisation for Gas
SOMO	State Oil and Marketing Company (Iraq)
SOOR	State Organisation for Oil Refining
SOR	State Organisation for Refining
SWF	Sovereign wealth fund
TAL	Transitional Administrative Law
Kbpd	Thousand barrels per day
TP	Transfer Point
TPC	Turkish Petroleum Company
TT	Technology Transfer
TTSF	Training, Technology and Scholarship Fund
Royalty	The consideration for use of an asset. Payment is made to the legal owner of the property.
SOMO	State Oil and Marketing Organization
Sovereignty	State control over resources
TSC	Technical Service Contract
UGSM	United States Gulf of Mexico (pricing)

Part I

1 Introduction

Oil and gas are owned by all the people of Iraq in all the regions and governorates.
– Article 111, Iraqi Constitution 2005

Oil is an integral part of the contemporary global economy and has been cited by many as the driving force behind the 2003 invasion of Iraq.[1] Revenue from the oil sector accounts for more than 90% of Iraqi government income.[2] In 2017, reserves were estimated at 148.8 billion barrels(bnb).[3] The same year, Iraq produced 4.520 million barrels per day (mbpd),[4] exporting around 3.8 mbpd to the value of over US$59 billion.[5] In August 2018, over 111 million barrels were exported at just over $69 per barrel (pb).[6]

OPEC estimates the global demand for oil to rise from 97.2 mbpd in 2017 to 111.7 mbpd by 2040.[7] At present, Iraq is the second largest OPEC oil producer after Saudi Arabia[8] and has the potential to become one of the largest global oil producers.[9]

This book addresses the development of oil legislation and the formation of contracts since the 2003 invasion. Since then, contracts have been entered into between international oil companies (IOCs) and the Iraqi government, and yet there has been no enactment of comprehensive legislation to govern these agreements. A draft oil law was published on 15 February 2007 and revised in 2011, but its enactment has stalled. How, then has the government legally entered into the current agreements? What measures are in place to protect the rights of the citizens as resource-owners?

Iraq is a unique environment for implementation of oil legislation due to the vast oil resources and political sensitivities in the country. When implementing a comprehensive legal framework, it is necessary to consider the practical environmental context for its operation in order to maximise the revenues for the reconstruction of the country and to allow the economy to prosper for the benefit of the Iraqi people. It is clear that when there is no comprehensive legal framework in place, the opportunities for exploitation and corruption are heightened and the legitimacy of contracts entered into can be questioned. The invasion had a devastating effect on a country capable of economic prosperity due to its vast natural resources.

In order to provide a comprehensive analysis of the position, it is necessary to consider the political implications influencing oil legislation and policy.[10] Understandably, there are very strong views about the international policies, primarily of the United States and Great Britain, in the conduct of the 2003 invasion, subsequent oil agreements and policies. As Engdhal observes:

> … the US occupation of Iraq is about control of global oil resources … the Iraq war is but the first in a major battle over global energy resources … It is about fixing who will get how much oil for their economy at what price and who not. Never has such a choke-hold on the world economy been in the hands of one power. After occupation of Iraq it appears it is.[11]

As demonstrated in the words of a former American President shortly before the Iraq-Iran war, US interference in Iraqi oil is not a new policy:

> Let our position be absolutely clear: An attempt by any outside force to gain control of the Persian Gulf region will be regarded as an assault on the vital interests of the United States of America, and such an assault will be repelled by any means necessary, including military force.[12]

Although at the time of writing, the draft oil legislation is yet to be enacted, major IOCs are currently engaged in production in Iraq.[13] In 2007, the Kurdish Regional Government (KRG) passed an oil and hydrocarbons law in the Kurdish region of Iraq. The majority of reserves are held in the south of Iraq but the central government has yet to implement similar legislation, despite having produced a draft oil and gas law in 2007. There has been an ongoing dispute between the KRG and central government about the validity of the Kurdish hydrocarbons law and contracts entered into without authorisation of the Oil Ministry and central government. The status of KRG contracts with IOCs is yet to be resolved and in itself presents significant legal implications for the parties. Clearly, the benefit of having a comprehensive and transparent legislative framework will assist not only the government but also oil companies to increase oil production and reduce corruption.

This research seeks to analyse the key factors in creating an environment where all parties can benefit from Iraq's oil so that its citizens are not disadvantaged by unfair terms in agreements with IOCs, thereby conforming with Article 111 of the 2005 Iraqi constitution. It is a common constitutional provision that natural resources are publicly owned, therefore even if the legitimacy of the Iraqi constitution is called into question this fundamental right should not be affected.

1.1 Research methodology

The research has been qualitative and doctrinal. The nature of this topic is open to political sensitivities and, as such, there has been an element of economic/socio-legal research through a brief analysis of political disputes and economic data surrounding the development and implementation of legislation relating to oil contracts. However, due to the focus on legal analysis in this book, there has been minimal economic and political commentary.

This book comprises six chapters across Part I and Part II. Part I provides background and context. To establish whether natural resources may be owned privately or publicly, Chapter 2 explores the legal foundations for state sovereignty and ownership from a property law perspective. This should determine whether the current government has authority to enter into oil agreements.

Part II focuses on Iraq. In order to understand the context of the current legal framework, it is necessary to look at the historical development of the oil industry in Iraq, particularly since the formation of the country, which is contained within Chapter 3. Chapter 3 also contains an analysis of the 2005 Constitution in the context of federalism and the differences in approach to the oil sector between the central government and the KRG. Chapter 4 discusses the current and draft legislation governing upstream oil contracts and the process of awarding contracts to IOCs. This is followed by an analysis of the terms and differences between the model contracts offered by the central government in Baghdad and the KRG until 2017 in Chapter 5. Finally, the book concludes in Chapter 6 with suggestions for further research and recommendations.

1.2 History

The historical aspects include development of regulation and oil exploitation, the colonial legacy and the political changes in Iraq before 2003. Chapter 3 covers the legal and political developments in the Iraqi oil sector from the establishment of the Turkish Petroleum Company (TPC) in 1912 to the US invasion in 2003.

A doctrinal historical analysis of legislation and policy since the first oil concession in 1925 provides background and context to the main arguments of the book concerning post-2003 developments. A review of key provisions in Chapters 3 and 4 provides perspective on the current legal disarray and exposes the legal foundations of the oil industry since 2003. Chapter 5 provides an analysis on various upstream contract terms.

The historical research was conducted through various library and online resources as the information is well documented. Since the unapproved US violation of Iraqi sovereignty, much of the information on the development of the legal system in Iraq is publicly available, particularly through the US government institutions. There has been coverage of Iraqi oil policies in the media, and it was necessary to trace information to the source of interviews and articles. Research by institutions concerned with the development of Iraqi oil law in the United Kingdom, Iraq, the United States and elsewhere has also been consulted.

1.3 Politics

In the context of Iraq, there can be no doubt that economics and politics drive the policy considerations behind legislation and the timing for the enactment of law. The current political situation means that there are many disputes between parties on numerous issues including aspects of legislation and policy. The religious and political sensitivities within the government cannot be overstated. In 2014, the Iraqi Parliament consisted of twenty-four political parties,[14] with the main parties comprising State of Law, Iraqiyya, Iraqi National Alliance and the Kurdish alliance.[15] There will be no general political commentary as Iraq is constantly in a state of flux, which will detract from the main theme of the book.

Although the focus of this book is on the current developments of oil legislation and contracts in Iraq, consideration must be given to the foundations of state ownership of natural resources. The relevant political and social aspects addressed include the validity of commercial agreements where the identity and structure of the government has changed, the status and legitimacy of transitional government participation in the development of the legal framework, the legal status of legislation in the previous regime and subsequent use in the new political and legal order.

1.4 Economic policy

It is essential that legislation supports the Iraqi economy in order to protect the oil industry from unnecessary exploitation and corruption of internal and external actors. It has been argued that economy drives the law and of the scholars who advocate this view, Weber states that:

> Obviously, legal guarantees are directly at the service of economic interests to a very large extent. Even where this does not seem to be, or actually is not, the case. Economic interests are among the strongest factors influencing the creation of law.[16]

Although there is a recent law for investment in Iraq, the Federal Investment Law of 2006, it does not apply to oil and gas extraction.[17] Foreign investment in the Iraqi oil industry is clearly taking place through the current agreements. Presently, there are three types of contract: production service contracts, technical service contracts and production sharing agreements (PSAs). The model contracts from the Iraqi Oil Ministry provide Iraqi law as the governing law of the agreements and Paris as the seat of any arbitration.[18]

1.5 Legal issues

In order to obtain detailed primary information on policy reasons behind relevant aspects of the Constitution and legislation, it has been necessary to review information from the government ministries in Iraq, the United Nations and the US Government departments and agencies.[19]

The analysis exposes minimal consideration afforded by provisional governments since 2003 to the regulation of oil agreements and shows that delay in implementing the draft oil law of 2007 is due to the political interests of those in power. At the time of writing there appears to be a lack of accountability for those entering and managing oil agreements on behalf of the Iraqi people.

1.5.1 Ownership and sovereignty of oil

Chapter 2 considers the issue of sovereignty and ownership in order to establish where the right to state ownership of natural resources originated. The issue of ownership is central to contractual rights and although concession agreements have taken different forms, it remains a concern. As Fan[20] points out, effective ownership of resources through decision-making allows a country to control the rate of extraction through sales whereas concession agreements pass the control to foreign investors.

The United Nations General Assembly resolutions of 1962, 1966 and 1974[21] enshrined the concept of sovereignty of natural resources and gave governments the right to manage their resources and nationalise where it is in the public interest to do so.[22] In essence the resolutions state that the rights of the people and States to sovereignty of natural wealth and resources must be upheld.[23] Further, exploitation of natural resources should be in accordance with national laws.[24]

1.6 Constitution

Key Constitutional provisions are addressed to determine the compatibility and legitimacy of legislation currently governing oil agreements. The documented discussions in the constitutional and legislative drafting process assist in determining the intended interpretation of the legal framework. For the purposes of this research it was therefore essential to assess whether the federal government's draft oil law of 2007 and the Kurdish Regional Government's oil law of 2007 (hereinafter collectively referred to as "the oil legislation") are in accordance with the 2005 Constitution.

Article 112 of the 2005 Iraqi constitution is a key provision for oil legislation, and an analysis is provided in Chapter 4 with a review of current legislation underlying the production and exploration contracts with international oil companies in Chapter 5.

The policy considerations should address how the federal and regional governments manage oil production. How does the central government cooperate with the regions? Who is ultimately responsible for managing production? What happens in the event of a dispute between the federal and regional governments? Article 112 second states that management and development should be "regulated by a law", what does this mean? What is the position where no law has been enacted?

1.7 Oil legislation

Since 13 July 2007, the Iraqi government has been drafting four separate pieces of legislation relating to the oil industry: (i) hydrocarbon framework legislation which establishes the structure, management and oversight for the sector; (ii) revenue sharing legislation; (iii) legislation restructuring the Ministry of Oil and (iv) legislation establishing the Iraqi National Oil Company (INOC). At the time of writing, all of these bills save for the last are yet to be enacted.[25] Legislation must be approved by the Council of Ministers (the Iraqi cabinet), the Shura Council (for conformity with the Constitution and Islamic principles) and then submitted to the Council of Representatives (Parliament). Once the laws are passed they become publicly available through publication in the Official Gazette.[26]

1.7.1 The draft oil laws

The draft oil and gas laws are analysed for adequate protection to the interests of the Iraqi people and economy: followed by consideration of the subsequent position of the IOCs. This leads to the issue of which fundamental provisions should be incorporated into the legislation generally and specifically within the Iraqi context.

On the documents considered, there is an issue between provisions for currently producing fields and those for unexplored fields, the legislation only protects existing fields therefore as the existing fields deplete IOCs gain a greater share of production. It has been concluded by some commentators that the draft oil law seeks to benefit IOCs and the terms of the legislation are "signing away Iraq's future".[27]

1.7.2 Oil concessions

Prior to nationalisation in 1972, the revenue structure of the TPC (Turkish Petroleum Company) and IPC (Iraq Petroleum Company) was problematic because, rather than for the Iraqi government, the IOCs produced and exported crude oil for their shareholders. Therefore the benefit of production rested with the predecessors to BP, Royal-Dutch Shell, TotalFinaElf, Exxon and Mobil, who would make a profit by selling the oil on the international market.[28]

The negotiations for the 1925 concession avoided terms to ensure that Iraq would receive substantial royalties, taxes and profits for the granting of the right to produce oil and gas. Although the 1952 agreement was more favourable, the Iraqi government only started benefiting substantially from its own resources when the IPC and oil and gas fields were nationalised in 1972.

1.8 Current agreements

The approval process for contracts as stated by the previous Iraqi Oil Minister is that the Oil Ministry has the right to sign contracts which only become legally binding once approved by the Council of Ministers.[29] However, there has been criticism by academics, such as Jiyad, about the actual process of entering into these agreements. As Jiyad states, the speed at which the current contracts were entered into did not allow sufficient time for the legal implications to be fully considered. In one instance, with the Rumalia field awarded to BP/CNPC, the legal adviser to the Prime Minister made sixty-five remarks on the contract within two days of instruction on the matter despite the award being granted 105 days earlier on 1 July 2009, which would have provided more than enough time for the terms of the contract to be reviewed.[30] The Council of Ministers (CoM) claimed not to have seen the contract prior to 13 October 2009, which implies that the Ministry of Oil did not provide the model contract in good time.[31] The CoM approved the contract on 13 October 2009 without the opinion of the legal adviser. Rumalia is one of the largest oil fields currently in production and combined with the other awarded fields in the first and second bid rounds amount to 62.7 billion barrels of proven reserves, approximately 54.5% of the previously estimated reserves of 115 billion barrels.[32]

Each oil field has a contract term of at least twenty years and contains forty-three articles, six annexes and four addenda. At least one of these contracts is comprehensively reviewed to check compliance with legislative measures and contractual justice. There are five main types of risk to be considered in oil agreements, namely, exploration, project, price, security and political risk. In order to avoid political risk, there is an increasing trend among IOCs towards internationalising oil agreements to provide a greater protection of interests as the contract will fall within international, rather than national, law.[33]

The current contractual models in Iraq are PSAs, used by the KRG, which are considered to be the least beneficial, and potentially damaging to the Iraqi economy, due to the amount of control provided to IOCs. There is much debate about the use of PSAs in countries such as Iraq as they are usually reserved for poor, developing countries with prospective oil and not in established oil producing countries.[34] PSAs are a form of oil sector privatisation where foreign companies develop a specific area of the host country's oil sector in exchange for a share in the profits.[35] They are usually used in high-risk developments where there is a possibility that oil may not be discovered. Iraq is not considered suited to PSAs as

> Iraqi oil is extremely inexpensive to extract; its development and production costs are among the lowest in the Middle East. Even with the security costs associated with extracting Iraqi oil in the near future, the average cost per barrel will be significantly cheaper than oil extracted almost anywhere else in the world: oil deposits in Iraq are near the surface and easily accessible.[36]

The central government uses development and production service contracts (DPSCs) and technical service contracts (TSCs). It will be necessary to review the terms of these types of contracts against the PSAs for a comparative analysis of terms to ascertain which are more suited to the Iraqi situation. In addition to existing contracts, it is necessary to research potential exploration contracts.

1.9 Research

The research was qualitative and doctrinal relying on a range of documents. Some primary sources were difficult to obtain and translate. Where primary sources could not be obtained, secondary sources were used and combined with information from key individuals willing to assist with this research.

1.10 Conclusion

There are many issues to be considered to assist the Iraqi oil sector to be effectively managed to benefit its citizens and economy. Further research must be conducted in order to address many of the issues raised in this book. It is hoped that this book will contribute to the process of improving the current position to provide greater stability and clarity to all parties involved in the exploration and production process. However, there are many economic, political, legal, developmental and sociological policies requiring substantive review, analysis and reform to positively develop a sustainable integral framework for Iraq.

Notes

1 See, as just one example, J. Ismael and T. Ismael, 'Iraqi Oil, the International System and Chimera of Democracy', (2007) 1 (3) *International Journal of Contemporary Iraqi Studies,* 287, 288.

2 EY, 'Iraqi Government Approves the 2015 Federal Budget' (20 April 2015), www.ey.com/Publication/vwLUAssets/Iraqi_Government_approves_the_2015_federal_budget/$FILE/2015G_CM5380_Iraqi%20Gvt%20approves%20the%202015%20federal%20budget.pdf, accessed 9 September 2016.

Ahmed Aboulenein and Ahmed Rasheed, 'Iraqi Parliament Approves Budget, Kurdish Lawmakers Boycott Vote' 'The Budget of 104 trillion Iraqi dinars ($88 billion) is Based on Projected Oil Exports of 3.8 million barrels per day (bpd) at a Price of $46, a Copy of the Final Bill Showed' *Reuters* (3 March 2018), www.reuters.com/article/us-mideast-crisis-iraq-budget/iraqi-parliament-approves-budget-kurdish-lawmakers-boycott-vote-idUSKCN1GF0PP, accessed 14 October 2018.

3 BP, 'BP Statistical Review of World Energy 2018' (12 June 2018), 12, www.bp.com/content/dam/bp/en/corporate/pdf/energy-economics/statistical-review/bp-stats-review-2018-full-report.pdf, accessed 14 October 2018. The Iraqi government estimated that the 2017 reserves to be around 153 billion barrels with a subsequent announcement in 2018 that this figure could be doubled, see John Everington, 'Iraq May Have Twice as Much Oil as Previously Thought, Says Minister' *Arab News* (29 March 2018), www.arabnews.com/node/1275391/business-economy, accessed 14 October 2018.

4 Supra n3 at 14. Rania El Gamal, Maha El Dahan and Stanley Carvalho, 'Iraq Nears Oil Output Capacity of 5 million bpd, Committed to OPEC Cuts' *Reuters* (13 January 2018), www.reuters.com/article/us-oil-opec-iraq/iraq-nears-oil-output-capacity-of-5-million-bpd-committed-to-opec-cuts-idUSKBN1F20E6, accessed 14 October 2018.

5 OPEC, 'Annual Statistical Bulletin 2018', 8, https://asb.opec.org/index.php/pdf-download, accessed 14 October 2018.

6 Iraq Oil Ministry, 'Crude Oil Exports', https://oil.gov.iq/index.php?name=Pages&op=page&pid=100 accessed 14 October 2018.

7 OPEC, 'OPEC World Oil Outlook 2018' (September 2018), 115, www.woo.opec.org accessed 14 October 2018.

8 OPEC, 'Annual Statistical Bulletin 2018', 8, www.asb.opec.org/index.php/pdfdownload, accessed 14 October 2018.
9 Iraq National Investment Commission (2013), 3, www.investpromo.gov.iq/wp-content/uploads/2013/05/oil_and_gas_sector_overview_en.pdf, accessed 3 February 2014. There has been recent speculation that the country's reserves could be considerably higher than recorded see John Everington (29 March 2018), 'Iraq May Have Twice as Much Oil as Previously Thought, Says Minister' *Arab News*, www.arabnews.com/node/1275391/business-economy, accessed 14 October 2018.
10 Politics will not generally be considered particularly in relation to the recent interference of ISIS in the country.
11 F.W. Engdahl (2004), 'Iraq and the Problem of Peak Oil', *Centre for Research on Globalisation, Current Concerns* 1/2004, www.globalresearch.ca/articles/ENG408A.html, accessed 25 February 2011.
12 James Carter, 'Third State of the Union Address', 21 January 1980, https://en.wikisource.org/wiki/Jimmy_Carter%27s_Third_State_of_the_Union_Address, accessed 28 January 2019.
13 The companies holding contracts with the central government include Royal Dutch Shell, BP, China National Petroleum, Total, Eni, Lukoil, Sonangol, KOGAS, JAPEX. In addition, the KRG has entered into production sharing agreements with inter alia DNO, KNOC, HKN Energy, Genel Energy, Hillwood, Repsol.
14 Global Security, 'Political Parties', www.globalsecurity.org/military/world/iraq/party.htm accessed 12 July 2014. Following the 2014 general election, nine parties are in the coalition government. There are two opposition parties and fifty-three independent members of parliament. In 2018, Muqtada al-Sadr in the Sairoon alliance party won the election and formed a coalition with Haider Abadi's Nasr alliance to govern the country.
15 US State Department 'Iraq Status Report' (3 March 2011), www.state.gov/documents/organization/157897.pdf, accessed 15 March 2011.
16 Max Weber, *Economy and Society* (Cambridge, MA: Harvard University Press, 1954), 334.
17 Sami Shubber, *The Law of Investment in Iraq* (Brill, 2009), 21. See also Article 29 First, Investment Law No. 13 of 2006.
18 Model Technical Service Contract clauses 37.1 and 37.5.
19 Preliminary information about Iraqi oil policy is available through: US Energy Information Administration (EIA), US Department of State, Government Accountability Office (GAO), Law Library of Congress, USAID, Iraqi Oil Ministry, Iraqi Council of Representatives (COR), Kurdish Regional Government (KRG), United Nations, International Energy Agency, OPEC, IMF and the World Bank.
20 Y.-K. Fan (1967), 'Ownership and Optimal Extraction of Oil Reserves' (1967), 47 sunzi.lib.hku.hk/hkjo/view/12/1200056.pdf accessed 4 February 2011.
21 UN General Assembly Resolutions: 1962 (Resolution 1803 (XVII)), 1966 (Resolution 2158 (XXI)), 1974 (Resolution 3281 (XXIX)).
22 Gregg Muttit, *Fuel on the Fire: Oil and Politics in Occupied Iraq* (London, The Bodley Head, 2010), 6.
23 United Nations General Assembly Resolution of 1962 (Resolution 1803 (XVII)), Article 7.
24 United Nations General Assembly Resolution of 1966 (Resolution 2158 (XXI)).
25 At a time when Iraq was producing over 4.5 mbpd, on 5 March 2018, (effective from April 2018) the Iraqi Parliament passed a law reinstating the Iraqi National Oil Company with the intention that it would 'serve as an umbrella organisation for Iraqi state oil firms'. Ahmed Rasheed, 'Iraq Parliament Votes to Create National Oil Company: Lawmakers' (5 March 2018) *Reuters*, www.reuters.com/article/us-iraq-oil/iraq-parliament-votes-to-create-national-oil-company-lawmakers-idUSKBN1GH1XB, accessed 1 November 2018. An analysis of this law by Ahmed Jiyad is available

on the Iraq Business News Website at www.iraq-businessnews.com/2018/03/12/inoc-law-dysfunctional-unconstitutional-and-disintegrative/, accessed 1 November 2018. See also Nick Butler, 'The Dangers of Iraq's Oil Law' (30 April 2018), *FT*, www.ft.com/content/da2b5cae-46d7-11e8-8ee8-cae73aab7ccb#comments-anchor, accessed 1 November 2018.

26 Iraqi Constitution (2005), Article 129.

27 Gregg Muttit, 'The Oil and Gas Law – Signing Away Iraq's Future?', *Carbon Web*, www.carbonweb.org/documents/oil_law_briefing.pdf accessed 2 February 2013. In October 2016, the MoO announced a further bid round to develop twelve small to medium size oil fields (four in Basra, five in Maysan and three in the central province) via direct negotiation with oil companies. Nineteen companies pre-qualified on the basis that they submit their own proposals for contractual terms. The bid round was postponed in November 2016 to mid-2017 due to a change in plans by MoO for it to develop some of the fields. [MoO announcement dated 10 November 2016] and Ahmed Ghaddar, 'Iraq Offers Oil Fields Under New Contract Terms' (24 October 2016) *Reuters*, www.reuters.com/article/us-iraq-oil-contract-idUSKCN12O1MV, accessed 25 October 2016.

28 Rex Zedalis, *Legal Dimensions of Oil and Gas in Iraq: Current Reality and Future Prospects* (Cambridge, Cambridge University Press, 2009), 7.

29 Ahmed Jiyad, 'The Legality of Iraqi Oil Contracts Remains Questionable' 53 (2) *MEES*, 1, January 2010.

30 Ibid., 2.

31 Ibid., 2.

32 Jiyad (n29). Current estimations have increased to just over 150 billion barrels as stated earlier in this paper.

33 Gregg Mutitt, 'Nationalizing Risk, Privatizing Reward: The Prospects for Oil Production Contracts in Iraq', 1 (2) *International Journal of Contemporary Iraqi Studies*, 17, September 2007.

34 Daniel Behn, 'Sharing Iraq's Oil: Analyzing Production-Sharing Contracts under the Final Draft Petroleum Law' (17 September 2007), http://ssrn.com/abstract=976407, accessed 6 July 2010.

35 Ibid., 3.

36 Behn (n33) 5.

2 Sovereignty and ownership of oil resources

> The first man who, having enclosed a piece of ground, bethought himself of saying This is mine, and found people simple enough to believe him, was the real founder of civil society. From how many crimes, wars and murders, from how many horrors and misfortunes might not any one have saved mankind, by pulling up the stakes, or filling up the ditch, and crying to his fellows, "Beware of listening to this impostor; you are undone if you once forget that the fruits of the earth belong to us all, and the earth itself to nobody." But there is great probability that things had then already come to such a pitch, that they could no longer continue as they were; for the idea of property depends on many prior ideas, which could only be acquired successively, and cannot have been formed all at once in the human mind. Mankind must have made very considerable progress, and acquired considerable knowledge and industry which they must also have transmitted and increased from age to age, before they arrived at this last point of the state of nature.
>
> – Jean Jacques Rousseau[1]

2.1 Introduction

The present position relating to property rights in natural resources on an international level is that the majority of countries, save for the United States,[2] place oil and mineral resources under public ownership.[3] This chapter will consider the legal position of the ownership of oil resources and subsequent property rights commencing with the historical foundations of public ownership, which should provide the context for subsequent analysis of the legislative and contractual framework in Iraq, particularly in light of the increasing hostility between the central government and the KRG.

It is often assumed[4] that ownership will change during the upstream and downstream process. Depending on the type of contract in place,[5] quite often oil remains state property until it reaches the well-head where proprietary rights are transferred to the counterparty to the production agreement. Usually an assignment of rights is justified by distinguishing between the ownership of, and rights to, subsoil resources and the assets of the oil companies. However, as hydrocarbons are extracted, the reserves are depleted thereby diminishing state or public control of the resource.[6] This ultimately places the oil company (as this is usually the entity which takes control of the resource) at a strategic advantage due to the increase in its assets to the detriment of the state and national sovereignty.

Iraqi law is a blend of Ottoman, French, Egyptian and Islamic laws. At the outset, reference must be made to the 1951 Civil Code, which provides for the sources of law in Iraq. In the absence of legislative provisions, courts consider custom and usage; Islamic Shari'a most consistent with the Civil Code; and, where there is no Iraqi precedent or jurisprudence, reference may be made to countries with laws proximate to Iraq.[7] These sources will be considered within this chapter in relation to the ownership of oil resources and the respective rights and obligations arising therefrom. Before analysing the legislative framework surrounding the Iraqi oil industry, it is necessary to consider land ownership and the state's authority to enter into agreements for the exploitation of natural resources. The issue of resource allocation and property rights has been both an historical issue and a source of contention in current political affairs.

There is considerable political tension between the KRG and the central government regarding the award of exploration and production contracts to IOCs for oil fields in the Kurdistan region of Iraq.[8] The current authority of the state to exploit natural resources for the benefit of the Iraqi people lies with Articles 111 and 112 of the 2005 Constitution. Establishing the historical rights of land ownership and state interference in the exploitation of oil will assist in ascertaining the current legitimacy of the Iraqi government's rights to deal with the exploitation of reserves on behalf of the people in accordance with these Constitutional provisions.[9]

The entitlement to exploitation and the allocation of general property rights has most recently been highlighted by the Exxon issue[10] between the central government and the KRG. This is of particular importance due to the KRG[11] dealings with IOCs. Therefore legal title to land and property rights are key concerns, along with the state mandate to deal with oil. Once the ownership issues are settled, this chapter will address the Constitutional division of power between the KRG and the central government. As part of this analysis it is necessary to consider federalism in Iraq and how the existing contracts should be dealt with.

2.2 Ownership

Where does the "right" to property and therefore oil resources derive?[12] Is it legitimate for the state to enter into oil agreements which may alter ownership entitlement to the resource?

Private property has been the central concern of philosophers and academics.[13] For the purposes of this chapter, public and common ownership will be assessed due to the historical development of the Iraqi oil industry and the 1972 nationalisation of oil resources. The conclusion to be drawn from the literature is that property ownership is a somewhat fluid concept and can be categorised as either public or private dependent upon the context and political motivation. This section should demonstrate that although private property is generally held to be the ideal state of ownership, there is, in fact, no obvious best or correct status of exclusive and unfettered private ownership.

2.2.1 Definitions

A generally accepted definition of land is 'immoveable property'.[14] Article 62(1) of the Iraqi Civil Code provides:

> The immovable (realty) is every thing which is fixed so that it would be impossible to move or convert it without causing damage thereto such as land … mines, and other real estate things.

Article 1115 of the Iraqi Civil Code provides that land is the private property of the state.[15]

Property is an ambiguous and elusive term with varying interpretations, which, according to Becker, is due to it being "*ubiquitous and complex, socially important and controversial*".[16] As defined in the Iraqi Civil Code, "property" is "every right having a material value".[17] The definition under the French Civil Code of 1804 at Article 544 is:

> Property is the right of enjoying and disposing of things in the most absolute manner, provided they are not used in a way prohibited by the laws or statutes.[18]

There is no concept of absolute property. Under the French Civil Code, specific reference is made to property in the soil at Article 552:

> Property in the soil imports property above and beneath. The proprietor may make above all kinds of plantations and buildings which he shall judge convenient, saving the exceptions established under the title "Of Servitudes and Services relating to Land." He may make beneath all buildings and excavations which he shall judge convenient, and draw from such excavations all the products which they are capable of furnishing, saving the restrictions resulting from the laws and statutes relating to mines, and from the laws and regulation of police.

Thus the right to the soil beneath the land has been recognised as belonging to the landowner save where there are minerals of value in the sub-soil, in which case legislative restrictions often apply. A concise definition of property is provided by Jeremy Waldron[19] as the "*… concept of a system of rules governing access to and control of material resources*".

Article 126 of the Ottoman Mejella[20] provides that "[p]*roperty consists of something desired by human nature and which can be put aside against time of necessity. It comprises moveable and immovable property*". The subsequent article of the Mejella provides that property "*of some specific value is spoken of in two senses (1) it is a thing the benefit of which it is lawful to enjoy; (2) the other is acquired property*".[21] The current Iraqi Constitution provides for the protection of private property, compensation for expropriation and a restriction on the ownership of immovable assets to Iraqi citizens unless exempted by law.[22]

"Rights" are interests "recognised and protected by the law, respect of which is a duty and disregard of which is a wrong".[23] By their nature rights have corresponding obligations.[24] Penner considers property more as a "bundle of rights" held as against the rest of the world.[25] Becker also refers to a "bundle of rights" and equates rights with ownership.[26] For the purposes of this chapter, when considering the issue of legal rights in hydrocarbons[27] the primary position is that oil is classed as immovable property to accord with the above references and arbitral precedents in industry.[28] Clearly there are circumstances where oil is categorised as moveable property, for example, once it is extracted from the subsoil for transportation.

The Ottoman Mejella provides a definition of absolute ownership as "… anything owned absolutely by man and may consist of either some specific object or of an interest therein".[29] A more detailed explanation[30] is provided in the Iraqi Civil Code[31], which appears to accord with the Shari'a law position, the most relevant of which is "[t]he ownership of land includes that which is above and below as far as can be usefully enjoyed in height and in depth".[32] The separation of the land is permitted under the Code and to some extent complicates the issue of ownership,[33] discussed further below.

The notion of "ownership" developed in Iraq according to political objectives, which shifted under the socialist era from a private function to an economic and social function in the public interest.[34] The leading form of public ownership was considered to be that of the state with private ownership conforming to "the prerequisites of the stages of building socialism".[35] Thus private ownership was only permitted to facilitate public ownership for the development of the nation.

2.2.2 Key concepts relating to natural resource ownership

The purpose of the previous section is to determine, at a fundamental level, whether the current government has the legitimacy and legal authority to enter into upstream agreements with private international oil companies. Thus the starting point for the purposes of the current chapter is the issue of ownership and whether the central government is capable of owning, and therefore managing, oil reserves. In order to answer this, it is necessary to determine whether oil, as a matter of legal analysis, can be publicly, privately or state owned. Once the issue of ownership is settled, it is then necessary to consider the allocation of rights to the oil resources as a matter of property law and then contractual terms. The issue of the KRG entering into oil agreements and claiming territories[36] with considerable oil wealth is a key concern in Iraq and thus the issue of federalism along with the ownership and management of oil will be analysed for legal legitimacy.

2.2.2.1 Property[37] rights

In general, property can fall under four categories of ownership namely, common, public, state and private.[38] Arguably, an ideal status of private property is where the owner has complete domination of his property and is free to do as he pleases without interference. In reality, as will become apparent, due to the principle of eminent domain, there is no such thing as complete private ownership or as referred to by Harris, "full-blooded ownership".[39]

At least since the time of Aristotle,[40] identifying the origins of property has caused much philosophical and academic debate. Religion has played a key role in the development of the notion of property.[41] The most widely accepted standpoint is that of divine ownership of the Earth with man being possessors in common.[42] Locke regards property as the fundamental basis of law and society. His theological standpoint, not unlike that of Islam and Christianity, is that all property belongs to God and used by man for a common purpose, thereby also subscribing to the Roman law concept of res communis.[43]

Locke considered that the earth and its fruits were provided to mankind in common and limited by the exception of individuals acquiring private ownership and by mixing their labour with the fruits in question.[44] Non-appropriated natural resources, unowned in their original state could be appropriated by anyone who will discover and extract them.[45] This concept is often accompanied with the analogy of the capture of wild animals.[46] Locke[47] considered res communis to be analogous to that of a wild beast, which is a free animal and can be hunted by anyone but once captured it becomes the property of the hunter.

Locke's explanation of appropriation can be applied to oil extraction,[48] as oil is of no use to man in the ground and requires labour in order for it to become useful and, according to the labour theory, ownership is acquired through extraction. This argument would lend itself to supporting the private ownership of oil, depending on whether an IOC or NOC is involved in the extraction process. In the alternative, Locke, when referring to nature, is primarily making reference to the humanitarian needs for survival and this is where a distinction may be drawn. When one considers oil or minerals in general, the supply far exceeds the needs of an individual and therefore a greater purpose for the common good requires the right to be extended for the benefit of society as a whole. Further, as the refinement process of oil into other products requires the labour of several entities and is often located in different jurisdictions, private ownership in a strict sense would pass by transfer of title. Although, according to Locke's argument, private rights only arise when labour is involved, prior to this the resource cannot be private and therefore must be natural, common or public.

When considering the issue of property ownership in relation to natural resources, the ends of the spectrum are that of complete private ownership against full public ownership. In jurisdictions subscribing to the notion of complete private ownership, there is always the opportunity for the government to appropriate private land where it is in the public interest. The notion of compensation for expropriation has been well rehearsed throughout history. Pufendorf, in 1673, refers to the notion in his writing on the duty of man and citizen when explaining the right of eminent domain.[49] In jurisdictions where the resources are considered common or public property, the benefit of the land is, more often than not, redistributed for the people. Although there may be some individuals proposing the strengthening of private ownership rights, the division of land will always contain a public interest safeguard.

Common property is previously unowned land and space incapable of appropriation and available for public use: examples include air, sunlight, the high seas, outer space and the moon.[50]

Public ownership is where property is held by public, rather than private, institutions usually for the benefit of the community. Quite often such property is state owned and managed through subsidiary institutions, which can be partly privatised by acting on behalf of the government and essentially performing the role of trustee. For the purposes of this book, public ownership refers to territorial land owned by the state or sovereign through government institutions for the benefit of citizens.

One can take the view that private ownership would be preferential to that of public ownership because where private oil companies generate profit from exploitation that revenue is often redistributed elsewhere within the global economy. Thus due to global economic dependence on the oil industry, private ownership will be the driving force behind market growth and as it is in the interests of IOCs to expand such economic activity, this works to the benefit of all. However, the growth of national oil companies and the emergence of resource nationalism in recent years acts as a counterbalance to the private exploitation of the industry on a global scale. The result has not had a significantly detrimental effect on the global economy and, in fact, it is suggested that the increase in national protection of resources has gone some way to stabilise the security of resources.

2.2.2.2 Authority of the state

As noted in Chapter 3, Iraq has only become a state relatively recently.[51] Since 2003, the nature of the state has changed, and this raises questions as to the legal validity of the Constitution and government in place.[52] It is sufficient to state at this stage that the Constitution was urgently passed in order to meet an external deadline set by the US administration[53]; therefore, due to the rapid changes in a country in turmoil the legitimacy of the Coalition Provisional Authority (CPA) and subsequent interim governments is questionable at best.

Although a system of government is in place in Iraq, one must consider the implications of external influences on the development of state structure; particularly the legal and political decision-making by the US and "allied" governments in the 2003–2005 period when the provisional Iraqi government and CPA operated without a genuinely legitimate mandate.

Under the 1951 Iraqi Civil Code, "perfect ownership" is defined as that which

> vests in the owner a right to dispose absolutely of that which he owns: through use, enjoyment, and exploitation he shall enjoy (avail himself of)

> the thing (ayn) owned as well as its fruits, crops and produce and may dispose of the thing itself (ayn) by all the allowable means.[54]

The formation of Iraq in the early twentieth century was, at the outset, intended to benefit the colonial powers.[55] In order to introduce some legitimacy to what would otherwise be the acquisition of land to which these powers would not be entitled, the League of Nations provided a vehicle for legal and political authority. Baker[56] notes that one of the founding principles of the Covenant of the League of Nations was the 'primacy of the Great Powers' which was 'admitted as of right' and:

> ... no Power, either while the Covenant was being drawn up, or since the League itself came into existence, has ever contested its validity. ... Had it not been for 'the Concert and the precedence which it had established by its spasmodic exercise of authority during a century, the Great Powers would not thus have been accorded, without dispute or even discussion, the special position which is theirs within the framework of the League of Nations.

The formation of Iraq emerged under a quasi-constitutional law through the League of Nations as highlighted by Baker:

> [f]or it must be remembered that the interventions of the Concert were those of a quasi legally constituted body which intervened by its own pretension, at least, as of right, which not only almost invariably received for its intervention and authority the de facto, consent of other States, but which even from time to time was formally appealed to by them, and that its intervention had been exercised for a century.[57]

The League of Nations introduced a more restrictive system in international law limiting the rights of independence under the international political system. Baker considers that the democratic development of international law rests on representative political participation by nations with the largest populations; one example is that even though the League of Nations was founded on inequality, it provided a "practical solution of the intricate problem of political representation".[58] The relevance of this for present purposes is that the law and the function of the state rest on politics at both national and international levels. Political institutions establish authority and prestige over a relatively short period of time which then permits them to set rules and regulations forming the basis of international law.[59]

Although arguably there is merit in creating a self-sufficient Iraq which would not require engagement with what are essentially US-dominated international institutions in order to protect Iraq's national sovereignty, to consider that Iraq may be unaffected by the international community would be an error given its significance in the global economy and the number of current and prospective oil and gas agreements with which the country is engaged on an international level. Whereas historically a state could act independently, in a modern increasingly interdependent and globalised world it is more difficult to retain extensive national sovereignty and authority. This does not mean, however, that Iraq should concede to terms that would erode her control over such a valuable resource and key asset for economic and political prosperity. In any event, over time the balance of power of the major international institutions[60] could change and if Iraq is to develop it must have access to such international fora.

A state can only be legitimate if guided by the general will of the people.[61] If the state lacks legitimacy, then it must follow that all legislation and legal frameworks including the Constitution are invalid until either rectified or redrafted by a government holding a legitimate, and not coerced, mandate of the people. One argument could be that due to the elections held in Iraq since 2003, the government in place is legitimate and therefore entitled to enact legislation and carry out its mandated functions. However, prior to the elections the 'government' was under the control of the CPA, which was in essence an extension of the US administration, which passed regulations central to the functioning of the future state of Iraq little or no form of consultation with Iraqis on the ground.[62] Unless all of these measures were to be revoked in order for the country to start anew it is difficult to see how the current government could be said to be legitimate. The shaping of the state of Iraq has been tarnished by external influence since 2003. So it is important to remember that it is not only the people but also external actors with vested interests seeking to maintain control and influence of Iraq for the purposes of exploitation who have formed the state of Iraq. Although this is a key topic for analysis, further consideration cannot be made at this juncture. In order to progress the analysis certain assumptions must be made, for example, the Constitution although questionable and likely to be amended in the future will be addressed in its current form as a starting point.[63]

2.3 The legal concepts of property ownership and sovereignty

In order to understand the subject matter of this book, it is necessary to consider the geological formation of oil reservoirs. Oil does not flow like rivers to the sea nor is it a vast mass of uncontrolled vapours such as air or a wild animal roaming free to be captured.[64] By natural law, common to all, of itself the use of oil is limited, unlike air and water, which can be consumed directly and therefore be legitimately claimed to be the common property of all. Oil requires processing for its extraction and use so although it is a natural resource in a pure sense as it is a formation under the subsoil, it can be distinguished on a practical level.

Article 23 of the Iraqi Constitution protects private property and provides for compensation for expropriation. Further, immovable assets may only be possessed by Iraqis unless there is legislative exemption.[65] The issue of whether oil can be classed as immovable property was briefly considered by Campbell J. in the case of the **Anglo-Iranian Oil Company v Jaffrate**,[66] which dealt with an action in detinue concerning the expropriation of Iranian oil cargoes in a vessel in the Gulf of Aden:

> It is true that oil can be classed as an immovable. But there is nothing to show that it must necessarily be so classed. It is merely necessary or convenient to do so in certain circumstances and for certain purposes. To extend what is really only a fiction would lead to obvious absurdities. The oil in this case is clearly in the category of moveables. Nor can I see that it makes any difference whether the action is in personam or in rem, though the defendants appear to attach importance to this point.

2.3.1 *Islamic law concepts underlying natural resource ownership*

Although it is not an Islamic state[67] the official religion of Iraq is Islam and Islamic jurisprudence is a source of law,[68] which is reinforced in the 2005 Constitution by Article 2, First,[69] and Second.[70] It is worth noting that the position of the reference to Islamic principles is in the second provision of the Constitution and that it is tied in with the principle of democracy and the guarantee of rights and freedoms.[71] Thus, it is apparent that the protection of Islam is considered of such vital significance to the political and legislative framework of Iraq that it was engrained in the Constitution at the outset. Article 2 is supported by Article 3[72] and Article 92, Second, which provides for experts in Islamic jurisprudence forming part of the Federal Supreme Court.[73] Iraq had an historical influence of Shari'a through Ottoman rule and, more recently, the 1951 Civil Code, which was compiled from the Shari'a and the Egyptian Civil Code.[74]

The population of Iraq is predominantly Shi'a[75] and the 2005 Constitution keeps the reference to Islamic law purposefully vague. When making comparisons with neighbouring states, the majority except for Iran are of Sunni population. The closest cultural neighbour of Iraq, Syria, follows the Hanafi School. Although they are Shi'a, Iraq has traditionally followed the Hanafi, Shafi'i and Maliki schools.[76] Given its significance to the legal framework of Iraq, it is important to provide the position under Shari'a law[77] relating to ownership and rights to natural resources, assets and economic return. This section will specifically seek to address the Islamic viewpoint relating to natural resource ownership.

Before considering general Islamic principles relating to natural resource ownership, the extent to which Article 2 of the Iraqi Constitution of 2005 affects the legal framework of the oil industry requires analysis. Islamic principles are a source of legislation, which makes it just one consideration of many to be taken into account. The other sources for consideration under the Iraqi Civil Code of 1951 are custom and usage, the laws of equity and precedent both in Iraq and proximate jurisdictions.[78] Provided that the oil legislation does not impose requirements contrary to the provisions of Islam,[79] it should not be considered unconstitutional.[80] The UN version of the Constitution provides Islamic principles as a foundation source of law.[81] During the drafting stage, the terminology of Article 2 varied between a fundamental source, a principal source, a basic source, a main source and a source among sources.[82] Towards the end of the drafting period the two terms mostly debated among the key parties were whether Islam should be a principal or fundamental source and the Arabic word of 'asasi' changed to 'asas', which can be interpreted as foundation or basis.[83] In any event, the Constitution does not refer to any alternative sources of law within Article 2, or elsewhere in the document, therefore a comprehensive list of legal sources appears to have been missed by the drafters with Islam as a single source of what should have specified a range of legislative sources. When compared with the Syrian,[84] Egyptian[85] and Libyan[86] Constitutions, the Iraqi version appears to be consistent in lacking definitive sources of law.

The Roman law concept of absolute ownership[87] is not recognised under Islamic law as all land belongs to God with man as mere trustee.[88] There are several verses in the Quran, which acknowledge ad interim and de facto ownership of property,[89] thereby indicating that private ownership is recognised on the basis of trust. This would, prima facie, appear to provide the relevant authority for natural resource management if not ownership per se. Under Islamic law, the legal legitimacy of the state to manage resources through the government and enter into contractual arrangements for their extraction and use is recognised, provided that the conduct of the state is just and equitable and the contracts are entered into in good faith. Thus, provided that the revenues from natural resource exploitation are used for the benefit of citizens and that the land remains under state control, on trust from God, concession agreements should not contravene the Shari'a in terms of ownership. Such agreements, in the form of usufruct in exchange for the payment of royalties and taxes, could provide the most beneficial use of the land.

Under Shari'a law it is an accepted concept that the land belongs to God and that the state and people are trustees.[90] Yamani refers to Al-Zamakhshari's explanation of the concept of trust:[91]

> The property you have in your hands is God's by virtue of Him making and creating it. He supplied you with it and permitted you to reap benefits, and made you his heirs and successors in disposing with it, but it is not really yours and you are only God's agents and representatives.

The protection of the community is paramount under Shari'a law, resources can be exploited to the benefit of the people provided that such exploitation is in the public interest.[92] According to Behdad,[93] "[t]he Islamic state will be the judge of interference and the abrogator of individual property rights". However, it must be remembered that Iraq is not an Islamic state and the Shari'a is not the sole source of law. The government is secular and religion, although an influence in the Constitution, legislation and politics is not the single basis of government. Even in non-Islamic states, the state is normally the actor in expropriation of property usually with the payment of compensation and will likewise abrogate personal property rights where necessary.[94]

According to Yamani, Shari'a encourages and protects private ownership provided that there is no detriment or injury to others or diversion from the social function within the community.[95] The right to private property is subject to some restrictions, the most relevant of which is that a private injury should be tolerated in order to avoid public harm and therefore the state may restrict private ownership for the public interest.[96] The concept of private ownership (dominium) and its relation to Islamic principles were considered by Dr. Mahmassani in the **LIAMCO v Libya** arbitration:[97]

> One of the fundamental rights universally recognised is the right of private ownership or property (Dominum). The Classical concept of this right defines it as the right to use, exploitation and disposal (usus, fructus, abusus) of the object owned. Although this classical definition has been tempered and limited sometimes by reason of public interest, nonetheless the inviolability of the right of property has remained throughout history as a sacred proposition confirmed and reaffirmed by a succession of Constitutional and international declarations and charters.[98]

It is accepted that, under Roman law, according to the ad coelum doctrine, the right to immovable private property extends to the subsoil:

> Applied to land (immovable property) the contents of this absolute right extended in theory to the air space above it and to things lying underground, as was often expressed in the Latin maxim "Cujus est solum ejus est usque ad coelum, et as inferos" (Whose is the soil, his is also that which is above and below it).[99]

The inviolability of the right to property is recognised under Islamic law through the prevention of unlawful appropriation.[100] This is evidenced in Article 97[101] of the Ottoman Mejelle, which provides that property is not to be taken "*without some legal reason*". This right was limited by Article 26, due to the duty of public interest under Islamic law and to avoid public nuisance, which provides that "*[p]rivate injury is tolerated in order to ward off a public injury*".[102] It can therefore be argued that for the benefit of public interest the oil-bearing land in Iraq should be owned and managed by the state for the benefit of the people even where such land may be privately owned provided that compensation is given to the landowner.

Despite reference to private property, which is generally accepted, there is some dispute about the ownership of mineral resources. The Maliki school maintains that such resources cannot be privately owned and thus belong to the state regardless of the extraction process or whether the state's consent was obtained.[103] Title to the minerals rests with the state. Jurists such as Abu Hanifa argued that "ownership of the land follows ownership of the surface" with the owner being obliged to pay a portion of the proceeds of sale to the treasury in the form of what is now commonly known as a royalty.[104]

Dr. Mahmassani[105] considered that, natural resource ownership is communal ownership and that the resources no longer belong to the owner of the land which accords with the Maliki school's view that "*mines and underground resources are the property of the Sultan (the State)*". According to the majority of Sunni Islamic schools,[106] natural resources belong to the state for the benefit of the whole nation. In Islam, a person can only own that which he has produced or developed as a result of his own efforts. According to the Hanafi school mineral ownership follows land ownership, whereas the Hanbali and Shafie schools state that apparent minerals cannot be privately owned but hidden minerals follow land ownership.[107] The Maliki school considers that all minerals are state owned and is followed by the Iraqi Constitution of 1965 which states:

> Natural wealth together with its resources and energies shall be the property of the state which shall properly dispose of them.

The 2005 Constitution of Iraq also holds that oil and gas are owned by the people but managed by the state.[108] The position, at the time of writing, therefore appears to be in line with Islamic principles provided that such ownership is used for the benefit of the nation. Article 112, First, provides for the fair distribution of revenues, with Article 112, Second, stipulating that policies for development of oil and gas wealth shall achieve "the highest benefit to the Iraqi people". This can only be achieved through proper use of the land and state ownership of oil resources. In the case of Iraq, adherence to Islamic principles relating to property ownership may assist in economic recovery, as emphasis is placed on public interest and benefit to the nation as a whole.

The primary objective of petroleum operations is to obtain maximum foreign exchange earnings to develop economic, social and political goals.[109] Thus, in order to attain these key developmental goals it is essential for the state to have a clear policy in place combining legislation, procedure and regulation so that there is a strong framework within which to work. As stated by El-Walid and El-Malik:[110]

> It is the primary duty of the producer state to formulate a clear policy stating whether the state is to be developed on the basis of a private, public or mixed system. Although the occurrence of minerals is an accident of nature its contribution to economic growth depends on the awareness of the choices and wisdom of the policies.

As the welfare of the people is paramount under Islam, it is for the state to develop petroleum and economic policies that do not breach the spirit of Shari'a. Although Ibn Khaldun[111] warned against state intervention in economic activities,[112] public interest is the exception and there can be no doubt that in Iraq state intervention is required for the management of natural resources and the regulation of the oil industry. In order to uphold Islamic principles regarding land ownership the most appropriate form of concession agreement would be a short-term possessory arrangement in consideration of royalty payments and taxes, which is likely to be a usufruct, where the state can withdraw such rights where it is no longer in the public interest.

The application of Islamic law to petroleum development is a recent concept as identified in the Aramco arbitration by Sheikh Mohammed Abu Zahra:[113]

> The regime of mining concessions, and, consequently, also of oil concessions, has remained embryonic in Moslem law and is not the same in the different schools. The principles of one school cannot be introduced into another, unless this is done by an act of authority.

The likelihood is that provided oil industry activities in Iraq are perceived to be operated in the public interest and that management does not become detrimental to the people, the enactment of legislation in accordance with Islamic principles can be justified. Yamani argues that the Shari'a is adaptable to environmental factors citing a principle which makes it possible for a "change of laws because of change of circumstances cannot be denied"[114] and provides an example of Imam Al-Shafie creating a new school of thought suited to the Egyptian environment which differed from his legal opinions and juristic thought in Iraq.[115] Further, Al-Hanafi and Quarafi confirm that where there is a conflict with public interest and an explicit and revealed provision, if custom has changed then the text may be modified accordingly.[116] Thus, it is unlikely that Article 2 of the Constitution will have a significant effect on the enactment of legislation or the terms of oil agreements provided that title to oil resources remains with the state, there are no provisions contrary to the interests of the Iraqi people and that the maximum benefit for the country as a whole can be achieved.

2.3.2 The principle of Permanent Sovereignty of Natural Resources (PSNR)

The principle of PSNR was established for the benefit of countries under former colonial rule, often referred to as "developing countries", to exercise their right to self-determination and for the encouragement of international co-operation in the economic development of these countries.[117] PSNR was a response to the unfair terms relating to profit and royalty payments[118] contained within existing concession agreements, which demonstrated the clear inequality of bargaining power between state governments and international oil companies (IOCs). This was due to the amount of power and control exercised by the colonial occupiers over natural resources often providing unfair terms in the concession agreements where very little profits were provided to the producing country's government. The companies established by the occupiers took the majority of the revenue out of the country of production thereby preventing investment in the economies and infrastructures of producing countries, in essence preventing the "developing countries" from developing in accordance with their economic potential.[119] On average, concessions lasted around seventy-five years, which restricted the right of producing governments to intervene in their own industries to improve their economic position. The IOCs held a superior bargaining position as a result of their technical know-how, capital and marketing capacity[120] in addition to their political influence.

An alternative interpretation is that PSNR is a method of controlling colonial interests in countries seeking nationalisation of resources by imposing compensation for expropriation on an international level. The principle of PSNR can be used as a legal point of reference in arbitration to counter reliance on the stabilisation clauses in the concession agreements.

PSNR was introduced in the early 1950s, initially through UN Resolution 523 (VI) of 12 January 1952. Later that year, UN Resolution 626[121] recognised the right of the people to use and exploit their natural resources inherent in their sovereignty. The resolution was passed to assist under-developed countries in the "proper use and exploitation of their natural resources".[122] The right of peoples to freely use their natural wealth and resources is inherent in their sovereignty. Article 2 recommends that all member states refrain from impeding, directly or indirectly, the exercise of sovereignty of any state over its natural resources.[123] The key provision relating to PSNR is the UN General Assembly Resolution 1803 (XVII) of 14 December 1962.

PSNR was introduced into international law through UN resolutions, namely:

1 Permanent sovereignty over Natural Resources, Resolution 3171 (XXVIII) December 1973
2 Declaration on the Establishment of a New Economic Order, Resolution 3201 May 1974
3 The Charter of Economic Rights and Duties of States, Resolution 3281 (XXIX) December 1974[124]

The right of state control over natural resources through equity and contractual joint ventures entered into in the late 1950s and 1960s were recognised following the passage of the resolution on PSNR. Consequently, in some jurisdictions, ownership of resources transferred from concessionaires to ownership in common or in accordance with additional contractual terms often in the form of production sharing agreements (PSAs). These new types of arrangement enabled the producing states to obtain control of operations and the development of national capabilities over and above the financial returns to the state.[125] The establishment of PSNR in the international arena provided states with an opportunity to renegotiate existing contracts or enter into new agreements. The principle assisted the progressive development of international law for more equitable exploitation of natural resources. The criteria for compatibility with the principle of PSNR are that (1) contracts must be in the context of national development and the well-being of the state concerned, (2) in accordance with the national legislation in force and (3) be freely entered into.[126]

There is academic debate surrounding the issue of whether or not PSNR is a legal concept. Duruigbo asserts that the PSNR principle was considered to be part of international law by the International Court of Justice in the East Timor case.[127] Consequently, Duruigbo considers that the principal legal character of PSNR cannot be denied.[128] Article 1 of the Resolution provides:

> The right of peoples and nations to permanent sovereignty over their natural wealth and resources must be exercised in the interest of their national development and of the well being of the people of the State concerned.[129]

To assist in the textual interpretation of international resolutions and treaties, Articles 31–33 of the Vienna Convention offer guidance.[130] Article 31 provides for an interpretation in good faith and in accordance with its ordinary meaning.[131] Article 32 provides for supplementary means of interpretation including reference to preparatory documents where the ordinary meaning is obscure, ambiguous, unreasonable or absurd.[132] Article 33 provides that where the treaty is in two or more languages, they shall be equally authoritative, unless otherwise agreed.[133] PSNR has the status of jus cogens in international law and cannot be defeated by treaty or contract.[134]

Hossain, Chowdhury and Schrijver all suggest that the principle of sovereignty of natural resources is settled under international law and that its validity is undisputed.[135] However, others such as Baslar[136] suggest that the principle is outdated due to the increased economic, political and financial interdependence of states.[137] In the debate of PSNR against the theory of the common heritage of mankind (CHM), nations must protect their resources and following the concept of CHM would, in essence, amount to a free for all to the detriment of the developing states.

Chowdhury suggests that the "natural wealth and resources located within the territorial jurisdiction of a sovereign state belong to the community".[138] According to Brownlie,[139] sovereignty can be defined as the 'reserved domain of domestic jurisdiction' or 'discretionary power within areas delimited by law'.[140] Jurisdiction includes the legal and legislative competence over national territory, which may be labelled 'sovereign rights'.[141] The sovereign rights of the people is supported in the 1970 UN Declaration concerning Friendly relations:[142]

> By virtue of the principle of equal rights and self-determination of peoples enshrined in the Charter of the United Nations, all peoples have the right freely to determine, without external interference, their political status and to pursue their economic, social and cultural development, and every State has the duty to respect this right in accordance with the provisions of the Charter.

Given the debate surrounding the issue of sovereignty and lack of clarity in attribution of responsibility for the exercise of the right, it would be somewhat dubious to cite PSNR as the premise upon which to base authority of the state to manage a country's natural resources. However, one argument is that, in a democratic society, the state will always act in accordance with the will of its people. This may be the case in an ideal democracy but in Iraq it is still difficult for the people to hold the government to account and particularly in light of the political instability, unemployment, lack of infrastructure and numerous complexities facing the country. It will take time for the issue of accountability to be established. The country is still at a very early stage of democracy and developing through a process to which it is unaccustomed, therefore the questioning of authority by the people is a mechanism yet to be fully developed.

This issue raises the next logical question of what is to be done in the interim period while Iraq is in its development phase. It cannot be justified to allow the country to develop organically whilst those in power are in a position to exploit and corrupt the resource wealth that is required for the economic development of Iraq. Protectionist measures should be put in place to facilitate hydrocarbon revenue distribution to the most urgent areas of the economy for development, particularly in light of the significant political turmoil throughout the country. An overarching framework independent of political influence could assist in effective revenue distribution until the economy has reached the necessary stage, with the appropriate foundations, to implement a system suited to its economy, for example, as has been achieved in Norway.[143]

Notes

1 'Discourse on the Origin of Inequality a Discourse on a Subject Proposed by the Academy of Dijon in 1751: What is the Origin of Inequality among Men, and Is It Authorised by Natural Law?' (1754) trans. G.D.H. Cole (Excerpted and adapted by A.C. Kibel), 29, www.ocw.mit.edu/courses/literature/21l-449-end-of-nature-spring-2002/readings/lecture10.pdf, accessed 8 September 2017.

2 The United States is the only modern state to assign private property rights to oil resources under the premise that the owner of the land is also the owner of the subsoil.

3 The United States is the only country to use the rule of capture, more commonly known as "finders keepers" in relation to its resources thereby safeguarding the private property rights of its citizens. Robert E. Hardwicke, a US oil and gas attorney, stated in 'The Rule of Capture and Its Implications as Applied to Oil and Gas', 13 *Texas Law Review*, 391, 393, 1935; 'The owner of a tract of land acquires title to the oil and gas which he produces from wells drilled thereon, though it may be proved that part of such oil or gas migrated from adjoining lands'. As cited by Bruce Kramer and Owen Anderson, *'The Rule of Capture – An Oil and Gas Perspective'* 35 *Environmental Law*, 899, 2005, www.repository.law.ttu.edu/bitstream/handle/10601/582/Kramer%2035%20Envtl.pdf?sequenc, accessed 8 September 2011.

4 This assumption is evidenced in the contractual terms of some upstream agreements where title to the resource passes from the state to the oil company. In some cases, the oil company involved is also a national oil company.

5 See later chapters for a discussion on contractual terms.

6 This is further discussed in Chapter 4.

7 Iraqi Civil Code 1951, Article 1.

8 Addressed in Chapter 4.

9 Ibid.

10 For an analysis of the implications of the Exxon decision to enter into agreements with both the central government and the KRG see Chapter 5.

11 Discussed in Chapter 4.

12 As we shall see, arguably there is no single right to property but rather a "bundle of rights" as referred to by academics such as Penner, see James Penner, 'The "Bundle of Rights" Picture of Property', 711 *UCLA Law Review*, 43, 1996–1997.

13 It is beyond the scope of this book to discuss extensively the views of Aristotle, Pufendorf, Kant, Locke et al. on the subject, their views are summarized later in this chapter.

14 Originating from the concept of natural law.

15 "Land uncovered by the sea, lakes or rivers will be the private property of the state; the neighbours may acquire it against payment of the comparable price."

16 L. Becker, *Property Rights: Philosophical Foundations* (Routledge & Keegan Paul Ltd, 1977), 6. For further reading many philosophers have written about the idea of property rights, a small example would be Harris, Penner, Hohfeld and Honore.

17 Article 65.

18 Property is further explained as "545. No one can be compelled to give up his property, except for the public good, and for a just and previous indemnity".

546. Property in a thing, whether real or personal, confers a right over all which it produces, and over all connected with it by accession, whether naturally or artificially. This right is termed the "*right of accession*".

19 Jeremy Waldron, 'What is Private Property?' 5 *Oxford Journal of Legal Studies*, 313–318, 1985.

20 C.A, Hooper, *Laws of Palestine and Transjordan*, Vol. 1, 34. The Mejelle is only a part codification of Ottoman law with the remainder resting in Islamic law principals.

21 Ibid. The example accompanying the article is "A fish while in the sea is not of any specific value. When it is caught and taken it becomes the property of specific value." Articles 128 and 129 of the Ottoman Majella define moveable and immoveable property, which does not differ from the current common definition.

22 2005 Constitution, Article 23:

> First: Private property is protected. The owner shall have the right to benefit, exploit and dispose of private property within the limits of the law.
>
> Second: Expropriation is not permissible except for the purposes of public benefit in return for just compensation, and this shall be regulated by law.
>
> Third: A. Every Iraqi shall have the right to own property anywhere in Iraq. No others may possess immovable assets, except as exempted by law. B. Ownership of property for the purposes of demographic change is prohibited.

23 Leslie Rutherford and Sheila Bone (Eds.), *Osbourne's Concise Law Dictionary* (8th Ed., Sweet & Maxwell, 1993), 293.

24 This is a settled point recognized by most academic writers including Becker.

25 For a detailed and interesting discussion on this see Penner (n47). Other philosophical perspectives are provided by Hohfeld and Honore.

26 Becker (n51) 18.

27 NB. Hydrocarbons and oil will be used interchangeably throughout this book.

28 This classification has been evident throughout legal history, seen in the Justinian Institutes and discussed in the Arbitration Award in the matter of the Libyan American Oil Company (LIAMCO) v The Government of the Libyan Arab Republic, 20 April 1977, 20 ILM 1, 1–87 (1981) at 89.

29 Iraqi Civil Code 1951, Article 125.

30 Which follows the French Code.

31 Iraqi Civil Code 1951, Articles 1048 and 1049.

32 Article 1049(2). Note that at Article 1049(1) "The owner of a thing also owns everything which is deemed by usage to constitute an essential element thereof such as it cannot be separated therefrom without the thing owned perishing, deteriorating or changing."

33 Article 1049(3) "The ownership of the surface of the land may by agreement be separated from that which is above it and that which is below it."

34 Law No. 35 of 1977 provided for the reformation of the legal system in Iraq in accordance with the new socialist agenda and national development plan. In the working paper it is clear that the legislation was created to empower the state to redefine and redistribute privately owned immovable property for the benefit of state ownership, to "widen the scope of public ownership". For a detailed commentary by N. Karam see the Iraqi Civil Code at 3.4-xvii et seq., http://gjpi.org/library/primary/statutes/, accessed 23 December 2011.

35 Ibid., 3.4-xviii.

36 There is an on-going dispute between the KRG and the central government over the jurisdiction of "transferred territories" which is subject to Article 140 of the 2005 Constitution. Discussed in later chapters.

37 Reference to property throughout this chapter, unless otherwise stated, is that of immoveable property as the concern is for sub-soil minerals.

38 Hereinafter referred to collectively as the property spectrum.

39 Jim Harris, *Property and Justice* (Oxford, Oxford University Press, 1996), 29.

40 Aristotle considered private property to be a cause of social injustice and writes about the communism of property as a solution to "the evils now belonging to regimes come about through property not being common. I mean lawsuits against one another concerning contracts, trials for perjury, and flattery of the rich." (*Politics* 1263b, 15–22, as cited by Mayhew in 'Aristotle on Property' at 808). Aristotle's solution seems to be that of making private property available for common use, enforced through legislation, in order to avoid the lack of productivity in truly common property –

> It is ... evident that it is better for possessions to be private, but to make them common in use. That they [the citizens] become such [as to use possessions in common], this is a special function of the legislator.
>
> (*Politics* 1263a 37–40, as cited by Mayhew at 816)

In describing "the best city" Aristotle acknowledges that the city-owned land would be required to support the institutions and generate revenues for the functioning of the city. (Mayhew 823). It would not be a stretch to consider that Aristotle may have been inclined to consider that oil and minerals would be state-owned for the benefit of the citizens of a country.

41 Given the strong influence of the Church and religious teaching at the time of the works of the great philosophers, it is perhaps understandable that the association of divinity with property was unavoidable. With the passage of time, philosophers sought to look beyond religion as the foundation of their theories although the mainstream views, which is built upon the earlier writings, continue to carry this influence.

42 According to Locke, Man, who is the "workmanship of one Omnipotent", through the use of his labour, acquires a right to the property for his own needs. This is the premise is commonly known as the labour theory of value. However, Pufendorf and Grotius hold slightly different views to this mainstream thought and assign the appropriation of property to universal agreement and not to labour.

43 In his second treatise, Locke rationalises this view:

> God, who hath given the world to men in common, hath also given them reason to make use of it to the best advantage of life and convenience. The earth and all that is therein is given to men for the support and comfort of their being. And though all the fruits it naturally produces, and beasts it feeds, belong to mankind in common, as they are produced by the spontaneous hand of Nature, and nobody has originally a private dominion exclusive of the rest of mankind in any of them,

as they are thus in their natural state, yet being given for the use of men, there must of necessity be a means to appropriate them some way or other before they can be of any use, or at all beneficial, to any particular men. The fruit or venison which nourishes the wild Indian, who knows no enclosure, and is still a tenant in common, must be his, and so his—i.e., a part of him, that another can no longer have any right to it before it can do him any good for the support of his life.

(Second treatise, §25/26)

44 Although revered for his labour theory Locke's concept can be traced to the Justinian Institutes, Book 2, Part 1, ss25–30.
45 Ibid.
46 Grotius supports this view in a maritime context where the sea is common property for all but that which is discovered in the sea only becomes the property of those who have expropriated it. Nature had given all things to all people and this was the argument used when introducing a regime for the freedom of the high seas – jus gentium verses jus naturalis. Hugo Grotius, *Freedom of the Seas* (MaGoffin trans., 1978), 29.
47 John Locke, *Two Treatises on Government*, 307–308, (1690).
48 For Locke, labour is the applicable test for appropriation:

Whatsoever, then, he removes out of the state that Nature hath provided and left it in, he hath mixed his labour with it, and joined to it something that is his own, and thereby makes it his property. It being by him removed from the common state Nature placed it in, it hath by this labour something annexed to it that excludes the common right of other men. For this "labour" being the unquestionable property of the labourer, no man but he can have a right to what that is once joined to, at least where there is enough, and as good left in common for others.

(para 26/27)

It is suggested that the "fruit" referred to by Locke, can be extended for present purposes to oil. Oil is a mineral produced by nature and therefore it is argued can have the same status so that "men … can make use of it to the best advantage of life and convenience".

49 Pufendorf, *On the Duty of Man and Citizen*, Book 2, Chapter 15, para 4, www.lonang.com/exlibris/pufendorf/puf-215.htm, accessed 1 May 2016.
50 For example, the UN charter on the Law of the Sea and the Moon Treaty.
51 Whether this original formation of the state of Iraq was legitimate is a matter for another publication. For ease of analysis it will be assumed that Iraq was a legitimate state at least until 2003.
52 Although some issues are raised later in this book, it is not the focus of the research.
53 Due to political pressure to demonstrate some measure of success of the operation. See Chapter 4.
54 Iraqi Civil Code 1951, Article 1049.
55 See Chapter 3 for the historical background. The British were interested in Iraq as a trading route to India in addition to the subsequent discovery of oil wealth.
56 P.J. Baker, 'The Doctrine of Legal Equality of States', 4 *BYIL*, 16, 1923/1924.
57 Ibid., Baker goes on to say that

Westlake was surely right in claiming that the special, position of the Great Powers … was at least becoming before 1914, a definite part of the legal relations between States which it was the duty of the rules of international law to define.

58 Ibid., 20.
59 The debate on validity of international law as true law or a concept is beyond the scope of this book.

60 Such as the IMF, World Bank, WTO among others. The BRIC countries are increasingly gaining influence in these organizations. For an insight into developments see 'Developing countries to the rescue at G-20' *Associated Press News*, http://m.apnews.mobi/ap/db_36972/contentdetail.htm?contentguid=uavwc1fa, accessed 20 June 2012.

61 The decision of the people through a sovereign assembly which is the subsequent source of law.

62 It appears that the US administration did consult with Iraqi exiles prior to and during the invasion, the prime example being Ahmed Chalabi, who was considered to be out of touch with events on the ground in Iraq. Sinan Salaheddin, 'Ahmed Chalabi: Politician Who Furnished Bush and Blair with the False Information that Led to the Allied Invasion of Iraq' (3 November 2015) *The Independent*, www.independent.co.uk/news/obituaries/ahmed-chalabi-politician-who-furnished-bush-and-blair-with-the-false-information-that-led-to-the-a6720136.html, accessed 9 December 2018.

63 To some extent chaos may ensue in an already volatile environment if it is not accepted that the current government is legitimate. This does not mean, however, that the issue should not be fully researched and analysed.

64 The rule of capture is the legal justification used for ownership of oil resources in the United States of America and is a principle applied in other jurisdictions. However, this method of obtaining property rights to oil is neither appropriate nor relevant to Iraqi oil.

65 Iraqi Constitution 2005, Article 23.

66 Anglo-Iranian Oil Company v Jaffrate & Others [The Rose Mary] [1953] 1 W.L.R. 246, 260.

67 Unlike the Islamic states of Iran or Saudi Arabia, Iraq is a secular state with the executive body comprising representatives of various ethnicities and religions, although non-Muslims are the minority.

68 2005 Constitution, Article 2, First (UN trans.).

69 Article 2, First, A, provides that "No law may be enacted that contradicts the established provisions of Islam".

70 Article 2, Second "guarantees the Islamic identity of the majority of the Iraqi people …"

71 Article 2, First, A and B.

72 Article 3 makes reference to Iraq being "part of the Islamic world."

73 Article 92, Second: "The Federal Supreme Court shall be made up of a number of judges, exerts in Islamic jurisprudence …"

74 See the Foreword to the 1951 Iraqi Civil Code, 3.4.i.

75 The religious demographic of Iraq as of March 2010 is 60–65% Shia, 32–37% Sunni, Christian or other 3% (CIA World Factbook, Iraq).

76 Majid Khadduri, 'Nature and Sources of Islamic Law', 3 *The George Washington Law Review*, 20–23, 1953–1954. For a summary of Shi'a legal theory see 20–23.

77 NB. The terms "Islamic law" and "Shari'a law" will be used interchangeably throughout this book.

78 Civil Code 1951, Article 1.

79 It should be noted at this juncture that the consideration of Shari'a, or as I have termed it here "Islamic principles", involves jurists interpretation of Quranic verses, the Sunna and fiqh. A good explanation of Shari'a and fiqh is provided by Kemal Faruki, *Islamic Jurisprudence* (Pakistan Publishing House 2962). There are varying interpretations of Shari'a and as an example, in Egypt in 1976 a draft code of fiqh was developed by Al-Azhar as there was no settled view on which principles of the Shari'a should be followed after the creation of Article 2 of the Egyptian Constitution which incorporated the Shari'a into Egyptian law (Lombardi 126). Clark Lombardi, *State Law as Islamic Law in Modern Egypt* (Brill, 2006) provides a good

analysis of the Egyptian position pre-2011. It is important to note that there are differing interpretations of Islamic principles between the Shi'a and Sunni schools of thought and most writings on Shari'a law refer to the Sunni interpretations which is not necessarily appropriate for the Shi'a majority in Iraq.

80 The Federal Supreme Court pursuant to Article 93 of the 2005 Constitution will consider the issue of constitutionality.

81 www.uniraq.org/documents/iraqi_Constitution.pdf, accessed 2 April 2012.

82 Ashely Deeks and Matthew Burton, *Iraq's Constitution: A Drafting History*, 40 (1) *Cornell International Law Journal*, 8, http://scholarship.law.cornell.edu/cilj/vol40/iss1/1, accessed 3 April 2011.

83 Ibid., 10. See also the Iraqi Constitution in Arabic, www.niqash.org/uploaded/documents/15.10.2005.htm, accessed 3 April 2011.

84 2012 Constitution, Article 3, 'Islamic Jurisprudence Doctrine is a Primary Source of Legislation', www.al-bab.com/arab/docs/syria/syria_draft_Constitution_2012.htm, accessed 11 April 2012.

Previous Constitution, Article 3(2), 'Islamic Jurisprudence is a Main Source of Legislation', www.mideastinfo.com/documents/Syria_Constitution.htm and www.law.yale.edu/rcw/rcw/jurisdictions/asw/syrianarabrep/syria_Constitution.htm, accessed 11 April 2012.

85 2011 Constitution, Article 2, 'The Principles of Islamic Law are the Chief Source of Legislation', www.egypt.gov.eg/english/laws/Constitution/default.aspx, accessed 11 April 2012.

86 1969 Constitution: Article 2, 'Islam is the Religion of the State and Arabic is Its Official Language. The state protects religious freedom in accordance with established customs."

> Article 8 [Property]
>
> Public ownership is the basis of the development of society, of its growth and of self- sufficiency in production. Private ownership, if it is non-exploitative, is protected. Expropriation will take place only in accordance with the law. Inheritance is a right which will be governed by the Islamic Shari'a.
>
> ...
>
> Article 35 [New Laws]
>
> Decisions, statements, and orders issued by the Revolutionary Command Council since Sep 1969 and before the issue of this Constitutional proclamation shall have the power of law and supersede all contrary provisions. They can be annulled or amended only in accordance with the procedure defined in the present Constitutional proclamation.
>
> (http://unpan1.un.org/intradoc/groups/public/documents/cafrad/unpan004643.pdf accessed 11 April 2012)

87 Being the Ad Coelum doctrine, that ownership extends from heaven to hell, see quote on p. 53.

88 El-Walied and M.H. El-Malik, 'Mineral Investment under Shari'a Law', 8 *Arab Law Quarterly* 106–107, 1993.

89 Quran, 10:55 "Unquestionably, to Allah belongs whatever is in the heavens and the earth ..." See also verses 2:255, 3:129 and 22:64, confirming this position. See also verses 2:261, 2:188, 9:103 and 4:7. See also Ibid.

90 Yamani explains the concept of trusteeship and God's ownership of property as a legal principle in 'Islamic Law and Contemporary Issues', Charles Malik Ed., *God and Man in Contemporary Islamic Thought* (Syracuse University Press, 1972), 62.

91 Ibid.

92 According to Yamani, at 55 "... there is no real issue or conflict among Moslem jurists as to the employment of public interest and welfare as a source of legislation ...".

93 Sohrab Behdad, "Property Rights in Contemporary Islamic Economic Thought: A Critical Perspective", 47 (2) *Review of Social Economy*, 185–211, 188, 1989.
94 Most Western and Middle Eastern countries follow the principle of compensation for expropriation. See, for example, the Fifth Amendment of the US Constitution (Bill of Rights) "No person shall ... be deprived of ... property, without due process of law; nor shall private property be taken for public use, without just compensation.", www.archives.gov/exhibits/charters/bill_of_rights_transcript.html, accessed 3 April 2012.
95 Yamani (n90) 67.
96 Walid and Malik (n86) 109.
97 Arbitration Award in the matter of the *Libyan American Oil Company (LIAMCO) v The Government of the Libyan Arab Republic*, 20 April 1977, 20 ILM 1, 1–87 (1981). [Hereinafter LIAMCO Award] See 89 & 93 of the award.
98 Ibid., 19.
99 El Malik (n86) 91.
100 Ibid., 92: "In comparison with these views on property, it is relevant to record that Islamic law recognised the inviolable character of the right to property on the basis of the Holy Quranic Verse: 'And do not appropriate unlawfully each other's property' (S II, 188)."
101 "No person may take another person's property without some legal reason." Hooper 26.
102 Article 26, Hooper 19.
103 Yamani (n90) 69.
104 Ibid.
105 LIAMCO arbitration 93.
106 Although reference here is made to the Sunni schools, namely, Hanafi, Hanbali, Maliki and Shafie, it is important to remember that the population of Iraq is predominantly Shia and therefore the Ja'fari jurisprudence requires consideration. It is worthy of note that the Iraqi Civil Code when drafted by Al-Sanhuri's committee purposely omitted a particular school of thought due to the diversity of the Iraqi population.
107 El Malik (n86) 114.
108 2005 Constitution Article 111.
109 El Malik (n86) 115.
110 Ibid.
111 A historian of philosophy and Islamic thought covering a wide range of disciplines including economic jurisprudence.
112 El Malik (n86) 116.
113 At 163. Saudi Arabia v Arabian Oil Co (Aramco) (1963) I.L.R. 117
114 Yamani (n90) 54.
115 Ibid.
116 Yamani (n90) 56.
117 United Nations General Assembly Resolution 1803(XVII) of 14 December 1962, preamble.
118 Which often resulted in the national economy suffering at the hands of the oil companies.
119 Which worked to the advantage of the IOC's and their home governments as it maintained the imperial advantage over the resource rich countries.
120 Kamal Hossain and Subrata Chowdhury, *Permanent Sovereignty over Natural Resources in International Law* (London, Pinter, 1984), x.
121 The right to exploit freely natural wealth and resources of 21 December 1952.
122 Preamble to Resolution 626.
123 In January 1955, the UN Human Rights Commission affirmed that the right of peoples to self-determination includes PSNR. The right was further incorporated

into the International Covenant on Economic, Social and Cultural Rights and the International Covenant on Civil and Political Rights 1966.

124 The principle is also referred to in other international instruments such as the European Energy Charter Treaty of 17 December 1974, the UN Convention on the Law of the Sea of 16 November 1994 Articles 56 and 93, UN Framework on the Convention on Climate Change 21 March 1994, Vienna Convention on the Succession of States in Respect of Treaties 22 August 1978, Article 13, International Covenant on Economic, Social and Cultural Rights, GA Resolution 2200 (XXI) 19 December 1966, Articles 1(2), 11(2)(a) and 25.

125 Hossain and Chowdhury, (n120) xi.

126 Ibid.

127 East Timor (Port v Australia) 1995 ICJ 90 (June 30), as cited by E. Duruigbo, 'Permanent Sovereignty and the Peoples' Ownership of Natural Resources in International Law', 38 *The George Washington International Law Review*, 33 & 39, 2006.

128 Duguibo 39.

129 General Assembly resolution 1803 (XVII) of 14 December 1962, "Permanent sovereignty over natural resources", Article 1.

130 The Vienna Convention on the Law of Treaties, 23 May 1969, http://untreaty.un.org/ilc/texts/instruments/english/conventions/1_1_1969.pdf, accessed 22 January 2012.

131 Ibid., Article 31.

132 Ibid., Article 32.

133 Ibid., Article 33.

134 Hossain and Chowdhury, (n120) 38.

135 Ibid., Nico Schrijver, *Sovereignty over Natural Resources: Balancing Rights and Duties* (Cambridge, Cambridge University Press, 2008).

136 See generally, Kemal Baslar, *The Concept of the Common Heritage of Mankind in International Law* (Brill, 1997).

137 Ibid., 132–133.

138 Hossain and Chowdhury 1.

139 Brownlie, *Principles of Public International Law* 289. See also UN Resolution 2625 (XXV) (1970) Declaration on the Principles of International Law Concerning Friendly Relations and Cooperation among States in accordance with the Charter of the United Nations.

140 Brownlie (n139) 290.

141 Ibid., 291.

142 UNSCR 2625 XXV (1970) 124.

143 Although reference is often made to Norway as a model oil system, it must be remembered that Norway only discovered oil as recently as 1969 and could look to Southern countries which had battled the oil majors and the difficulties of nationalisation decades earlier (such as Mexico in 1938 and Iran in 1951). By the time Norway had discovered oil OPEC had been formed and Norway had a welfare state in place with a sound infrastructure and economy which are favourable foundations not experienced by its "third world" counterparts. The Norwegian system is further explained in Chapter 3.

Part II

3 Historical background to 2003

3.1 Historical backgrounds

As the cradle of civilisation, Mesopotamia the country currently known as Iraq, has a rich historical tapestry spanning over 10,000 years. This chapter will provide a brief history of the development of the oil industry in modern day Iraq.

The Ottoman Empire controlled Mesopotamia from 1534.[1] As a result of British Government assistance in defending the Ottoman Empire against Muhammad Ali Pasha of Egypt who had sought to take over the Levant, British influence in the region commenced in the 1840s. The British Navy blockade cut Ali's supply line and in return the Sultan granted commercial concessions to Britain[2] through the Anglo-Ottoman treaty.[3]

The development of the global oil industry commenced in 1859 when the first successful drilling was achieved in the United States for what was known as "rock oil"[4] and by 1901 America had begun exporting petroleum products on a global scale. In 1873 the first production in Europe was in Russia followed by Galcia and Romania in 1898.[5] Following these discoveries, newly established companies commenced the refining process of oil.

In Mesopotamia, the trade agreements with the Sultan resulted in Britain becoming a preferential trading partner, which made it a leading foreign commercial partner of the Ottoman Empire.[6] However, following financial difficulties within the Empire, resulting in a loan default in 1875, Britain distanced itself from commercial dealings with the Ottomans and Germany took its place.[7]

The village of Hit, north-west of Ramadi, had been producing bitumen for approximately 5,000 years.[8] In 1871, German experts visited the vilayets of Mosul and Baghdad and provided a good geological report of the area.[9] In the 1890s a French expert surveyed seepage lands in Qayyarah[10] and Tuz[11] for development and distillation.[12] As a result, foreign interest began in the region by European observers M. de Morgan in 1892, A.F. Stahl in 1893, Colonel S.R. Maunsell in 1897 and Baron von Oppenheim in 1899.[13]

3.2 The first oil companies in Iraq, oil concessions and discovery

The first concession was granted to the German-owned Ottoman Railway Company of Anatolia in 1888, which provided Deutsche Bank with priority rights in mining developments including oil and petroleum.[14]

After 1890, Royal Dutch headed by J.B. August Kessler explored the resources of the Netherlands East Indies. Samuel Brothers, London merchants, began distributing petroleum products on a successful scale, leading to the building of their own oil tanker in 1892.[15] By 1897, Samuel Brothers founded Shell Transport and Trading Company and merged their marketing activities with the Asiatic Petroleum Co in 1903.[16]

In the same decade, in Istanbul, Calouste Gulbenkian studied reports of oil in Baghdad and Mosul and reported to the Ministry of Mines in Turkey.[17] This led the Sultan to decree a transfer of oil revenues, derived primarily from by-products such as lamp oil, from the Treasury to the Privy Purse in 1890 and 1899.[18]

On 28 May 1901, the Glasgow-based Burmah Oil Company[19] signed a concession agreement with the Persian government for the exploitation of oil resources throughout the Persian Empire.[20] This agreement covered an area subsequently known as the transferred territories in Iraq, where the International Frontier Commission of 1913–1914 transferred areas from Persia to Turkey. The territories included Naftkhana, which produced the first evidence of potential commercial oil production in Iraq.[21]

In 1903, following discussions in 1888, Germany secured a contract with the Sultan of the Ottoman Empire, Abdülhamid II, to build a railway from Berlin to Baghdad. As part of the contract, the Germans could exploit minerals 20 kilometres either side of the railway line.[22] Due to a destruction of Russian oil fields following riots in 1905, Germany and Royal Dutch collaborated on the railway project as a shared interest in developing oil fields in the Ottoman Empire.[23] At around the same time due to the widespread use of oil fuel in merchant navy steam vessels,[24] the British became aware of the need to move its naval fleet from coal power to oil. In 1903, trials commenced on vessels and submarines to improve efficiency.[25]

In April 1906 Calouste Gulbenkian[26] established the Dutch-British venture Royal Dutch Shell through discussions with Henri Deterding's Royal Dutch company and Marcus Samuel's British Shell Transport & Trading Company.[27] Three years later, Burmah Oil Company, which had operational control of a concession in Iran, formed the Anglo-Persian Oil Company (APOC) (predecessor to the Anglo-Iranian Oil Company, or BP), which shortly thereafter managed to find substantial crude oil deposits.[28]

Royal Dutch and Shell formed subsidiaries in 1907, comprising three-fifths Dutch and two-fifths British shareholding, the Anglo-Saxon Petroleum Company (ASPC) and Bataafsche Petroleum Maatschappij (BPM), with head offices in London and the Hague.[29]

By 1912, the British Government was ready to convert its fleet and entered into oil deals with companies including Royal Dutch Shell.[30] The same year, a Royal

Commission investigated a supply of fuel to the Admiralty by APOC.[31] These investigations into oil fuel led to the replacement of coal in warships by 1914.[32] The report suggested that the Treasury should acquire 51% of APOC's shares and two government directors should be appointed to the board. A fuel supply contract was agreed between the Government and APOC in May 1914.[33] The recommendations were converted to legislation, which received Royal Assent six days prior to the outbreak of World War I in August 1914.[34]

In 1912, in anticipation of oil and gas concessions from the Ottoman Empire in Mesopotamia as a result of the discoveries made by APOC, the Turkish Petroleum Company (TPC) was established through a collaboration between Royal Dutch Shell and British financiers controlling the National Bank of Turkey and Deutsche Bank which had formed the African & Eastern Concessions Ltd a year earlier.[35] A Protocol dated 4–17 November 1913 was entered into by the Ottoman government acknowledging APOC's rights under the Transferred Territories, areas transferred from Persia to Turkey upon the delimitation of the Turco-Perisan frontier.[36]

By 1914 oil was the main fuel in naval fleets, in addition to its use for lighting and the development of the combustion engine.[37] The following year, global oil production had reached 432 mb/y,[38] of which half came from the Middle East, a significant increase from just over 146 mb/y[39] in 1900 and just over 29 mb[40] in 1880.

In 1914 Gulbenkian, through discussions with the rulers of the Ottoman Empire engaged TPC in the first oil and gas concession covering much of Iraq. By 1914 the British government held a controlling interest in APOC, which purchased the British interest in the National Bank of Turkey. TPC's shareholding was divided between the National Bank of Turkey (50%), Gulbenkian (with a 5% non-voting shareholding) and the remaining 45% split equally between Deutsche Bank and Royal Dutch Shell.[41]

The Sykes-Picot Agreement[42] of 1916 sought to establish a division of the Middle East between the French and British in the event of victory in World War I. The terms of the agreement and division of the Middle Eastern territories were ratified in 1920 during the San Remo conference and signed as a peace treaty with Turkey, dividing the Arab countries under Turkish rule into British and French mandates.[43] The French mandate regions included Syria and Lebanon. The British mandate under the League of Nations included Mesopotamia and Palestine. The San Remo Agreement excluded US participation, to their subsequent annoyance, and Britain and France refused to allow US companies into the area until several years later. The US State Department protested on discovery of the agreement, through its ambassador in London, falsely claiming that Britain was attempting to dominate world oil supplies, even though in 1919 the United States controlled 82% of world oil.[44] In the correspondence, the United States reminded Britain that it had assisted in the war and therefore was entitled to a share of the spoils.[45]

In 1916, Mosul and the surrounding area had been assigned to the French region of the Sykes-Picot Agreement and later became the subject of an ongoing dispute between France and Britain. The matter was resolved in December 1918 by agreement between M. Clemenceau and Lloyd George by incorporating Mosul as part of British controlled Iraq which was later confirmed by the British Mandate from the League of Nations.[46] The key provision for Iraq's later admission as a member of the League, as will be explained later, is found under Article I[47]:

> Any fully self-governing State, Dominion or Colony not named in the Annex may become a Member of the League if its admission is agreed to by two-thirds of the Assembly, provided that it shall give effective guarantees of its sincere intention to observe its international obligations, and shall accept such regulations as may be prescribed by the League in regard to its military, naval and air forces and armaments.

The United States suggested an open-door policy to the British Foreign Office in an attempt to permit prospecting for oil in Iraq from 1919 onwards, which was refused by the British and French governments. A provisional agreement was reached in 1922 permitting US companies to enter Iraq through the acquisition of shares in TPC. In 1923, it was agreed that the US shareholding should derive APOC's 47.5% share in exchange for a 10% overriding royalty on all oil produced by TPC.[48]

The San Remo Agreement of 24 April 1920 provided for French participation in the event of oil exploitation in Iraq, by assisting with transportation pipelines through Syria in exchange for share capital in any private petroleum company created by "native" governments.[49] The Treaty of Sevres of 10 August 1920 was signed by the Turkish government and divided the Ottoman lands between the French and British, the treaty was subsequently replaced by the Treaty of Lausanne on 24 July 1923. The most significant issue arising from the Lausanne Treaty was the demarcation of Mosul which was divided between French Syria and British Iraq.[50]

Since the time of the British mandate, Iraqis have opposed foreign intervention in their government. Seven months following acceptance of the mandate, the British government[51] approved the High Commissioner, Sir Percy Cox, to manage the Iraqi government one month after his own appointment, on 11 November 1920.[52] The new state of Iraq was formed in 1921 combining the former Ottoman regions of Mosul, Baghdad and Basra.[53]

A provisional Cabinet known as the Council of State was appointed by Commissioner Cox in 1921, comprising eight ministers representing the ministries of interior, finance, justice, defence, education and health, public works and commerce and Awqaf.[54] Nine other ministers were also appointed without a portfolio. According to official British government reports[55] there was a "marked tendency in favour of a monarchy ...".[56] Amir Faisal was selected as "a candidate for the throne", probably due to his services to the Allies during World War I.[57] The lack of reference in the report to the consideration of any other candidates implies that there were no alternative recommendations for the post. In June 1921, the British Government announced its approval of the candidature following a referendum where the overall majority favoured Faisal and bestowed him with the title of King Faisal I of Iraq and his formal accession took place in Baghdad on 23 August 1921.[58]

The first Iraqi Council of Ministers, having been selected by Cox, was appointed by Royal Decree on 10 September 1921 and replaced the Council of the State.[59] In October 1922, a Treaty of Alliance was signed containing an article that the British government would secure the admission of Iraq to the League of Nations as soon as possible.[60] A protocol to the Treaty was negotiated in April 1923, providing that the Treaty would terminate upon Iraq becoming a member of the League of Nations and, in any event, no later than four years after the ratification of peace with Turkey (due to an ongoing dispute over the Iraq-Turkey border). The Treaty of Alliance was finally ratified on 10 June 1924.[61]

In 1923, definite proposals for exploration were provided to the Iraqi government by TPC, who were obliged to honour the 1914 Ottoman agreement. Initially the government demanded participation in share capital of TPC but in lieu of this they accepted royalty payments on a tonnage basis.[62] There was interference in the negotiations by the United States who insisted on their involvement in oil exploration under the open-door policy, which prevented TPC from obtaining exclusive rights over the vilayats and led to the introduction of a plot-based system of development permitting participation of the other companies to bid for plots and prospecting rights. The system was agreed and a Convention between the Iraqi government and TPC was concluded on 14 March 1925. This agreement would be supplemented on several occasions in the 1930s with subsidiaries and affiliates of the original companies to cover essentially all of Iraq.

When the Treaty was presented to the League of Nations, in September 1924, a resolution was approved which gave effect to Article XXII of the Covenant of the League. There was a definite acceptance that admission of Iraq to the League of Nations would terminate the mandatory obligations of the British government.[63]

On 21 March 1925, the Organic law, otherwise known as the first constitution of Iraq, was passed which provided that legislative power vested in a Parliament with a King. Parliament was to comprise a Senate, consisting of twenty members appointed by the King, and Chamber of Deputies, consisting of one Deputy per 20,000 male Iraqis.[64] The first Iraqi Parliament met under the new constitution on 16 July 1925. Ministers and deputies were elected pursuant to the electoral Law of August 1924, with the cabinet comprising six to nine ministers for a six-month seat unless they become a Senator or Deputy.[65]

On 30 August 1925, a concession agreement was entered into by the Iraqi government with APOC, under the name of its subsidiary Khanaqin Oil Company, which was later supplemented by an additional agreement dated 24 May 1926.[66] The same year, the TPC was provided with 24 rectangular plots each comprising eight square miles with the remaining plots put up for public auction.[67] By the end of 1926 the TPC had conducted surveys and selected ten locations for testing.[68]

On 16 December 1925, a resolution was passed by the Council of the League of Nations to provisionally fix Iraq's border with Turkey which would only become permanent if Iraq became a permanent member of the League and the British mandate continued for another twenty-five years. On 5 April 1927, test drilling began with the first oil being struck at Baba Gurgur near Kirkuk on 14 October 1927.[69]

The High Commissioner opened discussions with King Faisal in the spring of 1927 regarding the recommendation for Iraq's admission to the League of Nations. The British government subsequently examined the report of the High Commissioner but considered that a recommendation for membership would be premature and not in the best interests of Iraq resulting in the suggestion that the recommendation should be deferred to 1932 provided the country's progress was maintained.[70] This decision appears to relate to the investigation and subsequent discovery of oil. By spring of 1927 the British government would have been aware, through its participation in the TPC and reports from the High Commission in Iraq, of the potential production of oil and the subsequent contracts to be negotiated.

In order to gain access to the region, the United States negotiated with France and Britain. In October 1927, the American oil companies[71] formed the Near East Development Corporation to accept the transfer of half of APOC's shares in the TPC.[72] This was a strategic decision by the founding parties of APOC as a result of the open-door policy invoked by the US government when it realised that revenues could be made from the Middle East. The open-door policy provided for equal access for US capital and business and when combined with the US Mineral Leasing Act 1924 meant that the US government could deny "access to drilling rights on public lands to foreign interests who denied similar access to US companies and was aimed specifically at the Dutch in the East Indies and the British in the Middle East".[73] To formalise the change in shareholding of TPC, an agreement was signed on 31 July 1928,[74] famously known as the Red Line Agreement, which forced the company to act as a non-profit supplier of oil to its shareholders on condition that they would not operate independently in the region formerly controlled under Ottoman rule.[75] This agreement permitted the American companies to be represented in the Middle East. Gulbenkian maintained a 5% shareholding in all oil extracted from the countries under the agreement with the remaining 95% equally divided between Royal Dutch Shell, Anglo-Persian, Compagnie Francais des Petroles (CFP) (predecessor to TotalFinaElf) and the Near East Development Company[76] (headed by Walter Teagle, chairman of Standard Oil[77]).[78] Countries subject to the agreement included Turkey, Saudi Arabia, Iraq, Syria, Lebanon, Oman, Yemen and the Trucial coast but it excluded Iran, Kuwait and Trans-Jordan.[79] The Americans were allocated Saudi Arabia and subsequently exploited its oil,[80] while France maintained its mandate in Syria and Lebanon and Britain in Iraq and Palestine.

APOC drilled an area of approximately 40,000 feet in the Transferred Territories by 1929 covering the two sites of Chia Surkh and Naft Khana. In 1930, the total crude production was 894.26 million barrels[81] extracted from Baba Gurgur and Naft Khana.[82]

In November 1927, once informed of the refusal of the British government to support Iraq's admission for membership to the League, the Iraqi government reopened negotiations of the 1922 Treaty and its agreements.[83] A treaty was signed on 15 December 1927, which provided that the British government would secure the admission of Iraq to the League in 1932, conditional upon maintaining the rate of progress at the time. Copies of the Treaty were sent to the Council of the League of Nations but at their 54th session in March 1929 the issue was adjourned on grounds that negotiations were still in progress as the Financial and Military accords had still not been agreed.[84] The non-agreement caused the Iraqi cabinet to resign, and three months later a new cabinet was formed which decided to abandon these subsidiary agreements on the understanding that the undertaking of the British Government regarding admission to the League would not be withdrawn by them and relations between Britain and Iraq would be conducted in accordance with the 1922–1924 and 1926 treaties and agreements.[85]

Without qualification, on 14 September 1929 King Faisal was informed that Iraq would be supported by the British government for candidature for admission to the League in 1932.[86] Formal negotiations opened in April 1930, which concluded in June of the same year resulting in a treaty to regulate Iraqi-British relations and based generally on the proposals of the Anglo-Egyptian settlement published in August 1929 by the British government.[87] The treaty was ratified on 26 January 1931, and Iraq became a full member of the League of Nations on 3 October 1932.[88]

Following the attainment of full membership of the League of Nations, a seventy-five year concession was awarded to Mosul Petroleum Company (MPC) with a similar concession awarded to Basra Petroleum Company (BPC) six years later.[89] The three companies of MPC, BPC and Iraq Petroleum Company (IPC) were all owned in equal shares of 23.75% by the predecessors to BP, Shell, CFP, Mobil and the Near Eastern Development Corporation (owned by Standard Oil of New Jersey – now Exxon). The remaining 5% went to the Participation and Exploration Company owned by Gulbenkian.[90]

From the time of its creation, Iraq suffered internal weaknesses due to its diverse population comprising various ethnic and religious groups. In the 1930s, particularly following independence in 1932, the idea of pan-Arabism developed in Iraq as a means of obtaining legitimacy and domestic political support. There was significant anti-British sentiment in Iraq from the early 1920s which in 1941 resulted in a military clash with the British in 1941 during World War II.[91]

Beginning in 1934, the crude available as a consequence of the 1927 discovery was shipped by pipeline to the Iraqi town of Al-Hadithah, where the pipeline then split and sent on for export from Iraq to either the Lebanese port city of Tripoli or what was then the British Palestine mandate city (and is now the Israeli city) of Haifa. The latter route took the oil across British-controlled Jordanian territory and the former across French-controlled Syrian territory.

Internally, 1936 saw the commencement of military coups within Iraq and generally across the Arab world. The mildly conservative governments from 1921 to 1956 saw key violent military coups in an attempt to modernise the country in 1936 by Bakr Sidqi, 1941 by 'Abd al-Rahman 'Arif, 1952 by Abd al-Salamand and 1956 by 'Abd al-Karim Qasim.

In the early stages, export levels on the Haditha pipeline were low. However, by 1938, Iraq began exporting increasing amounts of crude over the route, reaching approximately 550,000 barrels annually, from 1938 until the commencement of major hostilities associated with World War II and the closing of the Mediterranean to commercial shipping.

3.3 Recent history

With the onset of World War II, exports of oil through Tripoli and Haifa ceased. IPC then became instrumental in the construction of crude oil refineries in Tripoli in 1939 and in Haifa in 1940. Due to the perilous nature of seagoing commerce in the Mediterranean severely restricting exports, oil was produced for regional use. Despite the expectations of the Iraqi government, TPC and its successor delayed wide-scale crude oil production until 1940 in an attempt to provide TPC and IPC with a means to better regulate total Middle East production and consequent price levels. The delay in wide-scale production as well as the revenue structure of TPC/IPC concession agreements, the building of refineries and Iraqi participation in IPC became sources of constant irritation with the Iraqi government.[92]

A glut would push oil prices downwards, so any single oil company was required to regulate its production to meet market demand at a price that would maximise profits and assist global investors in the industry.[93] The posted price was set at oil exporting terminals in the Perisan Gulf and Eastern Mediterranean with oil sold on a f.o.b. basis.[94] Due to the niche market of buyers, setting the oil price became an administrative decision rather than a reflection of market forces. United States Gulf of Mexico (USGM) set the foundation of the historical pattern for the posted oil price structure until 1941. A purchaser was billed the ruling price of USGM plus freight, irrespective of the source of supply.[95] Therefore, the Iraqi purchaser of oil would be charged prices issued on USGM quotations which did not reflect the fact that (a) crude produced in Iraq was low-cost, (b) it was refined locally and (c) it was marketed by a local company.[96] Thus the overall cost was far less than USGM production, which resulted in Iraqi purchasers paying an unnecessary premium and the oil companies gaining a significant profit.

In March 1947, Salih Jabr was elected as prime minister and was the first Shi'a head of government. Between 1939 and 1947 the cost of living increased by 800% while the unskilled wage increased by only 400%.[97] In addition, consecutive years of drought and a locust plague resulted in an unprecedented food shortage, which led to famine in the autumn of 1947 and winter of 1948.[98] Iraq demanded repayment of frozen assets held in London banks in addition to the debts incurred by Britain for Iraqi oil purchased during the war.[99]

The United Nations debated a partition plan for Palestine in the autumn of 1947 and Iraq led the Arab states in opposing the plan.[100] On 31 August 1947 the United Nations submitted recommendations for the partition of Palestine into Arab and Jewish states. Jabr, immediately sought to convene the Arab heads of state, undermining the status of Egypt and the Arab League. On 6 January 1948, an Iraqi delegation led by Jabr went to England for negotiations in Portsmouth, during the negotiations anti-British conflicts broke out on the Iraqi streets against the police.[101] Nine days later, a draft treaty was signed removing some of the restrictions on Iraqi independence.[102] Britain retained control of its military bases and the ability to sail warships in the Shat Al-Arab without prior approval of the Iraqi government.[103] The following day, news of the treaty in Iraq led to strikes and demonstrations by college and high school students demanding a rejection of the treaty.[104] The demonstrations escalated into riots where many demonstrators were injured on bridges over the Euphrates from 19 to 21 January 1948.[105] On 26 January 1948, one hundred people were killed in further escalation of the riots, which led to the resignation of Jabr on 27 January 1948 and the appointment of Mohammad Sadr.[106]

Following the conclusion of World War II, exports of crude and some refined products resumed. At the outbreak of the 1948 war in Palestine between Arabs and would-be Israelis, shipments of crude by pipeline to Haifa were interrupted and permanently ceased.[107]

From various analyses, the revenue structure proved problematic for two reasons. The first was that IPC and its predecessor were established as simple production and transportation enterprises that would deliver crude oil to their organisers[108] which would themselves sell the crude on the international market and retain the profit. Second, the 1925 concession for TPC failed to contain terms detailing a clear and transparent formula to ensure that Iraq would receive substantial royalties, taxes and profits for granting rights to produce oil and gas.

Prior to nationalisation,[109] IPC produced oil on behalf of its shareholders who determined the volume output. The 1948 agreement among IPC shareholders stipulated that each partner must submit its oil requirement for a five-year period, five years before the commencement of that period. This provided for delivery to be made at cost of production to shareholders' terminals in the Mediterranean.[110]

The United States became a net importer in 1948 and would rely upon importing low-cost foreign oil to meet its increasing energy demands.[111] The year 1949 marked the beginning of economic recovery for Iraq following the depression of World War II and the Wathba crisis of 1947–1948.[112] Income from oil increased from £2.3 million in 1945 to £4.388 million in 1949, increasing to £84.6 million in 1958. According to Eppel, two factors contributed to the escalation in revenue, namely (1) the recovery of the global economy and application of the US Marshall Plan, which resulted in the expansion of output as a result of increased global demand and (2) new agreements between the Iraqi government and IPC obliging IPC to increase Iraq's profit share through expanding output.[113]

By the 1950s, the combination of increasing post-World War II global economic development and the absence of opportunity to export through Haifa resulted in a push to produce crude from fields in the southern portion of Iraq, with discoveries in Zubair in 1948, Rumaila and Bai Hassan in 1953 and Jambur in 1954. From these fields, crude could be exported directly from Iraq, through the Persian Gulf port city of Basra, rather than having to pass initially through intermediaries such as Syria in order to reach the export point of Tripoli.[114]

In 1950, an agreement was negotiated between IPC and the government, which increased Iraqi government royalties from four shillings to six shillings per barrel. This agreement was revised and superseded by another agreement in March 1952 providing that 50% of IPC profits would be given to the Iraqi government, at least 30 million tons of petroleum would be produced annually, the royalties to the government would be at least £20 million per year in 1953–1954 rising to £25 million per year from 1955 onwards, and Iraqi citizens would be included at managerial levels within IPC.[115]

Price controls were removed by the US Office of Price Administration in 1950 and Middle East prices were publicly posted for the first time resulting in competition with United States' and Venezuelan oil. As a result of the United States losing its position as a key oil exporter, the Middle East broke links with USGM pricing.[116] The change in pricing structure coincided with the renegotiations and amendments to the seventy-five-year concession agreements in 1951 replacing fixed royalties with 50% profit through Iraqi government income tax. This resulted in the government obtaining a direct interest in crude prices for the first time.[117]

In 1951, the Iraqi Civil Code was enacted. Article 25 of the Code provided Iraqi law as a specific choice of law in commercial contracts and where the choice of law is silent, the place of contract would be the applicable law unless expressly agreed to the contrary. The same year, nationalisation of the industry in Iran led to negotiations between IPC, MPC and BPC resulting in an agreement in 1952 with the Iraqi government.[118] Two key provisions of the agreement were:

1 The fixed payment per unit of production was replaced by a new formula of profit sharing where the government would receive 50% of the annual profits of the companies, calculated on the basis of the difference between the posted price of oil exports and cost of production.
2 The government was entitled to receive f.o.b. seaboard terminal up to 12.5% of net production and to sell it on at whatever price it could obtain.[119]

In 1953, Zubair was the only producing field in Southern Iraq with three million tons per year rising to 4.5 million tons per year in 1954.[120] Late 1953 saw development in Rumaila with the commencement of production in 1954. By 1960, 38 wells had been drilled in Zubair and twenty wells in Rumaila. BPC produced 3.07 million tons per year in 1953 rising to 12.3 million tons per year in 1959.[121]

In February 1955, the Middle East Treaty Organization, also known as the Baghdad Pact, was formed. Iraq, Turkey, Iran, Pakistan and the United Kingdom were members. The organisation was intended to counter the threat of Soviet expansion into vital Middle East oil-producing regions.[122]

Outside Baghdad in 1955, work commenced on the Daura plant,[123] the first oil refinery in Iraq. In November 1956, the Syrian army destroyed the IPC's mid-desert pipeline stations disrupting exports for eighteen months[124] recovering to pre-1956 levels by June 1958 at approximately 25 million tons per year. A plan for an alternative pipeline through Turkey to a Mediterranean port was first considered around 1958 to increase exports.[125]

October 1956 saw the commencement of the Suez Crisis and riots occur in Mosul, Baghdad and Najaf.[126] Iraq sided with Britain, France and Israel in a failed attempt to seize back the Suez Canal from Egypt in 1956.[127]

Prior to the 1956 Suez Crisis, the price of Iraqi oil exported from Basra was $1.87 per barrel, which had been discounted by 11–13 cents per barrel by late 1958.[128] Following the attack on Egypt by Britain and France, Nuri Al-Sa'id attempted to distance Iraq from the colonial powers by breaking relations with France and excluding Britain from Baghdad Pact meetings.[129] However, the actions of Al-Sa'id to promote pan-Arabism came too late, as it could not prevent the public discontent with Iraq's association with Britain, which ultimately led to the revolution two years later.

In 1957, in order to protect its domestic industry from the effects of cheap Middle Eastern oil, the United States restricted oil imports primarily on a voluntary basis converting to a mandatory basis in 1959.[130] The global oil industry saw a further change in 1958, when Soviet oil re-entered the world market in an attempt to regain the 19% market share it held in the 1930s.[131]

In February 1958, due to hostilities between Iraq and Egypt following the Suez Crisis, Syria and Egypt formed the United Arab Republic (UAR). In retaliation, Jordan and Iraq formed the Arab Union as a defence to the UAR.[132]

In 1958, the IPC provided the Iraqi government with a loan of £25 million to assist in the maintenance of the development programme.[133] The revolution of July 1958 resulted in government emphasis on a political rather than economic relationship with the IPC.[134] Iraq began to establish links with the Soviet Union and Eastern Europe following the revolution by Abdul Karim Qasim, overthrowing the monarchy in 1958. In addition, one of the first measures brought in by the revolutionaries was to de-link the British pound from the Iraqi Dinar.

In September of the same year, the government communicated to the IPC group that greater revenues were expected from accelerated production and it would invoke the terms of its letter of September 1951, that in the event of a neighbouring country receiving higher average revenue per ton of oil than was received by Iraq, the government would claim a similar amount.[135]

Since the revolution, the new government took clear steps to increase political interference in the oil industry. In August 1958, the Government Refineries Administration was established to effect decisions under the Ministry of Economics and the Cabinet. In mid-1959, a new law was passed establishing a General Committee for Oil Affairs with a list of duties governing all aspects of the industry.[136] The same year the Iraqi government covered refining operations through the Government Oil Refining Administration (GORA) which was autonomous until 1959. GORA announced in July 1960 that it intended to build a large refinery in Basra at a cost of £20 million with two million barrels per year throughput.[137]

The Qasim regime did not have any meaningful planning which led to a plundering of wealth by foreign and local interests due to the dependency of the economy on foreign imperialism.[138] Iraq was seen as a market for foreign capital goods and an exporter of raw materials as well as low-cost oil.[139] There was heavy foreign intervention in the Iraqi oil industry including the composition of the Development Board, which increased Iraq's economic dependence on oil.[140]

In 1958, a decision was made by the government to construct an off-shore mid-sea loading terminal at the head of the Persian Gulf, twenty-four miles from Fao. The terminal was to consist of five platforms and connected to Fao by two, 32 inch pipelines. Fao would receive oil from Zubair through a new pipeline and the result would be two simultaneous tankers loading at a rate of 8,000 tons per hour.[141] Work commenced in 1959 with the intention of completion by 1961. By 1959, jetties and berths at Fao had been extended and strengthened.[142] In 1959, in an attempt to appease the Iraqi government, the BPC agreed to concede twelve miles of territorial waters to the Iraqi government.[143] Under the 1951 agreement with IPC, a proportion of IPC group royalties could be taken in kind. In 1959, the IPC agreed to permit the government to request payment at shorter notice.[144]

The two overriding goals of the Qasim regime, which may be gathered from announcements and official documents of the time according to Alnasrawi, were economic independence and an equitable distribution of wealth and income.[145] The main principles guiding economic policy at the time were:

1 Economic planning is important to guide and direct the whole economy.
2 Curbing monopolies and strengthening the middle class
3 Liberating the economy from imperialism
4 Abolition of the land tenure system
5 Establishing trade relations with all countries
6 Closer economic ties with Arab countries
7 Strengthening and expanding the public sector
8 Encouragement of the private sector
9 A higher rate of economic growth[146]

The Economic Planning Council was established in 1959, and the Ministry of Development was replaced by the Ministry of Planning. A provisional economic plan was adopted for continuity of existing projects to cover the period 1959/1960–1962/1963 with a total expenditure of ID 392 million.[147] A detailed economic plan was adopted in 1961 to cover the period of 1961/1962 to 1965/1966 with expenditure of ID 556 million and revenues of ID 424 million.[148]

On 24 March 1959, Iraq withdrew from the Baghdad Pact,[149] due to the nationalist policies of the new regime. The organisation was renamed the Central

Treaty Organization on 21 August 1959 with its headquarters relocated to Ankara. The impact of the organisation was further weakened by the Turkish invasion of Cyprus and the Iranian revolution of 1979 and was subsequently dissolved on 26 September 1979.[150]

In February 1959, BP reduced its Middle East oil price by 18 cents per barrel. A further round of price cuts ensued in August 1960 with oil at $1.74 at Basra and $2.21 at Eastern Mediterranean prices.[151] The Organization for Petroleum Exporting Countries (OPEC) was formed in reaction to the change in prices, with one of its earliest resolutions being a demand that prices be restored to pre-August 1960 levels and that they be stabilised.[152]

By the end of the 1950s, independent oil companies such as the Japanese Arabian Oil Co and the Ente Nazionale Idrocarburi (ENI) became involved in the Middle Eastern oil industry which displaced integrated oil from some markets resulting in increased surplus capacity and intensified pressure on posted prices.[153] In August 1959, oil was discovered in Bai Hasan and Jambur, 35 miles South East of Kirkuk. Four production wells were drilled from 1954 to 1959, producing oil for local use. Export production commenced in late 1959.[154]

Iraq's proven oil reserves in 1959 were estimated at 26.16 million barrels[155] with royalty payments ranging from £58 million in 1953 to £86.6 million in 1959.[156] The same year, legislation was enacted for the first authorised use of trade unions which provided increased involvement of Iraqi workers in the industry.

By 1960, there was a continued over-supply of global oil due to the investment and development of the industry. This had an adverse effect on prices and created further competition among the oil companies, which in turn resulted in lower oil production. Despite the market position, governments in the Middle East sought to increase production and contractual terms were not complied with.[157] Alternatives to the concession agreements were starting to be introduced, providing governments with more influence in the industry.

The idea of OPEC was created in Baghdad in 1960 and formulated and agreed in Caracas in January 1961, with Iraq as a founder member.[158] The IPC enjoyed almost a complete monopoly of oil production from 1960 to 1965.[159] In the summer of 1960, the government demanded an extra five shillings per ton in duty on crude exported from Basra.[160]

Development and drilling continued in Zubair and Rumaila in 1961 but was then suspended. The government modified the port surcharge at Basra on oil exports in June 1963 as a result of the new pipeline to Fao. Production from BPC fields increased from 83.48 million barrels to 131.72 million barrels from 1960 to 1965 with the major contributor being the Rumaila field.[161]

A series of laws in the 1960s designed to prevent a repeat of the 1925 concession meant that each oil contract would only come into force when parliament passed a specific new law to ratify it. These 1960s laws applied unless legislation was passed to repeal them. Contracts could be approved, amended and challenged by parliament but passing a law to delegate power to sign contracts to a delegate branch of government would arguably provide an element of protection from direct political uncertainty.[162]

In June 1961, Kuwait gained independence from British control, leading Qasim to demand its integration with Iraq. British troops were deployed to Kuwait and later replaced by an Arab League force in August.[163] In July, Barzani of the KDP demanded autonomy for the Kurdish region and fighting broke out in September between Barzani's forces and the Iraqi army.[164]

The many sources of long-standing Iraqi discontent with IPC, with the growing assertiveness around the world of former colonial nations and the rise of pan-Arab nationalism, resulted on 11 December 1961 in the adoption of Law No. 80 nationalising all non-producing fields held by IPC under the 1925 and all subsequent concessions. The enactment of Law 80 was a direct consequence of the conduct of the IPC companies which had worked against the interests of the country and the result of failed negotiations between IPC and the government since 1958.[165] The law permitted only the currently producing fields to be in the hands of the IPC and therefore immediately deprived the company of 99.5% of its concessionary area leaving it with 1,938 square kilometres of the original area of 435,780 square kilometres.[166] Law number 80 reclaimed 99.9% of unexploited areas under the IPC concession agreement and was the first step towards a strategic objective of oil policy in nationalising oil wealth.[167] By 1963, the resolution to restore oil prices to pre-August 1960 levels was abandoned and replaced with an attempt to raise per-barrel revenue. In April 1963, BPC completed work on a deep-water loading base at Khor al-Amaya, twelve miles from the Shatt al-Arab, at a cost of £22 million. By 1966, this base exported more oil than Fao.[168]

In February 1963, a coup d'etat led by the Ba'ath party took control of the country but the ideas of the party were too general and therefore no development programme existed. In November 1963, Abdel Salam Aref took control until his death in November 1966 when he was succeeded by his brother, Abdel Rahman Aref.[169] A five-year economic plan was created for 1965–1969 and was the most articulate to date. Its economic objectives included a rise in the standard of living at a rate of no less than 8% per annum, an annual growth rate of 7.5% for agriculture and 12% for industry in order to reduce dependence on imports and oil as a primary source of income; economic stability was necessary along with expediting the process of Arab economic integration, particularly with Egypt.[170]

In addition, the economic policies to be put in place were (a) full employment and the removal of structural and disguised unemployment, (b) expansion of social services to raise productivity to increase output and welfare (c) wider geographical distribution of planned expenditure to narrow the income gap between urban and rural population (d) economic growth to benefit the poorer classes with limited income.[171]

In February 1964, Law No. 11 was announced which created the Iraq National Oil Company (INOC). At the time, it was expressed by a government official, Al-Wattari, that it was hoped that IPC would co-operate with INOC and deemed its creation was a step towards nationalisation of IPC.[172] Following the enactment of Law No. 80, which was considered to be the most extreme action since the Iranian nationalisation of 1951, Iraq was considered to be the most radical country of OPEC at the time.[173]

INOC was vested with the right to control and produce those untapped fields reclaimed under Law No. 80, amounting to roughly 99.5% of lands formerly under IPC concession. INOC pursued this course through cooperative arrangements with other international oil companies. In response to the 1961 part-nationalisation, IPC threatened to institute lawsuits against anyone found to have purchased products from the Iraqi government or its operating company, INOC. Circumventing the IPC threat, INOC made sure its transactions were barter in nature. The tensions between Iraq and IPC following the 1961 nationalisation of non-producing fields may have suggested to some the wisdom of backtracking on Law No. 80 and attempting to improve relations.

The years 1963 to 1968 saw a steady increase in production except for a steep drop in 1967 due to controversy with Syria arising from pipeline charges and the war with Israel.[174] As part of the nationalist policy, in July 1964, in accordance with Law No. 100 all of the banks, insurance companies and large industrial firms were nationalised. At an international trade conference in Geneva the same year, Iraq presented a paper calling for more equitable distribution of earnings from crude oil sales.[175]

From August 1964 to June 1965 negotiations took place between the Iraqi government and IPC resulting in two draft agreements and two settlements being initialled in June 1965. One of the agreements was for a joint venture to create the Baghdad Oil Company (BOCO) to be owned by INOC and a consortium of CFP, BP, Shell and Mobil. The second agreement resolved issues including a single payment of £20 million from IPC to the Iraqi government to settle outstanding accounting issues.[176]

In 1965, a draft agreement was formed between the IPC and the Iraqi government. The company had accepted participation in a joint company to operate in areas expropriated under Law No. 80.[177] The same year, the INOC law was modified and a new draft was formulated in 1966, which extended the company's powers and authorised it to take over refining and distribution. The board of directors was reconstituted and its authority to borrow increased.[178] In autumn 1966, a national committee of oil experts was established with advisory functions and constituted nine members including two ministers, the governor of the central bank of Iraq and the chairman of INOC.[179] Article 2 of Law 97 revoked Article 3 of Law No. 80 of 1961, restricting areas where INOC commences exploration and any discoveries of oil. INOC could go into partnership "with others" only to the benefit of production with the requirement that all contracts are effected by law. Further, all material and data were to pass to INOC without consideration.[180]

Law No. 97 of 16 August 1967 provided exclusive rights to INOC to develop expropriated territories and specifically prohibited the restoration of expropriated territories in North Rumalia to IPC.[181] The relevant provisions provided that the "exclusive rights to exploit oil and hydrocarbon substances in all Iraqi lands …" go to INOC. Contracts with INOC would not affect public ownership of oil and hydrocarbons.[182] Perhaps unsurprisingly, given its effect, IPC protested claiming Law 97 to be in breach of international law.[183]

INOC was reorganised under Law No. 123 of 1967, which abolished the post of managing director and strengthened the power of the chairman who was to be appointed by Presidential decree and hold the rank of cabinet minister. As a result of Laws 97 and 123, INOC was brought under political control at the same time as discussions were ongoing with the Soviet Union, France and Italy for assistance to be provided to the company.[184] Thus Laws 97 and 123 of 1967 increased the role of INOC in the former concession areas.

On 10 April 1968, Adib al-Jadir announced that INOC would develop North Rumalia and all bids from external companies were rejected.[185] As a result, all IPC's connections with the North Rumalia field were removed. A general declaratory statement of petroleum policy in OPEC member countries was announced in June 1968.[186] The potential for Iraqi oil was recognised at the same time, when it was believed that Iraq would "prove a major and continuous oil provider for the world".[187]

In July 1968 a further coup d'etat saw the leadership change to Ahmed Hassan al-Bakr and the five-year economic plan in place at the time was allowed to run its course due to the absence of an immediate plan to put into effect.[188]

In November 1969, Saddam Hussein was appointed to the Revolutionary Command Council (RCC) and became vice-chairman, thereby propelled into the second most powerful office of the state.[189] On 16 July 1970, the Revolutionary Command Council adopted Resolution 792, the most recent constitution until 2005.[190] The same year, a law of commerce was passed, Law No. 149, later repealed by Law No. 30 of 1984, also known as the commercial code.[191]

In February 1970, the Iraqi government cancelled the remaining provisions of Law No. 80 which could allocate further territory to IPC and made the government position clear in its effort to avoid further dependence on international monopolies.[192] Four months later, Iraq presented a memorandum to an OPEC conference requesting support in its dispute with the IPC companies, which resulted in the adoption of a resolution to safeguard her legitimate interests.[193]

Law number 20 of 1970 dealt with the regulation of trade.[194] The RCC passed a provisional constitution in July 1970, which recognised Kurdish nationalism.[195] The same month, President al-Bakr threatened the BPC that if it did not increase output to approximately 36 million tons, the government would take over spare capacity and export oil itself.[196] The same year, the oil price issue was raised again when the Libyan government successfully negotiated an increase in its posted price and a rise in the tax rate from 50 to 54%. Following the Libyan settlement, the companies unilaterally announced an increase in Middle East posted prices in addition to an increase in the government share of profits from 50 to 55%.[197] Iraq wanted a similar increase in posted prices as had been agreed with Libya. The **LIAMCO v Libya arbitration**[198] set the international standard for nationalisation and provided that compensation must be given to the IOC although the sovereign right to nationalise is lawful and therefore protected.[199]

During that decade, major changes occurred in the world oil market, international monetary system, oil concession regime, oil prices and Iraqi's oil revenue. The United States emerged as an important oil importer, which led to a rise of independent oil companies and a gradual disappearance of excess capacity in oil producing countries.[200]

In addition, changes were taking place in the international oil market with a rapid increase in demand for oil being delivered to the Mediterranean due to the closure of the Suez Canal in 1967 and the war with Israel interrupting supply. Colonel Gaddaffi was engaged in confrontation with the IOCs in Libya. At the same time, Algeria took over a number of foreign oil companies and raised taxes on oil. Algeria and Libya were supported in their policies by OPEC.[201]

At the end of 1970, Standard Oil and BP announced increases in posted prices for Libyan crudes of 30 cents per barrel with effect from 1 September 1970 and an increase of 20 cents per barrel for Iraqi and Saudi crude at Mediterranean ports. OPEC supported Libya, Iraq and Algeria in an attempt to find a formula for application in Gulf countries for price and tax arrangements obtained by Libya and other terms applicable to oil shipped from Gulf ports that had an appropriate and stable relationship to shipments from Mediterranean ports.[202]

By 1971, Iraq and Libya succeeded in obtaining an appropriate and stable price relationship for export for the Mediterranean (separately negotiated) and Gulf ports.[203] In February 1971, a five-year price agreement was signed in Tehran by Iraq for Basra oil. At the same time, the Iraqi oil minister entered into a protocol with the companies reserving Iraq's rights regarding her outstanding financial claims against the IPC group, estimated at $200 million including back payments on account of royalty expensing and underpricing of Basra crude.[204] Libya believed the Tehran agreement to be too low and the term to be too long and therefore signed its own agreement on 2 April 1971 which provided for ten cents more per barrel on the basis of Libya having high-quality, low-sulphur crude (with Iraq and Saudi producing high-sulphur crude, thereby justifying the lower price).[205]

In July 1971 at an OPEC conference, Resolution XXIII 133 was passed providing that member countries should take immediate steps to implement the "principle of participation in existing oil concessions". Less than three months later, the companies were willing to accept participation.[206] Iraq at the time was mindful of the 20% participation promised but never realised under the 1920 San Remo Agreement.[207]

Iraq frequently accused IPC of using reductions in offtake as a means of bringing pressure on the government in negotiations. The National Action Charter was promulgated in November 1971 and declared that the "total liberation of the country's oil resources from foreign exploration and control their subjugation in every respect is a natural aim of the revolution".[208] At the end of 1971, Saddam Hussein announced that the oil companies had been asked to prepare for "decisive negotiations" during the first half of 1972.[209]

In 1971, the Tehran price agreement stabilised taxes and prices for the next five years, which increased per-barrel revenue for Arabian Light Crude from

\$0.91 in 1970 to £1.53 in 1975.[210] By the end of 1972, an agreement was reached by OPEC to change the concession system to allow member countries to purchase an equity interest in operating companies such as ARAMCO and IPC. Governments were allowed to acquire 25% in 1973 rising to 30% in 1978 and 51% by 1982.[211]

Iraq was insisting on moving the headquarters of IPC from London to Baghdad, a continuous audit of company accounts, agreement on the companies procedure manual, payments of expensed royalties from 1964 and agreement on an oil development programme.[212] Talks commenced on 15 January 1972 and were deadlocked despite a five-day adjournment and recommencement on 1 February 1972.[213] According to a Middle East Economic Survey (MEES) report, the IPC companies offered to increase BPC production and export capacity in 1976 by two-thirds.[214]

Oil prices were contentious between the Iraqi government and the oil companies. The consortia often sold the oil at prices favourable to their commercial agendas rather than in accordance with the terms of the concession agreements. In an attempt to address this, Iraq ratified an agreement for the establishment of the Organisation of Arab Petroleum Exporting Countries (OAPEC).[215] This was a logical move for the state given that it was central to the establishment of OPEC twelve years earlier. OAPEC is an organisation created to run alongside OPEC[216] which was established to harmonise the legal systems in Arab oil producing countries and to promote the cooperation and exchange of information between members.[217] This was followed by the ratification of the agreement on 20 January 1972 between six OPEC states of the Arab Gulf and the oil companies concerned dealing with the adjustments for posted oil prices.[218]

On 1 June 1972, Iraq bypassed the OPEC concession system by nationalising IPC and ending foreign control over its oil under Law No. 69 of 1972. Under this law, the Iraqi Company for Oil Operations (ICOO) was established to take over northern oil facilities.[219]

The 1967 Arab-Israeli War enhanced the standing of the pan-nationalist Baath Party in Iraq and other Arab countries. The complete nationalisation of all IPC operations within the country was achieved with the adoption in June 1972 of Law No. 69. The relevant provisions of the legislation are contained within Articles 1, 2, 3, 5, 7, 8 and 10.[220]

On 11–14 November 1972, Baghdad hosted an international seminar entitled, "Oil as a weapon in the struggle against imperialism and Israeli aggression and as a means to the development of an independent national economy".[221] The conference dealt with the issue of nationalisation and the importance of the sovereign right to oil without external interference. The Russians were held in high esteem throughout the conference but this was an opportunity for Iraq to fully vent its anger at the IPC and US dominance of oil with international support. All Iraq had ever wanted, it said, was economic independence and a diversified economy.[222]

Since 1972, Iran had supported the Kurdish rebellion against Iraq. The 1975 Algiers agreement at the OPEC conference resulted in the Shah of Iran renouncing his support for the Kurdish people in exchange for half of the Shatt Al-Arab.[223] For a short period following this agreement Iraq and Iran shared a common interest of driving up OPEC prices.[224]

From 1972 to 1979, six billion barrels per year were discovered by Iraqi exploration teams.[225] On 1 September 1973, the Libyan Revolutionary Command Council issued Law No. 66 nationalising 51% of concession rights of foreign oil companies.[226] On 8 October 1973, the OPEC governments increased oil prices unilaterally to $5.12 per barrel due to the continuing Arab-Israeli war and oil companies failing to respond to its demands to increase the price by $2 per barrel.[227] Following the price increase there was an oil shortage due to Arab producers lowering output and imposing an embargo on oil exports to the United States in a hope of influencing the outcome of the war. This led to panic buying, which in turn increased oil prices. OPEC decided to double the price of oil as of 1 January 1974 to $11.65 per barrel providing governments with revenue of $7 per barrel.[228] Iraq received a higher per barrel revenue as a result of the nationalisation.

On 17 October 1973, following the Arab-Israeli war, OAPEC[229] announced cuts of 15% in production and a 70% increase in oil prices along with an embargo on oil exports to the United States, Netherlands and West Africa due to these countries' support for Israel. OPEC also invoked the use of oil as a weapon against Israel's allies causing an oil price shock. This caused prices to increase 400% from October 1973 to May 1974.[230] The reaction of OPEC was unexpected and caused major concern to US security.

In 1973, the nationalisation of BPC commenced. The combination of nationalisation and OPEC pricing resulted in an increase in Iraqi oil revenue from ID 214 million in 1970 to ID 101.7 billion in 1974.[231] Negotiations between Iraq and IPC companies resulted in company acceptance of longstanding issues since 1955. IPC agreed to a deferred repayment of a £20 million loan provided in October 1970 to July 1971. BPC agreed to use its best endeavours to raise output to 29 million tons in 1971 to full capacity of 35 million tons by 1974.[232]

In 1975, the final step was taken towards complete nationalisation of the oil industry by providing INOC with full control of the oil and gas fields. The Ministry of Oil (MOO) was established in 1976, and by 1987 four entities had been created within the ministry. These were the State Organisation of Gas (SOG), the State Organisation of Oil Refining (SOOR), the State Company for Oil Projects (SCOP) and the State Organisation for the Distribution of Oil Products (SODOP).[233]

The spring of 1979 saw the success of the Iranian revolution. On 16 July 1979, Saddam Hussein confirmed his leadership of the Ba'ath party following the resignation of al-Bakr. To cement his control of the country, on 20 July 1979 at a conference a member of the party "confessed" to a plot against the regime. Two weeks later, five hundred high rank officials were executed by the other members of the party forming various firing squads, in order to test their loyalty to the regime.[234] The same year, Saddam Hussein, aware of the 1921 treaty between Iran and Russia whereby Russia had a right to invade Iran in the event of foreign troops entering the country, and in anticipation of the war with Iran,[235] drew up an Arab Charter, which was signed by six Gulf States to protect the Gulf region.[236] The United States would not move into Iran due to the 1921 treaty.

The overthrow of the Shah in Iran led to Khomeini making an enemy of Iraq. First, Khomeini saw Saddam as an enemy due to his expulsion from Najaf by Saddam at the request of the Shah.[237] Second, he supported Kurdish and anti-Ba'athist revolts in Iraq. Saddam, was worried about Khomeini instigating anti-Iraqi aggression in Bahrain which could hinder Iraq's access to the Indian Ocean and he also wanted to reclaim half of the Shatt Al-Arab which had been given to Iran under the 1975 agreement.[238]

In March 1980, for the first time since the overthrow of the monarchy in 1958, Saddam Hussein established a national assembly and a law was passed for the election of its members.[239] Ayotollah Muhammad Baqr al-Sadr was executed in April. In September, Iraq's military forces invaded Iran. The war escalated by 1984 and Iraq re-established diplomatic relations with the United States to combat Iranian action.[240]

In June the same year, fighting commenced between Iraq and Iran with Saddam officially declaring war in September and Iraqi troops crossing the Iranian border on 22 September 1980.[241] Within a short space of time, Iraq had achieved its military goals with minimal casualties. However, by September 1981 Iran, with a population three times more than Iraq, took on a human wave tactic motivating its army with martyrdom, which caused considerable damage to the Iraqi forces.[242] With US and Russian arms assistance the war continued until 1988.[243] In 1986, Iran captured the al-Faw peninsular.[244] On 20 August 1988, a UN ceasefire was agreed with Iran marking the end of the war.

In May 1987, INOC's activities were merged into MOO and SOG, SOOR and SODOP were disbanded. The same year, the North Oil Company (NOC) and South Oil Company (SOC) were established (similar enterprises to the IPC companies of MPC and BPC). An Oil Exploration Company (OEC) and Oil Distribution and Gas Processing Company (ODGPC) along with the State Oil and Marketing Company (SOMO) were also established.[245]

Throughout the 1990s Iraq's oil production was minimal due to sanctions, which hindered its impact on OPEC decisions during this period.[246] This was particularly painful for Iraq considering that Saudi Arabia was seeing a marked increase in output during this period. The rentier culture of previous decades had collapsed and some economists are of the view that the emergence of Iraq as a developing state rather than an oil rentier state would enable a repositioning of the oil sector without devaluing its importance to the economy. [247]

Saddam alleged that he had discovered that during the Iran war, Kuwait had almost doubled its production quota by stealing some of the oil from the Rumalia field.[248] In March 1989, Kuwaiti oil minister, Ali Khalifa advocated an increase in production to maintain the oil price at $18 per barrel.[249] This policy was rejected by OPEC in June.[250] Saddam saw this as a deliberate attempt by Kuwait to damage the Iraqi economy for its own benefit, particularly in light of the debts incurred from the Iran war. The actions of Kuwait therefore amounted to no less than economic warfare. On 10 July 1990, Gulf oil ministers met in Jeddah where they agreed to comply with OPEC quotas.[251]

In early 1990, due to some members of OPEC exceeding their production quotas, the oil price fell to $12 per barrel which resulted in Iraq having to cut its budget by $6 billion.[252] Saddam saw this as economic war against Iraq, which was trying to recover after the eight-year war. Although Saudi Arabia was the main culprit and greatest obstacle to an increase in oil price, Iraq signed a non-aggression pact in March 1989.[253] Kuwait was not included in the pact as Saddam believed that there was no alternative but to wage war on the Kuwaitis in order to drive up the price of oil to assist in Iraq's economic recovery.[254]

Despite being free from foreign debt since the 1950s, in the 1980s as a result of the Iran war, Iraq had a significant amount of foreign debt. By 1990, this was estimated to be $86 billion comprising $35 billion to western governments and banks, $11 billion to the former Soviet Union and Eastern Europe and $40 billion to other Arab countries.[255] Iraq treated the funds from the Gulf countries as a grant and specifically excluded it from its statement to the UN in 1991, where it claimed that its total external debts as of 13 December 1990, excluding interest, amounted to $42.1 billion.[256] In addition to foreign debts, Iraq later became liable for the reparations to infrastructure in Iran and Kuwait amounting to $97 billion (estimated) and $240 billion, respectively.[257]

The actions of Saddam following the Iraq-Iran war would set the foundation for the justification of the United States invasion fifteen years later.[258] However, the tipping point came on the fateful day in 1990 that Saddam decided to increase Iraq's oil reserves through the acquisition of fields in Kuwait. It was only at this stage that the United States government realised that there was a significant threat to the international oil supply if Iraq were to have a 20% control of global reserves. Inevitably, such a significant amount of oil would strengthen the economy of Iraq along with increasing the global power and influence of Saddam Hussein.

In 1990, Saddam sent his army to Kuwait on the basis that he believed that in addition to stealing oil from Iraq's reserves from the Rumalia field bordering Kuwait, the country was leading a conspiracy among members of OPEC to produce in excess of their national quotas, which would create a downturn in prices thereby preventing Iraq from trading its way to economic recovery following the war with Iran.[259] Having received support from the international community on the Iranian war, on 2 August 1990, Saddam ordered his troops to cross the border into Kuwait. Within 24 hours he declared Kuwait as the nineteenth province of Iraq. Saddam appeared to have seriously miscalculated international reaction to his invasion and on 6 August 1990, the UN Security Council demanded the unconditional withdrawal of Iraq from Kuwait by 15 January 1991 under UNSCR 678.[260]

The UN imposed a total trade embargo and sanctions on Iraq.[261] Operation "Desert Storm" commenced in January 1991 when the United States and allies bombarded Iraq by air resulting in the "liberation" of Kuwait. In April, UN Security Council Resolution 687 demanded Iraqi recognition of Kuwait and the destruction of all of Iraq's non-conventional weapons confirming economic sanctions until full compliance. The Kurdish region was placed under allied protection under UNSCR 688 in 1991,[262] which called for Iraq to end repression of its own population and created a "safe haven" of Erbil forbidding Iraqi aircraft from entering the Kurdish region.[263] Consequently, elections in the Kurdish region were first held in 1992.

On 26 February 1991, Iraqi troops were ordered to withdraw from Kuwait. Of the 40 UNSCRs adopted in 1991, thirteen were in relation to Iraq, twelve of which were the result of Iraq's invasion of Kuwait.[264] The previous year saw fifteen of the thirty-six resolutions passed by the UNSC relate to Iraq, of which three related to Iran and the remaining twelve to Kuwait.[265] By contrast the UNSC issued nine resolutions in total in the period 1980–1988.[266] The actions of Saddam in 1990 were to pave the way for his eventual downfall in 2003.

In 1996, Iraq accepted UNSCR 986 which permitted the export of crude oil every three months to the value of $1 billion in exchange for humanitarian products under the Oil for Food programme. By December, Iraqi oil distribution resumed through pipelines to Turkey and returned to the global oil market.[267]

In November 1998, US congress passed the Iraq Liberation Act where the intention of the US government to interfere with Iraq was made clear. The Act set the groundwork for the invasion and provided covert financial assistance to opposition groups.[268] The following month, the US military commenced "Operation Desert Fox" which comprised an air bombardment by US air force and the RAF in retaliation for non-co-operation with weapons inspections.[269] January to December 1999 saw weekly attacks on Iraq by US and British aircraft. In December 1999, the UNSC passed Resolution 1284 offering to suspend sanctions if Iraq co-operated with weapons inspections for 120 days.[270]

Prior to 1990, Iraq had a fluctuating but stable economy, which was paralysed by UN sanctions from August of that year which went on to cause "systematic destruction" of the economy.[271] The sanctions not only caused financial detriment, with debt and punitive sanctions threatening recovery, but also resulted in a "brain drain" from the country as many academics and well educated individuals moved to different parts of the world, which ultimately affected trade and technology transfer.[272] The UNSCR 661 of 1990 created powers akin to a supreme central planning authority for Iraq based in the United States. This meant that while other economies flourished during the decade, Iraq was isolated and unable to benefit from economic and technological advancement.[273]

3.4 Land ownership in Iraq and sovereignty

The importance of determining the issue of land rights and ownership of resources under public or private law cannot be overstated in the context of Iraq. The reason for this is the complex tribal system, which has been strengthened since the 2003 invasion, and the issue of territorial disputes within the national boundaries. The issue of federalism created by the 2005 Constitution further accentuates the prospective difficulties and scope for disputes over oil-bearing land. In addition, there are potential transnational disputes with Iraq's neighbouring countries.

The right to property has been protected historically through national constitutions worldwide along with international treaties, charters and declarations.[274] The right of ownership, or dominium, is defined as the right to use (usus), exploit (fructus) and dispose (abusus) of the property owned.[275] Since Roman law, the absolute right to property has been a private law right, confirmed by European civil codes which later influenced the civil codes of the Middle East,[276] particularly the French Civil Code in the twentieth century. As a private law right, the State could not appropriate moveable or immovable property without compensation, for the purpose of public necessity.[277] There is a distinction to be drawn between civil law and Islamic law.

Islamic law remains a subsidiary source of law in Iraq as evidenced in the Civil Code of 1951 and the Constitution of 2005.[278] Under Islamic law, property generally falls under the categories of public, state, and private property. These categories are further divided according to ownership through land tenure arrangements, such as private full ownership (*mulk*), state ownership (*miri*), endowment (*waqf*) and common land (*metruke*). Private ownership of property is recognised, although everything ultimately belongs to God. However, where it is in the public interest, private property rights may be infringed for the benefit of the majority. Under the provisions of the Iraqi Civil Code,[279] property is "*every right having a material value*". The Code states that everything is the subject of pecuniary rights except those things that are by their nature incapable of being so subjected (things to which no one may claim possession) or things that are by law excepted from being subject to pecuniary rights.

3.4.1 The Ottoman laws

For the purposes of the current analysis, the relevant legislation is the Land Code of 1858, the Mining Regulations of 1861 and 1888. The Ottoman Land Code of 1858 divides land into five categories of mulk, metruke, miri, waste land not in possession and of a distance of around 1.5 miles from towns and villages (mevat) and lands possessed by the Treasury and dedicated by Imperial sanction for some benefit (mevkufe).[280] Article 107 relates to the ownership of resources and states:[281]

> Minerals such as gold, silver, copper, iron, different kinds stones, gypsum, sulphur, saltpetre, emery, coal, salt and other minerals found on State land, by whomsoever it is possessed, belong to the Treasury. The occupier of the land cannot take possession of any of them, nor claim any share of any mineral which is discovered. Similarly all minerals found on mevqufe land of the takhsisat kind belong also to the Treasury; neither the occupier of the land nor the vakf authority can interfere with regard to it. Provided that in the case of both State and mevkufe land the possessor must be indemnified to the extent of the value of the land which ceased to be in his possession

> and under cultivation owing to the working of the minerals. In the case of metrouke land and mevat land one-fifth of the mines found belongs to the Treasury, and the rest to the person who finds them. In the case of true vakf land the minerals belong to the vakf. Minerals found in mulk land in towns and villages belong entirely to the owner of the soil. Fusible minerals found in tithe paying (uchrie) and tribute paying (kharajie) land belong as to one-fifth to the Treasury, and the rest to the owner of the soil ...

Thus minerals belonged to the state with some exceptions where the owner of the soil would be entitled to them. It is only where minerals are discovered on state land that the discoverer could not take possession as they belong to the Treasury, unless it is true waqf land and belongs to the waqf. Where the minerals are not fusible, then the entire find belongs to the owner of the soil. Minerals found in mulk lands belong entirely to the owner of the soil. Therefore, although the minerals are generally state property, there is scope for private ownership under Ottoman law.

Under the British mandate, the first Iraqi constitution was formulated in 1925. This set the precedent for the state's interaction with oil companies and appears to have been designed to prevent the government granting a monopoly over natural resources without following a stipulated procedure for which it is accountable:[282]

> No monopoly or concession shall be granted for dealing with or using any of the natural resources of the land, nor for any public service, nor shall the State revenues be farmed out, except in accordance with law, provided that where the period relating to them exceeds 8 years, they must in each ease (sic) be the subject of a special law.

The 1951 Civil Code repealed previous land laws in Iraq.[283]

3.4.2 Sovereignty and nationalisation

It is established that resources within territorial boundaries come under the sovereignty of the state. Since the establishment of Iraq under British mandate, the country essentially operated as an oil company for the shareholders of the IPC. Although it became a sovereign state in 1932, control of Iraq's oil was fought for by the government and achieved through the nationalisation of the industry in 1971. Under Law No. 80 of 1961, the government took control of approximately 99.5% of the exploration areas under concession agreements with the IPC and its subsidiaries.[284] These areas were later transferred to the INOC[285] under Law No. 97 of 1967.

Law No. 80 of 1961 set the foundation for the complete nationalisation of Iraq's oil industry a decade later. Iraq achieved full nationalisation of 99.1% of its oil reserves in 1971 pursuant to Law No. 97 of 1971. A common form of state ownership is nationalisation. An alternative form of state ownership is where resources are controlled by a state entity, which can lend itself to quasi-ownership.[286] In the case of the current Iraqi oil industry, it could be argued that the government bodies act as trustees for the citizens through various entities including national oil companies.[287]

Prior to the waves of nationalisation of natural resources, individual expropriation on the grounds of public necessity was an administrative law issue. A definition of nationalisation is provided by the Institute of International Law[288] as:

> Nationalisation is the transfer to the State, by a legislative act and in the public interest, of property or private rights of a designated character, with a view to their exploitation or control of the State, or their direction to a new objective by the State.
>
> (Annuaire 1952, II 279)

When the oil industry in Iraq was fully nationalised, the ownership of oil was under state control. Thus the industry has moved from private ownership to state ownership and the present position appears to be one of public ownership.

3.5 Ownership of Iraqi oil reserves post-2003

3.5.1 Federalism

Although it is written in the Constitution,[289] it is unclear whether Iraq is a truly federal state or whether the federal model is in the national interest. The Constitution divides the country into regions and governorates with a single semi-autonomous Kurdish region in the North. Consequently, Iraq comprises eighteen governorates[290] and the single region of Kurdistan.[291]

Prior to external intervention, predominantly by the United States,[292] Iraq's different religions and ethnic groups co-existed without significant conflict.[293] However, federalism introduced by the 2005 Constitution has sought to introduce a "divide and rule" culture in the country. It would appear that the concept of federalism and its consequences were not fully considered by the Coalition Provisional Authority (CPA) and US administration in the context of Iraq.[294] The initial proposal for federalism in Iraq was provided by Kurdish representatives suggesting a two-region system of Arabs and Kurds in September 2002.[295] The TAL of 2004 sought to provide a compromise position to this suggestion. The proposal for a federal Iraq was pushed through by the KRG as a step towards independence[296] and sought to take advantage of the political disarray to weaken the future control of Baghdad over the rest of Iraq.[297] The KRG appeared to be seeking to secure direct access to oil revenue and to deny Baghdad of a fiscal role as part of its own agenda relating to security concerns, long-term gains and future independence.[298] Control of licencing, collection and distribution of oil revenues is how the central government can maintain national authority. It is therefore critical to the KRG's long-term protection and plans for independence[299] to prevent Baghdad from having control over the Kurdish and other oil producing regions in Iraq.[300] Given the economic instability of the country, a centralised rather than federal system of government would be preferable from an economic, political and strategic perspective to encourage rapid redevelopment and growth but this does not suit the political agenda of the Kurd and to some extent Shi'a groups.[301]

Iraq is historically a secular society with the different religions and ethnic groups co-existing without significant conflict. Control of licencing, collection and distribution of oil revenues is how the central government can maintain national authority.

Introduced in the Constitution by the KRG and supported by the United States and CPA as a mechanism to protect against dictatorship,[302] the commitment to federalism by exiled Iraqis was put to the public for consideration with alternative forms of government even though many would argue that the resulting referendum provided deemed acceptance of the recent position. It is unclear what federalism means in Iraq as there is no definition of the term provided in the Constitution or elsewhere in official documentation.[303] The most effective path to resolving the oil standoff between Bagdad and Erbil and to prevent Basra from claiming political independence is for political cohesion, which will be difficult given the uncompromising stances of the politicians to date.[304] During his term of office, the majority of Iraqis supported Maliki's stance of an anti-Kurdish policy and strong central government.[305] The Council of Ministers took an anti-federal position and compromises within the government are only reached at times of crisis evidenced by action taken at the time of concerns of oil prices and risks to foreign investment.[306]

Writers such as Zedalis[307] have proposed various solutions to the issue. The primary argument being that the Kurdish region should exercise an element of independence from Baghdad in obtaining an automatic share of oil revenues provided that recognition is given to the central government's authority in revenue sharing and contractual drafting.[308] However, this solution is unlikely to be considered a desirable outcome by the central government[309] particularly in light of the fact that the Kurdish region's contribution to the country's revenue is minor and the KRG is already in receipt of what some view as an excessive share of the revenues generated primarily from the South.

3.5.1.1 The meaning of federalism, definitions and implications for Iraq

In Iraq, forced decentralisation occurred following the Iraq-Kuwait war, as a result of a no-fly zone established by the United States, United Kingdom and France over the Kurdish region in the north in April 1991 and August 1992 in the south.[310] This permitted the Kurds to enjoy a level of autonomy not experienced in recent history and reinforced notions of independence from Iraq.[311] The level of power attained is one for which they would fight to maintain and expand.[312] It was using this template provided by the "allied forces" over a decade earlier that set the backdrop post-2003. Despite its history,[313] Iraq appears not to be a country suited to federalism.

Federalism usually refers to a system of government combining regional self-regulation with the intention of accommodating unity and diversity among distinctive groups usually based on their collective religious or ethnic identity.[314] Dicey defines a federal state as "*a political contrivance intended to reconcile national unity and power with the maintenance of 'state rights'*".[315] The political system, rather than having a single central authority, has two or more levels of government "combining elements of shared-rule through common institutions with regional self-rule through the constituent units".[316]

As it is somewhat flexible, there are variations to the criteria for a federal state. Dicey[317] ascribes two conditions for federalism, first, a body of countries "*so closely connected by locality, by history, by race, or the like ... as to be capable of bearing ... an impress of common nationality*".[318] The second condition is the "existence of a very peculiar state of sentiment among the inhabitants of the countries which it is proposed to unite. They must desire union, and must not desire unity".[319] Federalism within a country can be further classified as either a federation or confederation. Federations enable elected general and regional governments to be accountable to their citizens as each possess powers delegated to it by the Constitution, which empower them to directly engage with the citizens in the exercise of taxation, legislation and administration.[320] Confederations occur where "polities are joined together to form a common government for certain limited purposes such as a defence or economy, but the common government is dependent upon the constituent governments".[321] In confederations, in order to conduct its functions, the common government requires the assent of member governments which act as intermediaries with the citizens:[322] this places the common government in a weaker position to deal decisively with contentious subjects or to redistribute resources.[323] Arguably, it is ultimately a confederation that is being sought by the KRG in order to permanently weaken the central government in Iraq particularly in light of its encouragement for other regions to seek independence from Baghdad.[324] The powers provided to the regions under the current Constitution may further this goal.[325] In addition, federacies can "*occur where a large unit is linked to a smaller unit or units, but the smaller unit retains substantial autonomy and has a minimum role in the government of the larger one, and where the relationship can be dissolved only by mutual agreement*".[326]

In order for federalism to occur successfully, national unity should be reconciled with state independence under a Constitution. For Dicey there are three main characteristics of federalism; "*the supremacy of the Constitution, the distribution among bodies with limited and co-ordinate authority of the different powers of government, [and] the authority of the law courts to act as interpreters of the Constitution*".[327] Upon reading the Iraqi Constitution it could be argued that all three conditions are satisfied through Articles 13, 93 and section five although it is evident that section five extends regional powers beyond reasonable expectation. Watts[328] identifies the common characteristics of federations as (1) "*At least two orders of government acting directly on behalf of their citizens*;" this is provided in Articles 1 and 116 of the 2005 Iraq Constitution. (2) "*A formal*

Constitutional distribution of legislative and executive authority and allocation of revenue resources between the orders of government that ensures some areas of genuine autonomy for each order" which is provided through the division of the Constitution in sections four and five where powers are divided between federal and regional levels. (3) "*Provision for the designated representation of distinct regional views within the federal policy-making institutions, usually including the representation of regional representatives in a federal second legislative chamber*" for which see Articles 49 and 65 of the Iraqi Constitution. (4) "*A supreme Constitution not unilaterally amendable and requiring for amendment the consent of a significant proportion of the constituent units either through assent by their legislatures or by regional majorities in a referendum*"; (5) "*An umpire, usually in the form of courts or by provision for referendums ... to rule on disputes over the Constitutional powers of governments*" this is satisfied under Article 93 of the Constitution providing for the federal supreme court to review Constitutional issues in addition to the remit of the Shura Council;[329] (6) "*Processes and institutions to facilitate intergovernmental collaboration in those areas where governmental powers are shared or inevitably overlap*", where Article 105 of the Iraqi Constitution provides for a public commission for this purpose and Article 65 provides for a federation council. There are some problematic provisions of the Constitution, which arguably take the notion of federalism too far, namely Articles 120, 121, 122, 146 and 142.[330]

For Livingston, the "essence of federalism lies not in the institutional or Constitutional structure but in the society itself. Federal government is a device by which the federal qualities of the society are articulated and protected".[331] Given that Iraq comprises essentially two regions, it is unlikely to be considered a truly federal state in accordance with Livingston's views:[332]

> If a society contains territorial groups that are so different from the rest of the society that they require some instrumentality to protect and articulate their peculiar qualities, then the society is likely to provide some means for the creation of such an instrumentality. One such circumstance doubtless does not make a society or a Constitution federal. But two or six or twenty may produce a result that may be properly so called.

It is not solely the Constitution that determines whether a state is federal as federalism is not achieved by labels alone. It is the practical mechanisms in place which create and maintain a federal state as a reflection of the general will of the population.[333]

> ... societies in which the demand for integration is stronger than ... decentralization will produce a set of institutions that is more nearly unitary ... in this sense that federalism is a matter of degree and not of kind ... what determines the federal quality of the government is not only the Constitution that draws the lines of the compromise but the whole pattern of instrumentalities that are employed as a result of these demands.[334]

Federalism is a political label and not a legal definition. There is no law providing the requirements of a federal state and the position becomes legitimised through Constitutional provisions,[335] which give rise to various rights between federal and regional governments. Therefore, on one hand, Iraq is not a federation but it may be considered as such as a matter of degree on a political basis. Thus, if Iraq is a federal state, it is likely to be a federation[336] rather than a confederation or a federacy due to the fact that there is only one region distinct from the rest of the country and the federal government retains substantial control of the governorates despite the powers provided to the region(s) under section five of the Constitution. This is the case as there is no definition provided for the requisite number of regions required to create a federation. In any event, there can be no question as to Iraq's sovereignty and despite the conduct of the KRG as an autonomous region it is not yet an independent state and thus is still subject to Iraq's sovereign rights.

3.5.1.2 The formation of a federal state

One view of federalism is that:

> Federalism is a function not of Constitutions but of societies. Viewed in this way, it will be seen that federalism is not an absolute but a relative term; there is no specific point at which a society ceases to be unified and becomes diversified. The differences are of degree rather than of kind.[337]

During the drafting of the Constitution:

> Kurdish and other secular negotiators slowly began chipping away at a Constitutional Council that could review laws prior to their enactment. … the Kurds were able to force the removal of any reference to prior review of laws.
>
> There is no doubt that ambiguities still remain with regard to how the Court will exercise its judicial review authority pursuant to these two provisions.[338]

Various solutions to the issue of federalism in Iraq have been proposed by academics such as Kelly, Katzman O'Leary, Galbraith and Kane.[339] The primary argument is that the Kurdish region should exercise an element of independence from Baghdad and obtain an automatic share of oil revenues provided that recognition is given to the central government's authority in revenue sharing and contractual drafting.[340] However, as mentioned earlier in this chapter, this solution is unlikely to be considered favourably by the central government, particularly in light of the fact that the Kurdish region's contribution to the country's revenue is relatively minor. The KRG is already in receipt of what some view as an excessive share of the revenues generated primarily from the South.[341] The selling point for federalism in Iraq has been that it prevents a return to the Saddam era position, which is a fallacy as conditions for dictatorship require more than a centralised state,[342] and thus cannot be the driving factor for such a serious division of a resource-rich country. The weakness of the arguments in support of creating a federal Iraq are compounded by the fact that such a situation would fall into the imperial notion of 'divide and rule'. It is perhaps trite to note that a divided country will take longer to make decisions and therefore regulation will be slower as consensus is required from the various regions which can result in political game-playing prolonging the decision-making process. In Iraq, due to its undeveloped oil wealth, it is necessary for a centralised government to be able to react quickly to the needs of the oil sector for the country's benefit as a whole as well as international market demands. Thus power should remain centralised for key economic decisions and control of all hydrocarbon resources, with legislative checks and balances through a strong oil law and competent committees to oversee sector regulation to prevent political abuse.[343]

3.5.2 CPA orders and transitional provisions

The CPA orders are not the first instance of US interference. There are many bills relating to Iraq, which passed through Congress in the period of 1990–2003.[344] It is beyond the scope of this book to engage in detailed analysis of their legitimacy as we are concerned with more recent events. However, it is worthy of note that there are commentaries on the authority of the CPA in Iraq in the transitional stage.[345]

The CPA took control of the political and administrative system in Iraq from 16 May 2003 to 30 June 2004 and in that time issued twelve regulations, hundred orders, seventeen memoranda and twelve public notices.[346] Section 2 of the first regulation, dated 16 May 2003 maintains the authority and enforcement of all pre-2003 legislation.[347] On 1 June 2004, political and administrative authority passed from the CPA to the Iraqi Interim Government[348] guided by the CPA,[349] TAL, preceding legislation and regulations pursuant to CPA Order 100. There are no CPA provisions directly regulating the oil industry or providing for contractual conditions, therefore the applicable legislation regulating oil agreements entered into post-2003 is the pre-existing legislation. The justification and authority provided for the post-2003 agreements are an exception under the INOC law of 1967.

CPA Order 36 makes it a criminal offence to breach the regulatory code requiring authorisation documents for the transportation, sale and export of oil. The CPA trade liberalisation policy does not apply to oil imports and exports.[350] Pursuant to CPA Order 87, the Office of Government Public Contract Policy was established to oversee the procurement of public contracts.

3.5.3 The 2005 electoral process and subsequent developments

Separate elections took place in all eighteen provinces of Iraq in January 2005. The TAL envisaged the separation of powers between all of the provinces and the federal government.[351] The Kurdish region is dominated by Erbil, Sulaimaniya and Dohuk which are part of the territories of the three other provinces of Ninevah, Diyala and Kirkuk. Thus in addition to being an autonomous region it also has a relationship with the federal government as part of Iraq's provinces thereby creating an overlapping jurisdiction in this two-tier system.[352]

It has been suggested that the TAL "*formed the basis of the permanent Constitution to such an extent that there was very little manoeuvre between the two iterations*".[353] However, there is a significant difference between the provision for the management of oil resources under Article 112 of the Constitution and Article 25(E) of the TAL in that the latter provided for exclusive federal authority over natural resources with management to be "in consultation with" the regions and governorates; these provisions are not found in the Constitution. The Kurds were so determined to influence the wording of the Constitution that they had a team of experts in place when Paul Bremer was negotiating the drafting process.[354] The difficulty of having US assistance in constitutional drafting is that problems inherent in the US Constitution were transferred. Kelly notes that Constitutional ambiguity remains in the United States despite attempts over two centuries to resolve it. The evolution of the US Constitution is a regular matter of debate in the US Supreme Court.[355] Thus, by creating a federal state in Iraq ambiguity has been created where it did not previously exist resulting in a lack of clarity which is likely to continue until the Constitution is amended. This creates instability for the oil industry which requires a solid foundation to foster development and growth. Continual debate as to the interpretation of Article 112 and related provisions would not be beneficial and likely to maintain instability. Article 141 of the Constitution protects Kurdish law and is considered an insurance policy by Kelly[356] even though it could be revised by a future review committee.

Prior to 2003, the oil in Iraq was nationalised and subject to the control of the regime, therefore ownership and exploitation of the resource was not an issue. When considering the expansion of the Kurdish authority regarding natural resources, Article 112 of the Iraqi Constitution must be considered alongside Article 25(E) of the TAL which places management of natural resources within the exclusive power of the federal government.

It is worthy of note that "in consultation with" in Article 25(E) of TAL was removed in Article 112 of the Iraqi Constitution. Thus the formulation of policies and management of oil and gas on one interpretation could mean that the federal government is unable to engage in activities relating to the oil industry without the involvement of the "producing governorates and regional governments". However, such a stringent interpretation would be absurd given the provision of Article 111. It is suggested that the intended interpretation of Article 112 is that the federal government is to take account of the viewpoints of the regional and producing governorates by way of consultation but this by no means results or implies that such views must be acted upon if it is not in the overriding interest provided under Article 111.

Several commentators promoting the Kurdish view[357] have stated that Article 112 was a resounding victory for the KRG, providing them with more power than originally set out in the transitional provisions, as it moves control of the industry away from the federal government towards decentralisation and sets the foundation for the road to Kurdish economic independence and control of oil resources within the region.[358] The commentators fail to address the fact that the wording of Article 112 was a compromise position in order to facilitate the passage of the Constitution. It was the intention of those involved in the process that a package of laws[359] would be produced in order to clarify the regulation of the oil industry and resolve outstanding issues.[360]

3.5.4 The 2005 Constitution

The problem of federalism and the diversity of interests is highlighted in the drafting history of the Constitution[361] and the legal advice provided to the KRG.[362] It is necessary to consider the legal opinion provided to the KRG which formed the basis for alleged legitimacy in signing contracts and regulating oil within the region.

In drafting the Constitution, Sunnis were excluded as a result of the exclusion of Arab nationalists as part of the United States imposed de-Ba'athification process forcing Sunni political activists to go underground.[363] Agreements concerning the structure of the state were made between the CPA and Kurdish parties forcing, to some extent, Shi'a agreement to the drafts and the interim constitution (TAL) preventing further alteration to the structure.[364] Arato argues that Sunni inclusion at the outset may have provided greater legitimacy to the constitution rather than imposition by the United States of Sunni inclusion in a Kurdish dominated and Shi'a majority constitutional assembly.[365] According to Arato, if the Sunnis had been included at the outset and

> if the process was kept fair and consensual, legitimacy could have been generated, and the parties probably would not have agreed to a confederal arrangement regarding Kurdistan, but would have perhaps compromised around a version of provincial federalism with some special autonomy rights for the Kurds.[366]

3.5.4.1 Comments on legal opinion provided to the KRG

As a key legal adviser to the KRG,[367] in his opinion to the Prime Minister, Crawford bases his analysis on the interpretation that the federal government may only manage oil provided it consults with or obtains cooperation from the regional government and governorates.[368] This appears to tip the balance of power in favour of the governorates and region and goes as far as to suggest that without the input of the governorates the federal government is somehow prevented from acting. Thus the qualification for Crawford is consultation. The starting premise appears to be incorrect particularly when read alongside the drafting history.[369] An alternative and better interpretation is that the federal government is primarily responsible for the management of oil and gas extraction, and this management is to be conducted with the regional governments in a manner most efficient and practical for the maximum benefit to the Iraqi people. Thus, the federal government requires the co-operation of the producing governorates for effective management.

It has been commented[370] that the KRG succeeded in influencing the drafting of Article 112 of the Constitution and preventing it from taking its natural place under Article 110 containing the exclusive powers of the federal government derived from Article 25(e) of the TAL.[371] To an extent, it may be regarded as a degree of success but it is not quite the shift in the balance of power concluded and suggested by many. Is the location of the provision significant? Yes. Given that oil is crucial to the Iraqi economy it is understandable that it would be dealt with under a separate provision in the Constitution but still within the remit of the powers of the federal government. The provision is within the section on federal powers in the Constitution[372] and does not fall within regional powers. Further, on an issue as important as oil, had the intention at the outset been to share control with the governorates and regions, an additional section of shared powers could have been placed after section four. No such section was added therefore, there is no categorical basis for asserting that the right of the federal government to manage oil and gas resources is a qualified one.

If Article 112 of the Constitution were to be given the weight attached to it by Crawford it would surely fall under the powers of the regions or at the very least there would be some reference to the regional authority to manage local resources. This is not the case because there was no such intention during the drafting stage and such a conclusion would be illogical, inefficient and detrimental to federal authority.

3.5.4.2 Analysis of Article 112[373]

Following the extraction of oil and gas, on Crawford's interpretation there is a requirement for joint management and cooperation with the producing governorates and regions "or at least with their approval" for federal government authority to manage the oil resources under Article 112, First.[374] Crawford concedes that the extraction and production process falls outside of the requirement for cooperation or joint management.[375] Thus its extent is limited to the post-extraction process.

Crawford's opinion suggests that Article 112 only relates to "present fields" which on his interpretation is limited to those fields under production in 2006, the date at which the Constitution entered into force, and not fields under exploration.[376] "On this basis, fields not producing, developed or even discovered – and the oil and gas yet to be extracted from them – fall outside Article 112. They fall under the Constitution to be managed by the relevant regional government alone".[377] Herein lies an error in the analysis. How can it be the case that the Constitution permits regional governments solely to manage future fields? The first provision of Article 112 also provides for the fair and proportionate distribution of revenues with the most damaged regions receiving a specified share of the revenue for development. The distribution cannot only relate to present fields as that would create a lacuna for the position on future fields along with uncertainty over future economic development. Crawford appears to have stretched the interpretation to its limit. It is clear that this provision is not placed in the category of the powers of the regions and remains within control of the federal government.

Even on the assumptions made by Crawford, future production will still be subject to Article 111. It cannot be denied that all of the oil within the territorial boundaries of Iraq belongs to the people as a whole and therefore any oil produced from the Kurdish region belongs to the whole of Iraq. In order to weaken the strength of Art 111, Crawford suggests that the provision must be read "in light of Art 112" and that ownership is "without prejudice to the "management" of oil and gas" either by the federal or producing governorates.[378] He further suggests that the redistribution of revenues provided for under Article 112 only applies to present fields! "*It is for the producing regional government, in the first place, to decide on the distribution of the revenues of new production from that region, subject to policies formulated under Article 112, Second*".[379] The fragmented position created by this analysis flies in the face of the spirit of the Constitution and ignores the drafting history. Just one example highlighting the flaws in the analysis lies in reading the preamble and Article 1 where the purpose of the Constitution is to be the "guarantor of the unity of Iraq". Crawford's suggestions would lead to disjointed management of the oil resources thereby creating not only political but logistical disputes arising from the discontented regions not in receipt of revenue for development thus creating disparity and a country divided between wealthy producing governorates and the rest of Iraq. The advice, if followed[380] would lead to fuelling and deepening existing divisions and general discontent, preventing unity among the governorates.

As for the footnote justifying the position adopted by Crawford, the interpretation of the Constitution could not be further swayed in favour of the KRG's sole management of oil. As

> the existing language of Article 111 affirms that there is a regional dimension to ownership oil and gas [sic]. … it might even support the view that the people of that unit own its oil and gas. But that denies effect to the term "all the people of Iraq".[381]

The better view is that Article 111 vests ownership of oil and gas in all Iraq's people, but that the distribution of that ownership must take account of Article 112. Thus, the Constitution as an instrument of "all the people" – authorises the respective federal and regional elements in revenue distribution and management according to the carefully balanced language of Article 112".[382] The reliance placed on Article 112 by Crawford is disproportionate and attempts to highlight its ambiguity, which is not as strong as suggested. There can be no doubt that Article 112 requires review to remove any risk of misinterpretation and place the management of oil firmly within the control of the federal government but permitting a level of consultation with the governorates to ensure that all future production is protected, monitored and managed in a coherent and unified manner so that all parties involved know where they stand at all stages of the exploration, extraction and production process.

As for Article 112, Second, Crawford advocates that the emphasis of the provision is on the formulation of policies rather than the management of oil and gas.[383] It is suggested that this provision does not provide for legislative authority to the federal government and that regional contracts are not dependent upon the formulation of strategic policies before they can become effective. Thus, Crawford goes some way to emphasise through this interpretation that not only is the management of oil not an exclusive federal power but there is inference that the regional government can enter agreements prior to the formation of a national oil policy which must be created in consultation with the regions and governorates.

Crawford dismisses Deeks and Burton's commentary[384] that the oil and gas provisions were specifically placed outside of the joint competencies for the very reason that they were to be treated differently from the other provisions. He uses Article 115 to support his argument that the KRG are entitled to formulate their own policies and legislation regarding oil and gas within the region. The crucial point here is that oil and gas is not subject to shared power, it is a federal power to be conducted in consultation with the governorates and regions. Article 115 bears a direct relation to Article 114 which makes reference to the shared powers or competencies. It cannot have been the intention of the drafters for Article 115 to be directed at the interpretation of Article 112. In addition, Crawford ignores the crucial elements of interpretation in the drafters' commentary that Article 112 is a compromise provision and therefore it would never have been the intention of the Shi'a and Sunni representatives, forming the majority representation, that Article 112 would give any measure of leniency to permit a handing over of management of oil resources to the KRG or to detract in any way from the authority of the federal government to manage national oil resources.

Crawford suggests that the central government can only deal with present fields and there is no federal right to manage non-producing and future fields. This is plainly wrong in principle, particularly as the right to manage oil is placed within the federal powers under the Constitution. There is only reference to present fields in the Constitution with no reference to future fields. Arguably there is an implied reference to future fields when considering strategic policies.

Given the drafting history, the location of the oil and gas provisions is fundamental to understanding the interpretation of Article 112. Oil and gas does not fall within the shared powers of the federal government and the regions. Had the intention been to provide the regions with some level of input, it would have fallen within Article 114 but it does not. The main provision relating to oil and gas requiring interpretation is Article 112 and this is located under the section on federal powers. Had it been the intention of the drafters to permit the regions to exercise power over the management and administration of oil resources then the Article would have fallen under the section relating to the powers of the regions or at least some other provision making reference to the administration of oil and gas within the regions would have been drafted in section five. This was not the case and the only provisions in the Constitution relating to oil and gas are found under the federal powers.

There is no reference in the advice to Article 25(E) of the TAL which provides the template for the current Constitution. The provision clearly provides for the management of natural resources to be within the exclusive competence of the federal government "in consultation with the governments of the regions and the administrations of the governorates". Further, the drafting committee interpretation of the federal position on management of oil and gas is that although one implication of Article 112(1) is that future fields are subject to different standards of management to present fields, this may not be an accurate interpretation due to the requirement under Article 112(2) that the regional, governorate and federal governments must work together to formulate policies to manage developing fields:

> ... federal legislation would be at least a plausible method by which strategic policies could be agreed upon and implemented. ... Article 112(second)'s failure to provide for legislation should not preclude it.[385]
>
> If the federal government actively involves itself in oil and gas development at the expense of regional or governorate influence, and a conflict arises, Article 93(fourth) gives the Federal Supreme Court jurisdiction over the dispute.[386]

The alleged lack of strategic oil policy by the federal government is a crucial aspect of Crawford's analysis as he premises many of his arguments on this in consultation with the KRG and governorates which means that it somehow lacks legitimacy. Further, he suggests that because the KRG have enacted an oil and gas law this somehow provides them with authority to enter into oil agreements and makes their conduct more legitimate than that of the central government. For Crawford the issue seems to be one of a race against time or because the KRG seems to have put its house in order it can dictate how oil and gas agreements can be dealt with and essentially regulate national resources in the region separately from the rest of the country. However, the KRG is bound by Article 111 as it is the overriding provision relating to oil resources and is unqualified. Thus the benefit of oil and gas from the fields within the geographical boundaries controlled by the KRG must be provided to all Iraqis, which can only be achieved effectively through federal distribution of revenues and the central collection of taxes, royalties and other payments under the relevant agreements.

3.5.4.3 Constitutional ambiguities and the section on federal powers

According to those present during the constitutional drafting, the intention behind federal governance is somewhat unclear:[387]

> Although this Section of the Constitution is entitled "Powers of the Federal Government," there is a wide spectrum of ways in which the federal and

> sub-federal governments can balance authority, such as exclusively federal, federally-led with regional participation, regionally-led with federal participation, and exclusively regional (or governorate). A number of these points along the spectrum are reflected in the negotiation and final structure of this section.

It has been suggested that there is potential conflict between Articles 115 and 121.[388] Authors in support of the federal position in Iraq, including Professor Crawford, have argued that Articles 115 and 121 (2) prioritise regional law over federal law because the Constitution technically provides for concurrent jurisdiction over these natural resources. However, Article 121(2) and 115 are not applicable to Articles 111 or 112 for the reasons outlined above, namely that the regional powers do not have authority to amend the application of Constitutional provision and subsequent federal legislation relating to oil and gas. The drafters also rightly disagree with the position as it not possible given the history of drafting Articles 111 and 112 whereby negotiations for other unresolved sections of the constitution were postponed for weeks until the oil and gas provisions were resolved:

> … It seems quite unlikely that the drafters, while undertaking painstaking efforts to agree that the federal government would manage oil and gas and distribute income "with" the producing regional and governorate governments, would have intended to upend such carefully negotiated language through the insertion of a last minute provision giving regional and governorate governments primacy over federal regulation in areas of concurrent authority.[389]

Deeks and Burton provide further historical context in that:

> … negotiators considered addressing oil and gas within provisions on exclusive and concurrent authorities in earlier drafts, but, with the final compromise, decided to address oil and gas outside of the exclusive-concurrent dichotomy. … the singular focus on resolving the distribution of authority over oil and gas, … suggests that the more reasonable reading is that the drafters did not intend Article 121 (second) to override the careful compromise on oil and gas.[390]

Thus, although commentators may provide a definitive analysis of the federal position on oil and gas and the rights of the KRG, it is clear that there was no intention at the time of drafting for control to move away from the central government on an industry at the heart of the national economy.

3.5.5 Future implications of federalism on oil revenues

Since the drafting of the 2005 Constitution there has been significant political tension within Iraq. Of the political parties involved in the creation of the 2005 Constitution, the Kurdish representatives made the most significant contribution to the division of Iraq, preventing a measured and long-term view of a unified country in its framework. It is perhaps unsurprising given the circumstances surrounding the drafting of the Constitution.[391] It is prudent to remember that at the outset there was significant objection to the intervention in Iraq for months before the military campaign was launched contrary to international law.[392] Amid all of the haste, disorganisation, inexperience and external international pressure placed on Iraq the military operation needed to be seen to be a success.

During the drafting of the Constitution, the main parties pushing for federalism and decentralisation, arguably to ensure that the country would not return to a Saddam style dictatorship,[393] were the Kurdish PUK and KDP parties and the Shi'a Supreme Council for Islamic Revolution in Iraq (SCIRI)[394] which had strong ties to Iran.[395] The Kurdish interests heavily swayed the elections and the adoption of the Constitution. More Kurds and Shi'a voters went to the ballot box resulting in lower Sunni representatives being elected.[396]

Literature on federalism and regionalism in Iraq lacks attention to the benefit of external powers and their influence upon making federalism and regionalism a key political issue. The benefits to the wider international community of dividing Iraq through the federal or regional form of government are all too obvious and yet there is a distinct lack of commentary on the issue in academic discussion. By weakening Iraq, the access to oil wealth is increased along with the additional benefit of gaining economic influence over regional governments thereby ensuring that the balance of power lies with individual regional politicians and international companies rather than a strong centralised government. A key aspect of the process of constitutional implementation is that the deadline was due to coincide with the US Presidential elections even though academics argue that there

> is little information about US pressure on Iraq to complete its constitution hastily by the end of August 2004 (so the Bush administration could claim political progress in time for the November presidential elections) and its role in pushing the regional federalism agenda.[397]

Generally, federalism lacks support among the population of Iraq except within the Kurdish region:

> Outside the Kurdish provinces, … regionalism has very little currency in Iraq. … If anything, hostility to the idea of regionalism seems to be growing … ISCI's efforts to create a "Shiastan" of Iraq's nine southern provinces have provoked strong opposition among the Shi'a themselves, who see this proposal as a bald-faced effort to establish a semi-independent state that would allow ISCI to control the south's vast oil wealth.[398]

Even at this stage, it is difficult to see how Iraq would ever become a truly federal state.[399] The best case that the Kurds could hope for would be to declare independence or perhaps to have a status akin to Quebec in Canada. In 2017, the KRG held a referendum for independence and despite a majority of over 90% voting in favour, the result was not entertained by the government in Baghdad which declared the vote unlawful. This view was supported by Ankara and Tehran in addition to wider international criticism for holding the referendum.[400] As for the rest of the country, it is highly unlikely that Iraqis will want their country to be divided, as there is no substantive basis for such division. It is often forgotten that Iraqis are nationalistic and despite sectarian violence, which is suggested to be a by-product of the transition from dictatorship to democracy, there is a sense of patriotism among Iraqis evidenced by a strong desire to rebuild the country. But what does this false notion of federalism mean for Iraq's oil industry and the political stalemate surrounding the draft oil and gas law? Due to the power associated with the regulation of oil it is likely that there will be continual argument until the balance of power within the central Iraqi government is proportionate to the population and oil reserve location, that is, when there is less Kurdish influence in the debate and passage of the legislation. The power to control oil resources must rest with the central government as any alternative is likely to cause ongoing tension thereby restricting the decision-making capabilities of the oil ministry and central government which could prove detrimental to the industry and any associated economic advantage. Clearly, this is not an option that would easily be conceded by the Kurds, as their ability to influence and essentially veto the development of federal oil policy would be severely diminished. The recent political balance is too far in favour of Kurdish control and as long as there are a number of Kurdish representatives in significant political positions[401] within the central government this is unlikely to change.[402]

It is necessary to consider the consequences of a disjointed government in the decision-making process and to question the capabilities of the level of government authorised to control key industries. Due to the various stages of the hydrocarbon extraction process the regulation, control and monitoring of the industry by the state must be cohesive, centralised and comprehensive in order to avoid complication and the risk of private companies finding alternative methods of operation outside control of the relevant authorised government agencies which could have a detrimental effect on economic development and income.

Federalism strengthens divisions and provides an opportunity for conflict, which would otherwise not exist. The implementation and promotion of the federal model of government in Iraq will have a detrimental effect on the growth and development of a country with exceptional potential. By creating a federal system with only two main sides, the Kurds and the central government, there has been significant political tension.[403] Iraq is not as ethnically divided as outsiders would like to portray and remains a secular society. There is a strong sense of attachment to local towns and villages regardless of religious or ethnic identity. When asked, traditionally many Iraqis will offer themselves, for example, as Basrawi, Baghdadi or Najafi before mentioning their religious or other allegiances; the people will usually consider themselves to be primarily Iraqi.[404] Thus this false and harmful division of the country legitimised through the 2005 Constitution, in its original state, is unlikely to foster significant political cohesion or progress on key legal and political issues as it was framed and enacted without due regard to the identity of the ordinary Iraqi on the street and is unlikely to change his views on the issue. It is therefore suggested that in order to make significant development in regulating the oil industry and passing a comprehensive oil law, the Constitution requires amendment to allow the appropriate political forum for debate and practical solutions for regulation rather than political trade-offs.

Dicey advocated the following when considering federalism; "[w]*hatever concerns the nation as a whole should be placed under the control of the national government. All matters which are not primarily of common interest should remain in the hands of the several states*".[405] This is an obvious notion to be considered in Constitutional drafting and is wholly applicable in the context of Iraq. The regulation of hydrocarbons must remain with the central government.

Notes

1 Courtney Hunt, *The Greenwood Histories of the Modern Nations: The History of Iraq* (Westport, CT, Greenwood Press, 2005), 52.
2 Stephen Pelletière, *Iraq and the International Oil System* (Westport, CT, Praeger, 2001), 23–24; P.T. Cain and A.G. Hopkins, *British Imperialism: Innovation and Expansion 1688–1914* (London, Longman, 1993), 397.
3 1838 Treaty of Balta Limani, provided for British merchants to have full access to the Ottoman markets on an equal basis.
4 Oil was discovered in Titusville, Pennsylvania by Colonel Edwin Drake, resulting in a sixty-nine foot well. However, the first oil well in North America was discovered in Ontario, Canada in 1858. The first modern oil well was drilled in Asia in 1848, on the Aspheron Peninsula north-east of Baku, by Russian engineer F.N. Semyenov, www.sjvgeology.org/history/index.html and www.arabianoilandgas.com/article-5817-10_events_in_oils_history_that_shook_the_world/.
5 Stephen Longrigg, *Oil in the Middle East* (Oxford, Oxford University Press, 1968), 11.
6 Stephen Pelletière, (n2) 24.
7 Ibid.
8 Naval Intelligence Division, *Iraq and the Persian Gulf* (Routledge, 2014), 28.
9 Ibid.
10 West bank of the Tigris.
11 55 miles south of Kirkuk.
12 Longrigg (n5) 14.
13 Ibid.
14 Ibid., 27.
15 Ibid., 12.
16 Shell, 'Our Beginnings', www.shell.com/about-us/who-we-are/our-beginnings.html, accessed 21 February 2016.
17 V. Necla Geyikdagi, *Foreign Investment in the Ottoman Empire International Trade and Relations 1854–1914* (I.B. Tauris Publishers, 2011), 122.
18 Ibid.
19 Established in 1886.
20 Longrigg (n5) 12.
21 Ibid., 43.
22 Ibid., 27.
23 Stephen Pelletière (n2) 23.

24 Longrigg, (n5) 16.
25 Anthony Sampson, *The Seven Sisters* (Kent, Hodder & Stoughton, 1993), 77.
26 A Turkish-born Armenian entrepreneur and British citizen since 1902. Longrigg (n5) 13.
27 Longrigg (n5) 12.
28 Sampson (n25) 83. The discovery was at Masjid-i-Suleiman in Iran.
29 Longrigg (n5) 16.
30 Ibid.
31 Ibid., 21.
32 Ibid., 16.
33 Ibid., 21.
34 Ibid.
35 Ibid.
36 Ibid.
37 Longrigg (n5) 16.
38 Reported as 59 million tons per year. Conversion calculated in accordance with BP conversion factors at 7.33 barrels per ton.
39 20 million tons per year.
40 Four million tons per year.
41 Rex Zedalis, *Legal Dimensions of Oil and Gas in Iraq: Current Reality and Future Prospects* (Cambridge, Cambridge University Press, 2009), 4.
42 Named after Sir Mark Sykes, an official of the British Foreign Office and Charles Picot, the French Ministry of Foreign Affairs.
43 Charles Tripp, *A History of Iraq* (Cambridge, Cambridge University Press, 2007), 40 and Sampson (n25) 97. The same year following disruption and riots in Baghdad the Prime Minister states at the British War Office in December 1920:

> Whether you go to Basra, or Nasariah, or Mosul, you are up against the same problem: you must have a boundary or a frontier somewhere. The point is, where are you going to fix that frontier? My Right Hon. Friend seems to forget that he is responsible for the Sykes-Picot Agreement. Under the Sykes-Picot Agreement the British – were to become responsible for the whole vilayet of Baghdad as well as Basra. That was the policy at that time. In view of the criticisms about the selfishness of our views about oil and grain, may I point out that under that agreement we claimed that Great Britain should have priority of right to enterprise and local loans, not merely in that area, but in the whole of that sphere of influence? That was the purpose of the authors of that agreement.
>
> (National Archives CAB/24/117, Image reference 0080)

44 Tripp (n43) 40.
45 Sampson (n25) 98.
46 Longrigg (n5) 44. The relevant provisions under the Covenant of the League of Nations are Articles XXII and I. Please see Appendix 1 for the full provisions.
47 The Covenant of the League of Nations, including amendments of December 1924, http://avalon.law.yale.edu/20th_century/leagcov.asp#art22, accessed 29 August 2011.
48 Longrigg (n5) 45.
49 *Special Report by His Majesty's Government in the United Kingdom of Great Britain and Northern Ireland to the Council of the League of Nations on the Progress of Iraq during the period 1920–1931* (London, HMSO, 1931), 217.
50 Mahmud Sami E., *The Quest for Sultan Abdülhamid's Oil Assets: His Heirs' Legal Battle for their Rights* (Istanbul, Isis Press, 2006). See also Article 3 of the Treaty of Lausanne. Available at wwi.lib.byu.edu/index.php/Treaty_of_Lausanne, accessed 11 November 2011, 4.
51 Through a treaty with the Iraqi government.

52 Tripp (n43) 44.
53 Ibid., 45. Michael Eppel, *Iraq from Monarchy to Tyranny* (Gainesville, University Press of Florida, 2004), 13.
54 Islamic charitable endowments.
55 *Special Report by His Majesty's Government in the United Kingdom of Great Britain and Northern Ireland to the Council of the League of Nations on the Progress of Iraq during the period 1920–1931* (London, HMSO, 1931), 14.
56 Ibid.
57 Ibid.
58 Ibid.
59 Ibid.
60 Special Report 16.
61 Ibid.
62 Special Report 218.
63 Special Report 31.
64 Special Report 30.
65 Special Report 16.
66 Special Report 222.
67 Special Report 219.
68 Ibid.
69 Special Report 219. Edith Penrose, *Iraq: International Relations and National Development* (London, Ernest Benn Limited, 1978) 67.
70 Special Report 18.
71 Jersey Standard, Socony, Gulf Oil, Pan-American Petroleum and Transport Company and Atlantic Refining – in the 1930s Jersey Standard and Socony took over the other companies in the consortium.
72 The TPC was originally the African & Eastern but changed its name in 1912 following the Young Turk revolution.
73 EGEE 120 Oil: International Evolution 'Opening the Door on the Middle East: the Turkish Petroleum Company' www.e-education.psu.edu/egee120/node/248 accessed 1 January 2016.
74 By France, Britain and the United States.
75 Longrigg (n5) 69–70.
76 Clifford Singer, *Energy and International War From Babylon to Baghdad and Beyond Singapore* (Hackensack, NJ, World Scientific Publishing, 2008), 135.
77 Now ExxonMobil.
78 Zedalis (n41) 5.
79 US Department of State Office of the Historian, 'The 1928 Red Line Agreement', https://history.state.gov/milestones/1921-1936/red-line accessed 1 January 2016.
80 Through Aramco.
81 122,000 tons.
82 Special Report 223.
83 Special Report 18.
84 Special Report 19.
85 Ibid.
86 Ibid.
87 Special Report 20.
88 H.A. Henry Foster, *The Making of Modern Iraq: A Product of World Forces* (London, Williams and Norgate Ltd, 1936), 1.
89 *Petroleum Press Service*, 1962, 7 as cited by Alnasrawi, *The Economy of Iraq: Oil, Wars, Destruction of Development and Prospects, 1950–2010* (Westport, CT, Greenwood Press, 1994), 2.
90 Alnasrawi 2.
91 Tripp, 102.

92 Longrigg 86–90.
93 Alnasrawi, *The Economy of Iraq*, 4.
94 Ibid.
95 Ibid.
96 FTC Report, 95. Also cited by Alnasrawi at 4.
97 Michael Eppel, *Iraq from Monarchy to Tyranny: From the Hashemites to the Rise of Saddam* (Gainesville, University Press of Florida, 2004), 73.
98 Ibid.
99 Eppel 74, Britain agreed to repay in pound sterling which was refused by Iraq due to the weakening of the currency.
100 Eppel 76.
101 Ibid., 78.
102 Ibid.
103 Ibid.
104 Ibid.
105 Eppel 78–79.
106 Ibid., 79–80.
107 Longrigg 180.
108 Companies that would eventually become BP, Royal-Dutch Shell, TotalFinaElf, Exxon, and Mobil.
109 In 1972.
110 Alnasrawi 3.
111 Ibid.
112 Eppel (n97) 93 – For the Wathba crisis see 73–80.
113 Eppel 93.
114 Ibid.
115 Eppel 93–94.
116 Alnasrawi 6.
117 Ibid., citing Hartshorn, *Politics*, 137.
118 Alnasrawi 2 citing Agreement with the Government of Iraq (Hertford, Austin & Sons, 1952), 4.
119 Alnasrawi 2.
120 Longrigg 273.
121 Ibid.
122 Tripp 135–136.
123 Longrigg 265.
124 Ibid., 262.
125 Ibid., 271.
126 Tripp 137.
127 Gregg Muttit, *Fuel on the Fire: Oil and Politics in Occupied Iraq* (London, The Bodley Head, 2010), 10.
128 Alnasrawi 8.
129 Tripp 137.
130 Alnasrawi 7.
131 Ibid.
132 Tripp 140.
133 Longrigg 263.
134 Ibid.
135 Longrigg 264.
136 Ibid.
137 Longrigg 265.
138 Abbas Alnasrawi, *The Economy of Iraq: Oil, Wars, Destruction of Development and Prospects, 1950–2010* (Westport, CT, Greenwood Press, 1994), 36.
139 Ibid.

140 Alnasrawi 36.
141 Longrigg 274.
142 Ibid.
143 Longrigg 267.
144 Ibid.
145 Alnasrawi 37.
146 Ibid.
147 Alnasrawi, 39 – the division of expenditure was 12.2% to agriculture, 12.4% to industry, 20% to transport and communication and 49% on building and construction.
148 Ibid.
149 Ruud van Dijk, *Encyclopedia of Cold War*, Vol. 1 (London, Routledge, 2008), 55–56.
150 Ibid.
151 Alnasrawi 8.
152 Ibid., 8 (fn38).
153 Alnasrawi 7 (fn28 citing Hartshorn, Politics, Chapters 7 & 22).
154 Longrigg 269.
155 3,570 tons.
156 Longrigg 268.
157 Ibid., 349.
158 Ibid.
159 Longrigg 353.
160 Ibid., 264.
161 Ibid., 362.
162 Muttit 188.
163 Tripp 159.
164 Ibid., 162.
165 Official justification for the legislation.
166 Longrigg 355.
167 Iraq National Oil Company (INOC) was created in 1964 and provided exclusive rights to exploit national resources in 1967 as a result of two laws being passed in 1964–1967. The success of INOC ensured the reliance of the Iraqi economy on oil and although it produced significant revenue it became the cause of economic detriment in the 1980s and 1990s. Alnasrawi 12.
168 Longrigg 363.
169 Alnasrawi 43.
170 Ibid., 44.
171 Ibid., 45.
172 Edith Penrose, *Iraq: International Relations and National Development* (London, Ernest Benn Limited, 1978), 386
173 Penrose 384.
174 Ibid., 399.
175 Ibid., 400.
176 Ibid., 387.
177 Ibid., 405.
178 Longrigg 356.
179 Ibid., 256.
180 Law No. 97 of 1967, Articles 1–4.
181 Law No. 97 of 1967.
182 Ibid., Article 3(4).
183 Further discussion in Chapter 5.
184 Penrose 394. Adib al-Jadir was appointed.
185 Penrose 396.

186 Ibid., 400.
187 Longrigg 275.
188 Alnasrawi 55.
189 Tripp 190.
190 Global Justice Project: Iraq, http://gjpi.org/library/primary/iraqi-constitution/.
191 This will be discussed in detail in a later chapter when considering the legal analysis.
192 Penrose 398.
193 Ibid., 401.
194 English version of this law available from Global Justice Project: Iraq at http://gjpi.org/library/primary/statutes/.
195 Tripp xiv.
196 Penrose 399.
197 Alnasrawi 9.
198 Arbitral Tribunal Award in Dispute between Libyan American Oil Company (LIAMCO) and The Government of the Libyan Arab Republic Relating to Petroleum Concessions, 20 (1) *International Legal Materials*, 1–87, January 1981.
199 Penrose 402.
200 Alnasrawi 9.
201 Penrose 401.
202 Ibid., 401.
203 Ibid., 403.
204 Ibid., 402.
205 Ibid.
206 Penrose 405.
207 Ibid.
208 Penrose 406 (fn28).
209 Penrose 406.
210 Alnasrawi 10.
211 Ibid.
212 Penrose 406.
213 Ibid.
214 Ibid.
215 Law 37/1972.
216 The agreement expressly stipulates that the decisions of OPEC are paramount.
217 Article 2 of the Agreement.
218 Law 51/1972, The agreement provides for an increase of 8.49% above the price on the effective date of the agreement.
219 Syria immediately issued Decree No. 46, which nationalised IPC pipelines and other IPC property in Syria including the Banias terminal. Penrose 409.
220 Law Number 69 of 1972.
221 See generally, "Oil as a weapon in the struggle against imperialism and Israeli aggression and a means to the development of an independent national economy", the Ministry of Information, Republic of Iraq, 1972.
222 Ibid.
223 Pelletière 158.
224 Ibid.
225 Muttit 18.
226 LIAMCO v Libya Arbitration 91.
227 Alnasrawi 10.
228 Ibid.
229 OAPEC, the Organisation of Arab Exporting Countries, was established by Kuwait, Libya and Saudi Arabia on 9 January 1968 in order to further the interests of its member producer states. In 1982 its membership expanded to Algeria (1970),

Bahrain (1970) (now Kingdom of Bahrain), Egypt (1973), Iraq (1972), Kuwait (1968), Libya (1968), Qatar (1970), Kingdom of Saudi Arabia (1968), Syria (1972), Tunisia (1982) and United Arab Emirates (1970). OAPEC Website www.oapecorg.org/Home/About-Us/History accessed 1 January 2016. Iraq originally formed closer formal links with Algeria and Egypt to counter the new organisation following its establishment.

230 This resolution was later amended by RCC Resolutions 567 of 1973, 247 of 1974, 928 of 1979, 385 of 1980, 836 of 1982, 196 of 1985, 1130 of 1985, 700 of 1987, 630 of 1988, 83 of 1991, 336 of 1991, 398 of 1991, 15 of 1993, 460 of 1992 and 112 of 2000. Nick Richie and Paul Roberts, *The Political Road to War with Iraq: Bush, 9/11 and the Drive to Overthrow Saddam* (Abingdon, Routledge, 2007), 10.
231 Alnasrawi 11.
232 Penrose 404.
233 Zedalis 198.
234 Muttit 22. Tripp 213–214.
235 Pelletière 104.
236 Ibid., 164.
237 Ibid.
238 Pelletière 191, 163.
239 Tripp 218.
240 Ibid., 221, 223–224.
241 Pelletière 163.
242 Ibid.
243 Pelletière 167.
244 Tripp 232.
245 Zedalis 198.
246 Abbas Alnasrawi, *Iraq's Burdens: Oil, Sanctions, and Underdevelopment* (Westport, CT, Greenwood Press, 2002), 132.
247 Kamal Mahdi, *Iraq's Economic Predicament* (Reading, PA, Ithaca Press, 2002), 12.
248 Alnasrawi, *The Economy of Iraq*, 117. This allegation was widely reported in the media at the time.
249 Ibid., 114.
250 Ibid.
251 Sampson 18.
252 Ibid., 17.
253 Sampson 18.
254 Ibid.
255 Alnasrawi, *Economy of Iraq*, 157.
256 Alnasrawi 158.
257 Ibid.
258 Over concerns that Iraq would be a potential military threat in the region and held "weapons of mass destruction" which later proved unfounded.
259 Terrance Daintith, *Finders Keepers? How the Law of Capture Shaped the World Oil Industry*, (Routledge, 2010), 370.
260 Tripp, 244. UNSCR 678.
261 UNSCR 661 (1990).
262 Tripp 248. UNSCR 688 (1991). The resolution condemns Iraq's action in the "Kurdish populated areas" and provides under Article 4 for the UN to intervene in the protection of the Kurdish population.
263 Tripp 248.
264 The other resolution related to Iraq–Iran under UNSCR 685. See www.un.org/Docs/scres/1991/scres91.htm, accessed 5 August 2011. The relevant resolutions are: 686, 687, 688, 689, 692, 699, 700, 705, 706, 707, 712 and 715.

265 Iraq-Iraq Resolutions: 676, 671 and 651. Iraq-Kuwait: 678, 677, 674, 670, 669, 667, 666, 665, 664, 662, 661 and 660. UNSC Website: www.un.org/Docs/scres/1990/scres90.htm, accessed 5 August 2011.
266 Resolutions 479 (1980), 514, 522 (1982), 588, 582 (1986), 518 (1987), 612, 619 and 620 (1988). See generally www.un.org/Docs/sc/unsc_resolutions.html, accessed 5 August 2011.
267 Tripp 252.
268 Section 2 (12):

> On 1 May 1998, President Clinton signed Public Law 105–174, which made $5,000,000 available for assistance to the Iraqi democratic opposition for such activities as organization, training, communication and dissemination of information, developing and implementing agreements among opposition groups, compiling information to support the indictment of Iraqi officials for war crimes, and for related purposes.

Section 3 continues:

> It should be the policy of the United States to support efforts to remove the regime headed by Saddam Hussein from power in Iraq and to promote the emergence of a democratic government to replace that regime.

Section 7 provides the intention of Congress once Saddam Hussein is removed from power:

> It is the sense of the Congress that once the Saddam Hussein regime is removed from power in Iraq, the United States should support Iraq's transition to democracy by providing immediate and substantial humanitarian assistance to the Iraqi people, by providing democracy transition assistance to Iraqi parties and movements with democratic goals, and by convening Iraq's foreign creditors to develop a multilateral response to Iraq's foreign debt incurred by Saddam Hussein's regime.

269 Tripp 254.
270 Ibid., 269.
271 Mahdi (n241) 3.
272 Mahdi 4.
273 Ibid., 9.
274 For example, the Magna Carta 1215, French Declaration of the Rights of Man and Citizens 1789 (incorporated into the French Civil Code of 1958), the US Constitution 1789, the Hague Conventions of 1890 and 1907 and the International Law Association Declarations of 1926 and 1932.
275 LIAMCO 89.
276 Particularly Iraq, Egypt, Syria, Libya and Lebanon.
277 LIAMCO 91.
278 See Article 2.
279 Iraqi Civil Code 1951, Article 6.5.
280 The Land Code 1858.
281 Ottoman Land Code 1858, Article 107. Translation from Fisher M., *Ottoman Land Laws Containing the Ottoman Land Code and Later Legislation Affecting Land, with Notes and an Appendix of Cyprus Laws and Rules Relating to Land*, 35.
282 Constitution of 1925, Article 94, http://gjpi.org/wp-content/uploads/iraqiconst19250321.htm#(1), accessed 10 November 2011.
283 Discussed in the next chapter.
284 Alnasrawi, *The Economy of Iraq*, 139.
285 Established under Law No. 11 of 1964 and expanded powers through Law No. 123 of 1967 following the enactment of Law 97 of 1967.

286 For more detail on quasi-ownership see Harris, Property and Justice 106.

287 In the case of Iraq, the key entities these include are the North Oil Company (NOC), South Oil Company (SOC) and the State Oil Marketing Organisation (SOMO) among others.

288 Kenneth S. Carlston 'Concession Agreements and Nationalization', 52 (2) *The American Journal of International Law*, 260–279, 272, April 1958.

289 2005 Iraqi Constitution, Article 1: "The Republic of Iraq is a single federal, independent and fully sovereign state in which the system of government is republican, representative, parliamentary, and democratic, and this Constitution is a guarantor of the unity of Iraq."

290 The governorates are, Baghdad, Basra, Babil, Najaf, Misan, Karbala, Qadisiyah, Wasit, Anbar, Dhi-Qar, Diyala, Salahuddin, Ta'mim, Muthanna, Ninevah, Suleimaniyah, Erbil and Dohuk.

291 Article 117 of the Iraqi Constitution.

292 Although there was a peace agreement in March 1970 which established the Kurdish region in Iraq with autonomy granted in 1974, in 1991 the United States facilitated the development of the Kurdish region by establishing a no fly zone in the area. They were also instrumental in the drafting of the 2005 Constitution.

293 Dr. F. Jabar speaker at Post-American Iraq Conference, Chatham House, 24 March 2010.

294 R. Schneller, speaker at Post-American Iraq Conference, Chatham House, 24 March 2010. Perhaps this was the desired outcome and it was in fact considered by the US administration as disarray means more flexibility to take advantage of the oil resources by pursuing contracts when they may not otherwise be given.

295 The suggestion was provided in a document entitled Stansfield and Andersen "Constitution of the Federal Republic of Iraq" 372.

296 Ashley Deeks and Matthew Burton, 'Iraq's Constitution: A Drafting History', 40 (1) *Cornell International Law Journal*, 79–80, 2007. Unknown, Press TV, *Iraqi Kurdistan Threatens to Declare Independence*, 21 March 2012.

297 R. Alkadiri, speaker at Post-American Iraq Conference, Chatham House, 24 March 2010.

298 Ibid. See also, 'Iraqi Kurdistan Threatens to Declare Independence', www.presstv.ir/detail/232718.html, accessed 17 April 2012.

299 A. Yee, 'Iraq Oil Hopes Slide on Legal Limbo', *The National*, 20 June 2012, 'UPDATE 2-Baghdad, Kurdish Oil Clash Deepens Rift', *Reuters*, 2 April 2012. Vivienne Walt, 'Why Iraq's Oil Law Remains Deadlocked Three Years On', *Time Magazine*, 10 October 2009. Ben Lando, 'Erbil, Baghdad Still at Odds over Oil', *Iraq Oil Report*, 3 December 2010.

300 Ibid.

301 Deeks and Burton 64. There was talk of a 'Shiastan' in the south of Iraq during the drafting stage of the Constitution.

302 R. Alkadiri and F. Jabar, speakers at Post-American Iraq Conference, Chatham House, 24 March 2010.

303 R. Alkadiri, Ibid.

304 Ibid.

305 Ibid. Maliki held office as PM 2006–2014. In September 2014, Haider al-Abadi became PM. In April 2017, prior to a KRG call for a referendum for independence on 25 September 2017, Abadi publicly stated that he respected the Kurdish right to call a referendum but it was not the right time, as it would cause further instability in the country. The government is therefore not willing to recognize the call for independence in the referendum. *Al-Jazeera*, 'Iraqi Government Rejects Kurdish Move for Independence', 9 June 2017, www.aljazeera.com/news/2017/06/iraqi-government-rejects-kurdish-move-independence-170609093336816.html, accessed 14 July 2017.

306 Ibid.
307 Rex Zedalis, *The Legal Dimensions of Oil and Gas in Iraq* (Cambridge, March 2014) Chapter 4.
308 Joost Hiltermann, Sean Kane and Raad Alkadiri, 'Iraq's Federalism Quandry', *The National Interest*, 9, www.crisisgroup.org/en/regions/middle-east-north-africa/iraq-iran-gulf/iraq/op-eds/hiltermann-iraqs-federalism-quandary.aspx, accessed 6 March 2012.
309 Recently, there has been what could be argued as a slight softening in the stance of the central government towards the KRG in order to boost oil revenues. See *Al Jazeera*, 'Iraq: Baghdad and Kurds Strike Deal to Resume Kirkuk Oil Exports' 16 November 2018, www.aljazeera.com/news/2018/11/iraq-baghdad-kurds-strike-deal-resume-kirkuk-oil-exports-181116170010040.html, accessed 5 January 2019.
310 Deeks and Burton 75. British Ministry of Defence document provided to the Iraq Inquiry. Available at: www.iraqinquiry.org.uk/media/38010/mod-no-fly-zone-r1.pdf, accessed 18 June 2016.
311 Ibid. A Kurdish Parliament was elected in May 1992 and installed a cabinet in September 1996.
312 Throughout the drafting process of the Constitution the Kurds sought to expand their control and weaken the federal power. See generally Deeks and Burton. One of the root causes of current political difficulties in Iraq is the level of control provided to the KRG through the Constitution and is an issue which needs to be addressed in order for Iraq to progress economically and politically. They managed to go beyond the powers provided under the Transitional Administrative Law 2004 (TAL).
313 Iraq has historically been divided among its regions and it was only in the early twentieth century that the current Iraq was formed.
314 Ronald Watts, 'Models of Federal Power-Sharing', 53 (167) *International Social Science Journal*, 23–32, 2 March 2001.
315 A.V. Dicey, Federal Government, 1 L.Q. Rev 80 1885, 82.
316 Watts 2.
317 A.V. Dicey, Federal Government, 1 L.Q. Rev 80 1885, 80.
318 Ibid 81.
319 Ibid.
320 Ibid.
321 Ibid.
322 Ibid.
323 Ibid.
324 R. Alkadiri, speaker at Post-American Iraq Conference, Chatham House, 24 March 2010.
325 Section 5 of the Constitution.
326 Supra n763. There are, of course, hybrids of these models, which is beyond the scope of this book. Hybrid systems are discussed by Watts.
327 Dicey 82.
328 See n771.
329 Even though no reference is made to the Shura Council, which was established in 1933, it is the administrative and Constitutional safeguard in Iraq vetting legislation for Constitutional compliance before it is provided to the Council of Representatives. Its authority is derived from Article 101 of the Constitution "A State Council may be established, specialized in functions of the administrative judiciary, issuing opinions, drafting, and representing the State and various public commissions before the courts except those exempted by law."
330 See the next section and the following chapter.
331 William S. Livingston, 'A Note on the Nature of Federalism', LXVII (1) *Political Science Quarterly*, 84, March 1952.
332 Ibid., 89.

333 "The Constitution, which endows the states with the characteristics of diversity, treats them indiscriminately and thus tends to create diversity where none previously existed. The Constitution with its federal plan, though designed as an instrumentality, has become a part of the complex of sociological and psychological values that constitutes the pattern of diversities. It is no longer merely an instrumentality serving to protect and articulate the diversities; it has itself become a part of that complex of values which is the pattern of diversities and which determines the pattern of the instrumentalities." Ibid., 95.
334 Livingston 90.
335 Although not necessarily through a written Constitution, for example, see the United Kingdom and Australia.
336 Although this may change to a confederation if the KRG gains increased autonomy and its hydrocarbon legislation is recognised by the federal government.
337 Livingston 88.
338 Deeks and Burton 50.
339 Kelly, … Katzman, … Kane see below.
340 Kane et al., 'Iraq's Federalism Quandry', *The National Interest*, 28 March 2012, 9, http://nationalinterest.org/article/iraqs-federalism-quandary-6512?page=1, accessed 4 March 2012.
341 The KRG enjoys a 17% share of national oil revenue deriving mainly from Basra without contributing to the economy outside the Kurdish region which means that around $5–6 billion of the national budget is provided to the KRG per annum. F. Jabar, speakers at Post-American Iraq Conference, Chatham House, 24 March 2010. P. Cameron, *Managing the Politics of Oil Reforms: Lessons from Iraq: Keynote Address at the Oil and Gas in Federal Systems Conference, March 4, 2010*, Washington DC, CEPMLP, March 2010, 12.
342 A discussion of the criteria for dictatorship is beyond the scope of this book. There are many democratic centralised states, just one example is the majority of European countries.
343 Although to return to a centralised state would require an amendment to the existing Constitution.
344 For further information see Jeremy Sharp, CRS Report for Congress, Iraq: A Compilation of Legislation Enacted and Resolutions Adopted by Congress, 27 March 2003, http://fpc.state.gov/documents/organization/17330.pdf accessed 2 May 2011.
345 Ibid.
346 See www.iraqcoalition.org/regulations/#Regulations, accessed 11 August 2012.
347 CPA/REG/16 May 2003/01, www.iraqcoalition.org/regulations/20030516_CPAREG_1_The_Coalition_Provisional_Authority_.pdf, accessed 11 August 2012.
348 CPA/REG/9 June 2004/10. Section 1(1), www.iraqcoalition.org/regulations/20040609_CPAREG_10_Members_of_Designated_Iraqi_Interim_Government_with_Annex_A.pdf, accessed 11 August 2012.
349 Supra, section 1(2). The Governing Council dissolved on 1 June 2004 pursuant to CPA/REG/9 June 2004/09.
350 CPA Order 54, s3(2).
351 TAL Articles 52, 55–57.
352 Liam Anderson and Gareth Stansfield, 'The Implications of Elections for Federalism in Iraq: Toward a Five-Region Model', 35(3) *Publius*, 359–373, 2005.
353 Kelly 726 (infra) citing Arato, Constitution Making under Occupation: the politics of imposed revolution in Iraq. 2009, CUP. New York. According to Arato the imposed constitution making was opposed by Sistani-led Shi'a clerics requiring sovereign constitutional assembly ratified by a referendum.
354 The team of experts was led by Peter Galbraith and Brenden O'Leary. Michael Kelly, 'The Kurdish Regional Constitution within the Framework of the Iraqi Federal

Constitution: A Struggle for Sovereignty, Oil, Ethnic Identity, and the Prospects for a Reverse Supremacy Clause', 707 *Penn State Law Review*, 727, http://ssrn.com/abstract=1608334, accessed 3 September 2012.

355 Kelly 729.

356 Ibid., 732.

357 Kenneth Katzman 'The Kurds in Post-Saddam Iraq' (6 April 2009) Congressional Research Service, Kelly et al.

358 See Kelly, Deeks and Burton.

359 Namely the Oil and Gas Law, the Revenue Sharing Law and a law re-establishing the Iraq National Oil Company.

360 Deeks and Burton 55–58.

361 Ibid.

362 James Crawford, 'The Authority of the Kurdistan Regional Government over Oil and Gas under the Constitution of Iraq', dated 29 January 2008, www.krg.org/uploads/documents/James_R_Crawford_Kurdistan_Oil_Legal_Opinion_English__2008_07_09_h11m23s26.pdf, accessed 22 February 2012.

363 Andrew Arato, 'Post-Sovereign Constitution-Making and Its Pathology in Iraq', 51 *New York Law School Law Review*, 535–548, 2006–2007.

364 Ibid. The amendment rule of the TAL is ¼ of deputies of constitutional assembly being provided with a veto to block all revisions. In addition, two-thirds of the voters of three provinces could veto a permanent constitution if enacted by the constitutional assembly. Arato, 550.

365 Arato 552.

366 Ibid.

> In summary, three factors – the nature of the Saddam regime; American historical opposition to regional, i.e., Arab, nationalism; and the aggressive nature of the war – all conspired to turn the strategy of imposition into an especially mindless one, under the circumstances. These three factors were given, and could have been in large part neutralized only by the kind of internationalization entirely unacceptable to this particular American government. Whether or not there was theoretical knowledge and moral conviction available to institute a version of post-sovereign constitution-making that would have had a chance to contribute to the rebuilding of Iraq, the three factors worked against the possibility.
>
> (Arato 554)

367 On the basis that the advice is published on the KRG website.

368 James Crawford, 'The Authority of the Kurdistan Regional Government over Oil and Gas under the Constitution of Iraq', dated 29 January 2008, 7, www.krg.org/uploads/documents/James_R_Crawford_Kurdistan_Oil_Legal_Opinion_English__2008_07_09_h11m23s26.pdf, accessed 22 February 2012.

369 Deeks and Burton.

370 Kelly, Deeks and Burton.

371 See previous section.

372 Section 4.

373 Article 112:

> First: The federal government, with the producing governorates and regional governments, shall undertake the management of oil and gas extracted from present fields, provided that it distributes its revenues in a fair manner in proportion to the population distribution in all parts of the country, specifying an allotment for a specified period for the damaged regions which were unjustly deprived of them by the former regime, and the regions that were damaged afterwards in a way that ensures balanced development in different areas of the country, and this shall be regulated by a law.
>
> Second: The federal government, with the producing regional and governorate governments, shall together formulate the necessary strategic policies to develop the oil

and gas wealth in a way that achieves the highest benefit to the Iraqi people using the most advanced techniques of the market principles and encouraging investment.

374 Opinion 7.
375 Ibid.
376 Opinion 7.
377 Opinion 7.
378 Ibid.
379 Ibid.
380 The advice appears to have been followed by the KRG to date as it is engaging a number of IOCs in production sharing agreements contrary to the authority of the federal government who have blacklisted oil companies entering into agreements with the KRG from obtaining contracts in the rest of Iraq.
381 Crawford 8 (fn 9).
382 Crawford 8 (fn 9). An Arabic version of the Committee's report is available at www.parliament.iq/dirrasd/des.pdf accessed 15 February 2012.
383 Crawford 8.
384 Crawford 8 citing Deeks and Burton 58.
385 Deeks and Burton 69 (fn 393).
386 Ibid., 69–70.
387 Deeks and Burton 54–55.
388 Ibid., 65–66, see also Prof. Crawford's Legal Opinion.
389 Deeks and Burton 65–66.
390 Deeks and Burton 65–66.
391 It was at the behest of the US administration, no doubt realising that it was out of its depth in involving itself in Iraq in the first place, that a Constitution needed to be put in place as soon as possible as a mark of US and allied success and justification for the invasion to be demonstrated to the international community. An alternative view is that the United States had no intention of assisting with or imposing a Constitution on Iraq as the political disarray was commercially and economically advantageous to US companies who could dictate terms on obtaining access to oil and reconstruction projects. It was only at the request of the Iraqi's themselves that the Constitution became a priority (Anonymous source, interview dated 3 July 2012).
392 The legality of the war in Iraq has been an ongoing question with the Chilcot Inquiry taking place in London from 2009 to 2011. In any event, the legality of the war is a moot point given that the intention was to bolster the US economy by securing oil resources and long-term contracts in the rebuilding of the infrastructure of the country which is clearly evidenced by the number of American companies involved in Iraq and the delayed withdrawal of US troops.
393 Dr. F. Jabar speaker at Post-American Iraq Conference, Chatham House, 24 March 2010.
394 Which is now known as the Islamic Supreme Council of Iraq (ISCI).
395 A Shi'a group with direct funding from Tehran, www.globalsecurity.org/military/world/paa/sciri.htm, accessed 3 February 2011.
396 In the National Assembly results,

> Sunnis hold only 17 seats (about 6% of the total seats), leaving them underrepresented relative to the population, and Kurds and Shiites overrepresented. There are about 90 women in the Assembly. In provincial elections, the Kurds won about 60% of the seats in Tamim (Kirkuk) province (26 out of 41 seats); Sunni Arabs hold 6 and Turkomens hold 9 seats. This has strengthened Kurdish attempts to gain control of oil- rich city of Kirkuk and provoked an Arab and Turkmen boycott of that council, according to press reports. Pro-Sadr candidates won pluralities or

majorities in several Shiite provinces (Wasit, Dhi Qar, and Maysan) while SCIRI (running separately) won in Najaf, Karbala, Qadisiyah, and Muthana province.

(– K. Katzman, CRS Report to Congress, 'Iraq: Elections and New Government', 5)

397 Eric Davis, 'The Puzzle of Federalism in Iraq', 247 *Middle East Report*, 42, 2008, http://fas-polisci.rutgers.edu/davis/ARTICLES/DavisPuzzleIraqFederalism-MER.608.pdf, accessed 15 January 2013.

> Nor, in a related problem, is there much discussion of the influence of Washington's local and expatriate allies, particularly the Kurds, the Islamic Supreme Council of Iraq (ISCI) – formerly the Supreme Council for the Islamic Revolution in Iraq – and Ahmad Chalabi's Iraqi National Congress, who have much to gain from the implementation of regional federalism.

398 Ibid.

399 The author is not considering the recent implications for Iraq's recent turmoil with Da'ash.

400 For further information about the vote see Michael Eppel, 'A Future for Kurdish Independence?', 2 (25) *Middle East Quarterly*, Spring 2018, www.meforum.org/7226/kurdish-independence, accessed 8 January 2019. See also, Loveday Morris, 'How the Kurdish Independence, Referendum Backfired Spectacularly' *Washington Post* (20 October 2017), www.washingtonpost.com/world/how-the-kurdish-independence-referendum-backfired-/2017/10/20/3010c820-b371-11e7-9b93-b97043e57a22_story.html?noredirect=on&utm_term=.9e582ac723a2, accessed 8 January 2019.

401 There were three Kurdish members of the Council of Ministers following the 2014 elections.

402 The Iraqi President is Kurdish: Jalal Talabani, who in public interviews has maintained that Kurdish independence is unlikely and a united Iraq is more beneficial to the Kurds. A stance which is perhaps unsurprising given the official position held by Talabani. Interview with Al-Jazeera dated 15 April 2012, www.aljazeera.com/indepth/features/2012/04/2012415183347330127.html, accessed 11 July 2012.

403 There are, of course, other disputes between the various political parties in Iraq but the oil dispute is a key issue of contention between the KRG and federal government.

404 Author's personal experience of interaction. This was the situation prior to the recent extensive issues with Da'ash.

405 William S. Livingston, 'A Note on the Nature of Federalism', LXVII (1) *Political Science Quarterly*, 82–84, March 1952.

4 The legislative framework of the Iraqi oil industry

4.1 Current laws governing the oil industry

Although Iraq's current constitution refers to conformity with Islamic principles,[1] it is not stated to be the sole or main source of legislation. According to Article 2 of the Constitution, no laws may be enacted in contravention of Islamic principles, which require consideration when addressing and formulating legislation, but it is not an issue directly relevant to commercial activities within the oil industry.[2]

Since the invasion in 2003, Iraq's legal framework has been in disarray, causing confusion and reluctance of international companies seeking to invest in the oil industry and wider economy.[3] Key considerations for foreign investors include the legal landscape and security when selecting jurisdictions so as to be confident that contracts will be upheld and the location of operations will be secure enough to conduct commercial activities without significant interruption.[4] Laws governing oil prior to 2005 remain effective "unless annulled or amended in accordance with the provisions of [the] Constitution".[5] There have been subsequent attempts to create legislation for the oil industry although many agreements are still governed by pre-2005 laws.[6]

When considering the transition to the current Constitution, it is clear that the central government had a stronger control of hydrocarbon resources under the TAL which diminished as a consequence of accommodating requests by the KRG for increased autonomy during the constitutional negotiation process.[7] Control of hydrocarbon resources in Iraq is a fundamental issue given that, in 2017, it held approximately 148.8 bnb of oil reserves.[8]

4.1.1 Pre-2003

Following the formation of modern Iraq, the domestic framework[9] commenced with the 1925 Constitution.[10] Prior to 1951, Iraq's legal system comprised many different sources of law due to the influences of various occupiers.[11] Work commenced on the Iraq Civil Code shortly after independence following the British Mandate. In 1933, a committee of Iraqi jurists compiled a report for the codification of Iraqi law, and three years later a second committee, chaired by the acting Minister of Justice,[12] was appointed to determine the sources of law for the code and to provide a preliminary draft.[13] The committee considered the Egyptian Civil Codes of 1875 and 1883,[14] adopted from the French Civil Code.[15] The then Dean of the Iraq Law College, Abd al-Razzaq al-Sanhuri, was selected to lead the committee of Iraqi jurists in drafting the code. However, al-Sanuri's work was suspended due to a military coup and subsequent political interruptions but he later returned at the request of the Iraqi government in 1943 to complete the task.[16] The Civil Code was enacted on 8 September 1951 and came into effect on 8 September 1953.

One of the most interesting aspects of the Iraqi Civil Code is found in Article 1(2):

> If the Code does not furnish an applicable provision, the court shall decide in accordance with customary law, and failing that, in accordance with those principles of Muslim law (Shari'a) which are most in keeping with the provisions of this Code, without being bound by any particular school of jurisprudence, and, failing that, in accordance with the principles of equity.

This provision was drafted to assure the majority Shi'a population that the Hanafi principles, which had formed the basis of the Ottoman Mejelle, would not be the dominant source of Shari'a. It would appear that in an attempt to obtain uniformity across the region, al-Sanhuri's influence in the Code comes through in Article 1(3):

> In all of this, the Court shall be guided by judicial decisions and by the principles of jurisprudence in Iraq and in foreign countries whose laws are similar to those in Iraq.

The clearest interpretation of the reference to "similar laws" is to those drafted by al-Sanhuri, namely Egypt and Syria, with reference to the French Civil Code.

The relevant oil legislation pre-2003 includes:

- Law 80 of 1961; Law 11 of 1964;
- Laws 97, 123 and 130 of 1967 on INOC;
- Law 84 of 1985 for the preservation of hydrocarbon resources;
- Law 101 of 1976 organising MoO;[17]
- Resolution 272 of 1987;
- Law 3 of 1997 for the Protection of the Environment;
- Income Tax Laws 113 of 1983 and the State Companies Law 22 of 1997.

Those laws relevant to this chapter will now be addressed in turn. In terms of practice and procedure, the Iraqi Civil Code[18] remains a fundamental component of the legal system along with the Iraqi Code of Civil Procedure.[19]

Although the road to nationalisation of the oil industry was paved prior to 1961, Law No. 80 of 1961, often referred to as the nationalisation law, is the most well-known due to it stipulating the relinquishment of 99.5% of land retained by the IPC group which remained unexplored since the establishment of TPC's Iraqi operations in 1921. This set the foundation for INOC to commence production under a nationalised plan. Subsequently, Law 11 of 1964 established INOC, providing for its objectives and functions and was the first effort of the state to take control of the oil industry and prevent further interference of IOCs. As Law 80 had reclaimed a significant proportion of the nation's resources, it was necessary to implement a commercial structure to control reserves and further the national development plan for exploration and production.[20] Given that the whole issue in hand was nationalisation, Law 11 was a clear sign of efforts being made to create a state-run industry to benefit the national economy. To strengthen state control over national revenues, the same year legislation was passed[21] to regulate the distribution of companies' profits for all companies on the basis of 25% allocation to "labourers and staff" of the relevant company.[22] However, it was subsequently amended[23] to exempt its application to oil and hydrocarbon profits.[24]

INOC was granted ownership of the "geological and geophysical materials and data" for the land transferred under Article 1 of Law 80[25] in addition to the "exclusive rights to exploit oil and hydrocarbon substances in all Iraqi lands including Territorial Waters, Continental Shelf and Iraqi interests in the Neutral Zone". Articles 2(2) and 2(3) of Law 11 provide for INOC to enter into contracts with "companies or bodies undertaking work connected with its purposes. It may also buy or amalgamate them". Thus, for the first time, the capacity to enter into agreements with other oil companies in order to effectively exploit the resources for the benefit of the nation has been available since the establishment of INOC. Parliamentary approval and the maintenance of state funding for operations were the conditions upon which the contracts could be entered. Further, INOC could not compete with other government institutions for refining and distribution of oil products and state ownership of resources was not to be assigned.[26] In 1967, INOC was authorised to directly undertake the exploitation of the resources and, where necessary, with assistance from external companies "by way of partnership with others if it finds this better for the realisation of its purposes".[27] In an attempt to prevent complete monopoly over the oil industry, Article 3 prohibits INOC from exploiting oil in all areas allocated to it by way of concession agreement and confirms that public ownership rights to oil and hydrocarbons cannot be transferred or breached by contract, nor can "any principal or accessory right thereon" be created. Thus, authority is granted under this provision for IOCs to engage in the oil industry and it is this provision that remains in force for the post-2003 contracts, as it has not been repealed to date.

Law No. 123 of 1967 repealed Law 11 of 1964 and re-established INOC as a public body wholly operated by state funds. Pursuant to Article 3(4) INOC "may cooperate with companies, organisations or establishments engaged in operations related to its objectives" thereby permitting agreements with external oil companies in order to maximise production and achieve efficiency in managing resources but retaining the requirement of parliamentary approval for the contracts. The aforementioned legislation was supplemented by regulations including Regulation 41 of 1969 stipulating that the Ministry of Oil and Minerals (MoOM) shall comprise a private bureau, diwan,[28] directorates general of oil affairs, technical affairs and economic affairs.

In 1970, an interim constitution came into effect, lasting until 2005, outlining the competencies of the various political institutions including the RCC which had, inter alia, authority to ratify treaties and international agreements.[29] Article 13 provides that "*[n]ational resources and basic means of production are owned by the People. They are directly invested by the Central Authority in the Iraqi Republic, according to exigencies of the general planning of the national economy.*" An Oil Administration Law was passed the same year assigning offices to be attached to MoOM and the duties and functions of the same.[30] Further, for non-compliance with its provisions for the import or sale of oil, the law provided for criminal sanctions of one year imprisonment or a fine up to double the value of the import or sale.[31] There are subsequent minor pieces of legislation relating to the administration of the oil industry which are not relevant to this book.[32]

During the nationalisation process, attempts were made by the Iraqi government to obtain funds from the IPC group of companies for its share of revenues since the commencement of commercial production. Law 198 of 1970 ratified the agreement between the government and oil companies in Iraq for the payment of an advance in the sum of £20m and set out conditions for government quarterly repayments.[33] In 1971,[34] to address environmental and economic issues which had occurred during the history of IPC dominance, legislation was enacted to provide for the conservation of petroleum resources and hydrocarbon materials.[35] This was the overriding legislation to be considered by companies engaged in operations throughout Iraq stipulating precautions to be taken to prevent damage to property, land or life and that equipment should meet "recognised standards" for efficiency and safety.[36] There were also periodic reporting requirements of proposals and operational data to MoOM (Ministry of Oil and Minerals). Permission from MoOM was required at most stages of operations and criteria for proposals and reporting[37] were set out in the legislation evidencing greater control by the government over the conduct of the E&P process. One example of greater interference in the operations is a requirement for the use of dry holes which may only be plugged with consent from MoOM.[38] There were financial penalty provisions in place for breach of the legislation by operators to be applied at the discretion of the Minister.[39] The legislation was, however, open to abuse in that there was an exemption provision from all or part of the law which could be invoked by the RCC.[40] The protection of national resources was further strengthened the same year when oil operations were to be conducted exclusively by INOC with an express prohibition on concession agreements throughout Iraq save for the non-relinquished fields stipulated in Law 80 of 1961.[41] From the perspective of the IPC group, Law 97 of 1967 marked the end of their freedom to operate in Iraq and was arguably the most significant piece of legislation for Iraqi nationalisation. The implementation of the law sparked correspondence threatening and eventually leading to arbitrations against the Iraqi government. This law tipped the balance of power in the industry to INOC as it could now enter into partnerships[42] with oil companies, where necessary; thereby potentially opening up the industry to foreign companies beyond the IPC consortia. This was in fact the result of the legislation, with INOC entering into agreements with Russian, Venezuelan, Brazilian and Italian international companies.

To facilitate the administration of operations, Law 13 of 1972 established the State Consulting and Planning Company for Oil Projects (SCPCOP)[43] to conduct "technical and economical studies" for installations and projects "and laying down their specifications and designs".[44] SCPCOP was authorised to acquire land "free of charge" and enter into partnerships with other companies and charge service fees to government departments.[45] As a state company, it also enjoyed exemptions from taxation and was governed by a board of directors[46] under the supervision of the Minister of Oil and Minerals.[47] The law overrides any conflicting legislation.

As previously mentioned,[48] Law 69 of 1972 completed the nationalisation of IPC with the state claiming the installations and operational rights.[49] The companies' funds were to be frozen with immediate effect.[50] The Iraq Company for Oil Operations was established to acquire all of the IPC "funds, rights and assets".[51] Following nationalisation on 1 June 1972, the first oil marketing organisation was formed through the General Directorate for oil marketing "to manage and run the entire marketing operations related to crude oil and products".[52]

In 1976, INOC was attached to MoO[53] thereby bringing it under the organisation of the oil industry's entities and centralised control of the supply chain providing for the functions of MoO and INOC. In an effort to further control and protect Iraq's oil wealth, Law 84 of 1985 was passed for the preservation of hydrocarbon resources which provided for a range of stipulations for regulating the industry, including the requirement of producing and maintaining records for operations and the use of efficient scientific technology with the "newest techniques" to be used for exploration. In the main, the legislation provides for the use of an annual plan and reports of each stage of the exploration, extraction and development process. Law 84 is still in effect given that there is no comparable recent legislation. This Law deals with the technical aspects of the industry including procedures for development, production and refining.[54] The same year, legislation was passed organising MoO to administer the industry and structure it into a centre, comprised of the Minister of Oil responsible for the Department of External Relations and Investments and the Administrative Department, the Oil Board, the Under Secretary of Oil for Planning and the Under Secretary for Oil Establishments. The law provides for the functions of INOC[55] and allocates state establishments for oil and gas production, exploration and drilling; oil and oil products marketing and transport as attachments to INOC.[56] The level of detail in the Law extends to issues such as the role of Department of External Relations in "[s]upervising the execution of oil service contracts signed between the Ministry, of the one part, and the oil companies in the Arab Homeland and the world, of the other part".[57]

Law 35 of 1977 is the Legal System Reform Law which aimed to change "the whole structure of the old society"[58] and outlined the "nature and goals of the July revolution 1968".[59] Given that the socialist ideology at the time was that laws are "a reflection of ideas and economic interests prevailing in the society" reconsideration of the old system of legislation was required "in order to change, improve or repeal any one thereof".[60] The aims of this law bear some relevance to the current situation in Iraq, in that if the

> legal rules need "administration" which maintain and implement them, then it is necessary to have legislations which organise this "administration" and define the policy of the leadership towards the total social and economic questions. But the rules laid down by the political leadership … may be violated and consequently, it is necessary to ensure the integrity and respect of these rules through promulgating penal legislations springing from the same comprehensive concept of society.[61]

The current weakness in Iraq's economy is due to a lack of comprehensive state machinery to oversee the economic and commercial activity for the national benefit. The state structure is severely fragmented with a wide gap between government and society. For the purposes of the oil industry, the relevant explanations for this legislation are found in its Explanatory Memorandum, which provides, inter alia, that the management and development of commodities should achieve national development goals and implement rules for the distribution and re-distribution of national income to conform with national economic requirements.[62] Existing commercial legislation was seen in the document to be of a capitalist nature promoting certain interest groups to the detriment of society as a whole, citing as an example the partiality towards creditors "even on the account of public interests".[63] There are suggestions for commercial legislation to be reformed to protect the weaker party to the agreement by imposing penalties for defects or exploitation in contractual obligations.[64] The key issue of rights and ownership is to further the national development and consider state ownership as the key component of public ownership.[65] Many suggestions for reform are contained within the document and suggest reframing the country's legal system from a socialist viewpoint. However, for present purposes there is no necessity for a detailed analysis of it due to a minor implementation of the recommendations.

The 1984 Law of Commerce[66] relates to transportation, international sales and transactions in the midstream sector and is not considered further here. A marketing body for the oil industry was established in 1987,[67] the State Organisation of Oil Marketing (now known as SOMO). The following decade the state recognised the need for environmental legislation and passed Law 3 of 1997 for the Protection of the Environment which created a framework primarily to prevent pollution.[68]

State Companies Law 22 of 1997[69] provided for the restructuring and organisation of state companies with the aim of improving national economic growth.[70] It sets out guidelines to the relevant ministry for the establishment of new state companies requiring cabinet approval. The company's capital will be provided by the state treasury, and company registration will be published in the official gazette. Up to 30%[71] of the net profits of the company[72] are to be divided between the state treasury,[73] company employees,[74] research and development,[75] social services[76] and capital reserve.[77] In the event of corporate losses amounting to more than 50% of the company's capital, an economic appraisal will be conducted by the relevant ministry and provided to the cabinet for approval.[78] Cabinet approval is required for investment outside Iraq of surplus funds by the company, but internal investment does not require this approval.[79] Four members of the board of directors of the company shall be selected by the relevant minister.[80] Following cabinet approval, the state company may be changed to a shareholding company.[81]

4.1.2 Post-2003

Following the regime change in 2003, the Coalition Provisional Authority (CPA) formulated legal documents designed to privatise the majority of key economic sectors to attract foreign investment. Consequently, Iraq's business environment has improved for investors due to a gradual change in the legal landscape. Some key legislation includes:

- The Central Bank Law No. 56 of 2004
- Law No. 64 of 2004, amending Company Law No. 21 of 1997
- The Banking Law No. 94 of 2004
- Kurdistan Region Investment Law No. 4 of 2006
- Private Investment in Crude Oil Refining Law No. 64 of 2007
- Decree No. 329/2008
- Law 27/2009 an Environmental Law

Some of the investment laws are not applicable or relevant to the oil industry for the purposes of this book. The Trade Liberalization Policy Law No. 54 of 2004 suspended all customs imports and export tariffs pending notification from the transitional Iraqi authority with the exception of crude oil which is governed by SOMO.[82] Oil contracts are exempt from Law No. 13 of 2006. Order 39 permits complete foreign ownership of businesses except in the sectors of natural resources, banking and insurance. Some degree of property protection is provided as foreign ownership remains prohibited but renewable licences for the use of real property may be granted for up to forty years.[83]

Key legislation relating to the oil industry is yet to come into effect. It was originally suggested that a package of laws should be provided to address the issues of the industry, these laws drafted in 2007 being the Federal Oil and Gas Law (FOGL) (later amended on 2011); the Iraq National Oil Company (INOC) Law[84]; Ministry of Oil Law (MoOL); Revenue Sharing Law (RSL) and the Public Commission to Audit and Appropriate Federal Revenues Law (PCAAFRL).

Federal oil and gas law drafts have been in existence since 2007 with the last revision in 2011. It is essential for legislation to govern the industry in order to promote stability and security for both the state and investors, although the current ambiguity provides both the state and IOCs with flexibility to negotiate and renegotiate contractual terms where necessary. There has been political deadlock in passing the draft legislation, which is considerably affected by the KRG acting independently of the central government, contrary to the Constitution. The KRG has its own version of a hydrocarbon law which is not recognised as valid by the central government due to the differing interpretations of the constitutional provisions providing for the assignment of control over oil resources.

Before addressing these issues, it is necessary to provide some context to understand the importance of a legal framework. Between 2005 and 2015, there have been over forty PSAs entered into by the KRG with IOCs and fourteen SCs by the federal government, through three licensing rounds. Due to an increasing rift between the central government and the Kurdish region since 2005, the Oil Ministry has created a blacklist of international oil companies dealing with the KRG preventing them from operating in the rest of Iraq. Pursuant to Article 130 of the current Constitution, no contract will be valid unless authorised by Parliament.[85]

4.1.2.1 The TAL

Under international law, allied forces in Iraq only had power to issue rules necessary to protect the occupied territories and no authority to change the constitution. However, the US administration in Iraq, under the guidance of Paul Bremer,[86] cancelled the 1970 interim constitution and issued the Transitional Administrative Law (TAL).[87] The steps taken by the CPA were to ensure wholesale US administrative dominance, with impunity, over fundamental aspects of Iraq's political, legal and practical infrastructure. The CPA orders

> included banning the Iraqi courts from considering claims against US soldiers or security contractors, appointing a national security adviser, appointing a US adviser for each ministry, and regulating the media. Bremer took control of Iraq's financial resources, dissolved the Iraqi armed forces, and disbanded the Ba'th Party, resulting in the disenfranchisement of hundreds of thousands of Iraqis.[88]

It may be argued that the cause of current frictions in the Iraqi political and legal sphere are a consequence of CPA governance. The TAL refers to "sect" in Articles 12 and 20 which is the first time the word has been incorporated into any Iraqi constitutional document and, according to Jawad was rejected by most Iraqis.[89] This is understandable given that generally the objective of a constitution is to unify a nation rather than divide it.[90]

The Governing Council (GC)[91] for the first time in Iraqi history comprised "*25 people selected according to their sect, ethnic background, and, most importantly, their loyalty to the US. This was the first time in the history of Iraq that appointments were made on sectarian and ethnic bases*". In the GC, 65% of members held other nationalities in addition to their Iraqi nationality and, excluding the Kurdish parties, "*only five members of the GC were living in Iraq before 2003*".[92]

> In most cases, merit and qualifications were not taken into consideration. The GC was asked to approve the TAL, and did so with only minor modifications. The Council's main objection was that the new law did not refer to Islam as the official religion of the state and on their insistence, Article 7 was included.[93]

Clauses 60 and 61 stated that the permanent constitution should have been drafted before 15 August 2005 by the new unelected National Assembly and presented for approval in a general referendum "*no later than 15 October 2005*". If the referendum were to result in the approval of the constitution permanent government elections were to be held by 15 December 2005 with the new government taking office by 31 December 2005 at the latest.[94]

The special committee to draft the constitution was formed only two months prior to the October deadline.

A review of the drafting process of the TAL and 2005 Constitution reveals a concerted effort to weaken the central government and strengthen the provinces in a misguided approach to federalism which was inappropriate in the Iraqi context.[95] The TAL was drafted by individuals inexperienced in constitutional law with no real connection to, or understanding of, Iraq at the time.[96] For example, Article 10 attempts to acknowledge democratic governance and national input into the Iraqi structure and hides the context in which the document was drafted[97]:

> As an expression of the free will and sovereignty of the Iraqi people, their representatives shall form the governmental structures of the State of Iraq. The Iraqi Transitional Government and the governments of the regions, governorates, municipalities, and local administrations shall respect the rights of the Iraqi people, including those rights cited in this Chapter.[98]

As for the maintenance of legal order Article 26 provides:

> (A) Except as otherwise provided in this Law, the laws in force in Iraq on 30 June 2004 shall remain in effect unless and until rescinded or amended by the Iraqi Transitional Government in accordance with this Law.
>
> (B) Legislation issued by the federal legislative authority shall supersede any other legislation issued by any other legislative authority in the event that they contradict each other, except as provided in Article 54(B).
>
> (C) The laws, regulations, orders, and directives issued by the Coalition Provisional Authority pursuant to its authority under international

> law shall remain in force until rescinded or amended by legislation duly enacted and having the force of law.[99]

Despite the negative commentary above, the position of the central government was stronger under the TAL than the current Constitution as it provided centralised control of oil resources which withered during the constitutional negotiation process.

The relevant provision for the oil industry under the TAL 2004[100] provided the Iraqi Transitional Government with exclusive competence in:

> (A) Formulating foreign policy and diplomatic representation; negotiating, signing, and ratifying international treaties and agreements; formulating foreign economic and trade policy and sovereign debt policies; …
>
> (E) Managing the natural resources of Iraq, which belongs to all the people of all the regions and governorates of Iraq, in consultation with the governments of the regions and the administrations of the governorates, and distributing the revenues resulting from their sale through the national budget in an equitable manner proportional to the distribution of population throughout the country, and with due regard for areas that were unjustly deprived of these revenues by the previous regime, for dealing with their situations in a positive way, for their needs, and for the degree of development of the different areas of the country;

Article 2 of the TAL 2004 provided for a permanent Constitution to enter into force no later than 31 December 2005. On 15 October 2005, by controversial referendum, the constitution was ready for enforcement by publication and the sitting of the first Parliament.[101] Due to the speed at which the constitution was drafted and implemented, the National Assembly permitted a short extension to the original timetable.[102] Commentators, such as Brown, note that there is no clear explanation for the tight drafting timetable being due to political or partisan concerns for such an important document. Instead:

> They present the process of writing a constitution—as President George W. Bush recently described it—as an opportunity for Iraqis to "bind their multiethnic society together in a democracy."[103]

Brown notes that, instead of reflecting the short-term political interests of parties or groups, Iraqis have spoken of writing a document expressing the entire public will for 'the future generations'.[104] Former Prime Minister Al Jaafari has described the political process as 'worth a thousand tanks.'[105] This view was echoed by Richard Jones, the Iraq coordinator in the US Department of State, in his testimony before Congress on 29 June 2005 that, "*[g]enerally speaking, Iraq needs to move from ethnic to issue based politics. This evolution will require national political dialogue among Shi'a, Sunni, and Kurdish groups and the involvement of other minority populations*".[106]

4.1.2.2 The Constitution – oil, disputed territories and related issues

Far from being a lengthy and considered process for a new state democracy following regime change, the current constitution was drafted, approved and published in the official gazette in 2005 and entered into force upon the first sitting of parliament in 2006. All existing legislation in place prior to enactment remains in force unless amended or annulled. The legislation prior to 2003 requires consideration of its effect on any subsequent provisions for the legal framework as a whole. Although there are many laws connected with the development of the oil industry since the 1925 Convention with the TPC, it is only the fundamental provisions that will be addressed here. The 1925 Convention provided exclusive rights to TPC for a seventy-five-year term for the exploration, exploitation and production of oil with all property belonging to TPC reverting to the Iraqi government on the expiration of the term.[107]

4.1.2.2.1 DRAFTING OF THE CURRENT CONSTITUTION

As noted above, after some debate between the US administration and Iraqi political interests, the TAL provided the National Assembly with a deadline of 15 August 2005 for completion of the drafting of the permanent Constitution with the final deadline of 15 October 2005 for a general referendum and the interim period to be used for public awareness and debate of the document. In order to ratify the Constitution through referendum, there had to be a majority approval and two-thirds of the voters in a minimum of three governorates must not reject the document. Although controversial, the document was approved in the referendum albeit for some Iraqis their vote for the document was on a conditional basis. As Ali notes

> there is no dispute that the vast majority of the Iraqi population never had the opportunity to review the 2006 Constitution's final draft before the referendum date, as a result of the fact that a number of changes were introduced two days before the referendum date. Iraqis therefore approved a text that they had not seen, let alone read.[108]

A common issue raised by those involved in the constitutional drafting process is the restrictive time frame in which the document was to be compiled. The drafting committee was appointed on 10 May 2005 by the National Assembly, and given just over three months in which to construct the Iraqi constitution.[109] Upon reading contemporaneous documents it becomes clear that certain interested parties were more organised and dominant than others, most notably the Kurdish representatives, which explains the ambiguity within the document particularly in relation to the balance of power between the central government and the regions.[110] As observed by Brown, the dialogue during the constitutional drafting process did little to encourage a unified political community. In fact, since 2003, political divisions were exacerbated by "*the process of constitutional design*". For example, the Presidency Council "*was designed by the TAL, with Shiite, Kurds, and Arab Sunnis each laying claim to one of the seats*". The fundamental error in the process appears to be due to the fact that

> [m[ost of the bargaining over the permanent constitution has been carried out in ethnic, religious, and regional terms, and initial indications are that the constitution being drafted will reflect the interests of the various groups without resolving the many differences among them—or even provide clear tools for resolution.[111]

Prior to the August 2005 deadline, great importance was placed on having a draft constitution as a benchmark of progress in Iraq so it was crucial that a constitutional document emerged in order to show some element of success for the coalition forces as well as the Iraqi political elite at the time. Advisers to the drafting committee state that in relation to the section on federal powers[112]:

> … there is a wide spectrum of ways in which the federal and sub-federal governments can balance authority, such as exclusively federal, federally-led with regional participation, regionally-led with federal participation, and exclusively regional (or governorate). A number of these points along the spectrum are reflected in the negotiation and final structure of this section.

It would seem that given the political differences during the drafting process, where at times parties were at a stalemate, the solution provided ambiguity in order that each side might interpret the document to suit their interests. However, this was a mistake as it merely postponed the difficulties and tensions by translating and cementing them in such a crucial and fundamental document. As noted by comparative law observers, the way in which the constitution was drafted and the difficulty in amending provisions relating to federalism aimed to create a confederation rather than a truly federal state due to the regions having considerable autonomy[113]:

> … regional authorities are residual lawmakers who are also entitled to amend federal law in matters that are not exclusively in the federal realm. Other than foreign, defense and monetary policy, the category of exclusive federal powers is fairly small … Amendments would require local consent, through the local legislature and a local popular referendum, as well as the difficult national process of legislative approval, referendum and presidential signature.

The key provisions of concern in the Constitution for the oil industry are the ownership and management of resources, scope of federal powers, geographical and boundary provisions and the legal system and judiciary. The fourth section of the current Constitution contains the powers of the federal government and significant reference points for the administration of natural resources with the central provision being Article 111 providing that "[o]il and gas are owned by all the people of Iraq in all the regions and governorates". However, when one looks to the exclusive powers of the federal government there is an absence of reference to the management of natural resources or oil and gas which is often found in other constitutions.

There is an unusual provision under Article 115 whereby the regional laws passed by local governments may supersede any conflicting federal provision as regional law takes "priority" over federal law. This can be seen as an absurd attempt by the drafters with the influence of the more organised and adversely affected sections of Iraqi society under the previous regime to seriously weaken the power of the central government and enforce a policy of significant decentralisation of the country. The effect of such a provision could only ever lead to chaos and conflict within Parliament which has played out in the political arena since 2006. Article 115 is a poorly drafted and misplaced provision which upon close reading was formulated in order to appease the conflicting interests at the drafting table and when combined with Article 121, which provides for the regions to amend the application of national legislation for matters outside the exclusive authority of the federal government where it conflicts with regional law and significantly weakens the powers of the central government. These provisions have been used by the KRG to maintain their position that they have constitutional authority to manage and export oil and gas in the region. Given the amount of negotiation over many of the provisions, a strong counter-argument advanced by those present during the drafting process is that by separating the provisions for oil and gas from Article 114, they remain within the remit of federal law and there was no intention for the laws of the regions or governorates to take priority over the issue. As observed by Deeks and Burton in agreement with the counter-argument that the drafters would never have intended for Article 121(second), which derived from Article 54(B) TAL, to override the carefully drafted compromise on oil and gas by inserting a last-minute provision handing over a key area of federal regulation to the regions and governorates.[114] This provision was included in the constitution before Article 115, which entered into the draft constitution on 21 August with hardly any prior debate.[115] All unresolved areas of the constitution were held-up by the negotiations on the oil and gas provision which took weeks of compromise to resolve, with the drafters "painstakingly" ensuring that oil and gas management remained with the federal government and that revenue distribution would be 'with' the producing regional and governorate governments.[116]

Although there has been some recognition of the Kurdish region as being somewhat semi-autonomous from the rest of Iraq, with the first constitutional reference in 1970 and further assistance in 1991 by the external imposition of a no-fly zone over the region during the Kuwait war, the most recent Constitution expressly provides for the separation of the Kurdish area into a region thereby unnecessarily giving away elements of key central government control and ultimately facilitating Kurdish independence. This position was further cemented through Article 141 which provides for Kurdish regional legislation since 1992 to remain effective

> and decisions issued by the government of the region of Kurdistan, including court decisions and contracts, shall be considered valid unless they are amended or annulled pursuant to the laws of the region of Kurdistan by the competent entity in the region, provided that they do not contradict with the Constitution.[117]

Among the Iraqi representatives at the drafting table there appeared to be no foresight into the consequences of the provisions to be enacted save for the Kurdish agenda to secure decentralisation, which appeared to pass without significant resistance from others in the process. However, the provision for regional division of the country caused concern among advisers at the time of drafting, such as Nicholas Haysom, the 2005 director of the Office of Constitutional Support in Baghdad, who wrote an internal report prior to the conclusion of the constitutional negotiations stating that

> the provisions for the conversion of governorates into a region outside Kurdistan create a model for the territorial division of the State which in our view leaves the central government underpowered and possibly under-resourced.[118]

At the time of writing, the only "region" in Iraq designated as such is the Kurdish area in the north, the boundaries of which are disputed. There have been calls from the south of the country for the Basra area to become a "region" but this call has been intermittent and dependent upon the political climate in the country as a whole. Ten months following the implementation of the new constitution, legislation was passed to assist in the formation of regions entitled the "Law of the Executive Procedures Regarding the Formation of Regions Pursuant to Articles 117(second), 118, 119, 120, 121 of the Constitution". On this, Deeks and Burton have the following comment:

> … the law determined how a province might accede to an existing region. The law assigned to Iraq's Higher Electoral Commission the role of conducting requisite referenda… explained how citizens in a province are to make known their desire to join a region; described what happens if the Electoral Commission received competing requests for different regional configurations; and defined a successful referendum as one that received a majority of affirmative votes …[119]

The overriding concern about the drafting process is the apparent exclusion, unwillingness or non-incorporation of Sunni representatives which appear to have only been present as a token gesture in the proceedings. This has hindered the political process since 2006 with a significant proportion of Iraqi society feeling excluded from the state structure and development of the country. As noted by Deeks and Burton[120]

> [v]irtually none of the compromise ideas that had arisen during constitutional negotiations to appease Sunni fears of regional formation appeared in the final law. The COR gave the federal government no substantive role in approving the formation of regions … There is no limit on the number of governorates that may merge into a region. And region formation requires only a simple majority approval by voters in the referendum.

4.1.2.2.2 THE 2005 CONSTITUTION AS ADOPTED

Article 23 of the 2005 Iraqi Constitution protects private property and provides for compensation for expropriation in addition to stating that possession of immovable assets is restricted to Iraqis unless there is a legislative exemption. As in the case of many other states, Iraq's oil resources belong to the people with a duty on the government to preserve the sovereignty of the state. Article 111 is often referred to by the KRG as providing legitimacy for an autonomous oil industry in the region. However, this argument fails at the outset given that the benefit of oil wealth is for the whole country and not merely the northern region. The attempt by the KRG to independently sign oil agreements due to the central government failing to provide them with their share of the national budget, which has been calculated at 17%, bears no coherent relevance to the federal government's duty to protect the security and sovereignty of national resources.[121] The withholding of the proportion of the budget by the central government[122] was a direct consequence of the KRG's attempt to bypass the federal legislation and create a separate industry independent of Baghdad and in direct competition.[123] The different contractual terms were seen by some oil companies to be more preferential than those contained within the contracts awarded by MoO, thereby damaging the sovereignty and unity of the country.

Article 110 on exclusive authority of the federal government does not make any reference to natural resources or oil and gas. It provides for "[f]ormulating foreign policy and diplomatic representation; negotiating, signing, and ratifying international treaties and agreements; negotiating, signing, and ratifying debt policies and formulating foreign sovereign economic and trade policy".[124] Although there is no specific reference, the remit of this provision extends to the particular operations of the hydrocarbon industry. Thus the federal government is exclusively responsible for authorisation of oil agreements with international companies, treaties relevant to the industry, economic planning and distribution.[125] As the oil sector is a key component of the Iraqi economy, the planning of the national budget, investment budget and fiscal policies will bear some relevance to the industry along with the policies for water sources, water flow and distribution which are necessary requirements for the extraction process.

A fundamental provision causing significant debate and differing interpretations, with some commentators and advisers placing more emphasis than others on the significance of cooperation with the governorates and regions, is Article 112. Powers shared between the central government and the region are stipulated in Article 114 where no reference is made to hydrocarbons thus indicating that there was no intention for the oversight, authorisation and management of natural resources to be shared with regional governments or governorates. The extent of coordination is limited to a consultative process in the management and policy planning but not governance of the industry, including the allocation and award of contracts, which is to remain with the central government.

An arguably ambiguous provision lies in Article 115 and has been cited on numerous occasions by the KRG to justify their independent and illegal award of PSAs to foreign companies without consultation with MoO or approval from Parliament.[126] On one view, Article 115 is problematic as Article 110 specifies exclusive federal powers and the management of oil resources is not listed. The provisions relating to the management of oil resources are specified immediately after Article 110 and before the section of the Constitution relating to regional powers. Therefore they were placed in a compromise position in order to get the Constitution through a referendum resulting in ambiguity and causing significant difficulties for the KRG and federal government. The problem is further compounded by the fact that Article 121, second, provides the regions with power to amend the application of national legislation where it contradicts regional legislation. However, the answer is clear as the oil and gas provisions in the constitution fall within the section on federal powers. Had the drafters sought to weaken or share the governance of the hydrocarbon industry with the regions or governorates then these provisions would have been placed in the following section relating to regional powers.

Pursuant to Article 120, any region in Iraq has authorisation to adopt its own constitution to assist in structuring the authorities in that region provided that there is no conflict with the federal constitution. The KRG has its own constitution but any conflicting provisions with the 2005 federal constitution would be void, including the authorisation of petroleum operations without consultation with or ratification through the federal Parliament. Further guidance on regional regulation is provided in the next provision which provides a significant amount of autonomy to these authorities as they "shall have the right to exercise executive, legislative, and judicial powers in accordance with this Constitution, except for those authorities stipulated in the exclusive authorities of the federal government".[127] Article 121 contains the provisions to make the regions mini-states within Iraq and cements the decentralisation and diminishing control of the central government particularly in circumstances where the regional governments can amend national legislation to suit their policies in the event of conflict where the matter does not fall within the exclusive authority of the federal government.

The Kurdish representatives at the drafting table managed to protect their existing legal position through the negotiation and acceptance of what became Article 141, which when combined with Article 121 gives a considerable amount of legislative control to the KRG on issues outside of the exclusive control of the federal government, but for the reasons stated above does not include the regulation and administration of the hydrocarbon industry.

4.1.2.2.3 PROPOSED AMENDMENTS: THE CONSTITUTIONAL REVIEW COMMITTEE

Iraq's Constitution has several issues questioning its legitimacy which has led to considerable dispute between the KRG and the central government in relation to the management of oil resources and the allocation of contracts. This disagreement arises from the formulation of the key constitutional provisions relating to oil resources and the scope of interpretation between the KRG and central government. The KRG's position is that it has a constitutional right to enter into agreements with IOCs to exploit hydrocarbons in the region.[128] However, the position of the central government is that the management and control of oil and gas is a federal power, which is undoubtedly the clearest literal interpretation of the 2005 constitutional provisions. Given the disagreement over its provisions, the obvious solution would be to amend the constitution but this is not as simple as it first appears due to the wording of Article 126, Fourth:

> Articles of the Constitution may not be amended if such amendment takes away from the powers of the regions that are not within the exclusive powers of the federal authorities, except by the approval of the legislative authority of the concerned region and the approval of the majority of its citizens in a general referendum.

The above provision may be suspended for the purposes of constitutional review. As a protection mechanism and to appease the conflicting interests during the drafting process, Article 142 was incorporated to provide an opportunity to amend the constitution. The process commenced shortly after the constitution was ratified. Pursuant to Article 142, First, a report containing a review of the constitution with suggested amendments was to be presented to the Council of Representatives (CoR) within four months of the commencement of its work. The recommendations were to be approved by an absolute majority of votes in the CoR and then within two months of the vote, the amendments were to be presented for public referendum. The amendments are effective upon approval "by the majority of the voters, and if not rejected by two-thirds of the voters in three or more governorates".[129] Article 142, Fifth may save the federal government because the committee which was due to provide proposals for amendment to the constitution have not yet submitted their report and suspended their work.

A first report of the Constitutional Review Committee (CRC) was dated 23 May 2007 but many issues were unresolved resulting in the CoR extending the timeframe for completion of a report to 2009.[130] The first report suggested that Article 110 expands the exclusive powers of the federal government with the agreement of the 'related governorates' to, inter alia; auditing the federal government accounts, federal power system, state liabilities, quality control, regulating work and safety standards in the oil fields and mines, protection of the environment and national geological surveys.

In its report dated 7 July 2008, the CRC, comprising twenty-nine members, identified forty-five areas that require amendment but could not resolve matters relating to the Preamble; Article 41 on Civil Status; powers of the President, Prime Minister and ministers, powers of the Federal Council, redrafting oil and gas provisions unanimously with a single proposal; providing a single proposal for the powers of the regions and governorates and Article 140.[131] The report states that "[f]or all of the aforementioned issues, there are convergent or adversary views for which alternatives and proposals have been developed".[132]

It is evident that consensus on amendments comprehensive enough to provide the federal government with power to exclusively monitor and control the hydrocarbon industry is unlikely. The Committee in 2008 recognised the political difficulties in amending the Constitutional provisions as suggested and provided an alternative suggestion that[133]:

1 In case of not amending the text or if the amendments were not ac cepted, this suggestion might be considered.
2 Changing the sequence of the Articles, as Articles (111 and 112) on oil and gas shall follow Article (115) and the exception might be omitted.

It is not entirely clear as to the intent behind this suggestion. It might be that by placing Articles 111 and 112 after Article 115 and within the section on federal powers the oil provisions are highlighted as being federal and separate from the shared powers. By deleting the first sentence of Article 115, which appears to be the reference to "exception" above, there is clarity in the event of there being powers shared between the regions and federal government, as it is only in these circumstances that regional law will take priority in the case of dispute thereby ensuring that any reference to oil and gas is outside of this scenario.

By making amendments to the constitution the foundation of the legal framework of the state can be improved to provide more credibility to the original formulation process described as "remarkable in the way in which members of the assembly, though legally charged with responsibility for writing the draft, were not involved".[134]

4.1.3 The Kurdish region

In drafting the Constitution the "clear favouritism towards the Kurdish parties" has been noted by Jawad through Articles 53, 54 and 58.[135] The de facto authority of the KRG extended beyond the recognised Kurdish areas of Dohuk, Erbil and Sulaimaniya to the disputed areas of Kirkuk, Diyala and Nineveh (Mosul). Baghdad and Kirkuk, unlike other provinces, were prevented from establishing federal status.[136]

Due to the strength of the Kurdish representation, an opportunity appears to have been seized to extend the remit of the region during the constitutional drafting process as

> [t]he oil rich Kirkuk province became a very difficult issue. Historically, Kirkuk was not predominantly Kurdish … Yet following the 2003 invasion and the domination of the Kurdish parties of Kirkuk, the Kurdish regional

government moved Kurdish families into Kirkuk, claiming that they had previously been living there. These moves have been consistently opposed by the Turkoman and Arab inhabitants of Kirkuk.[137]

The Kurdish region has its own elected parliament and President. On 11 March 1970 an agreement was signed between the Iraqi central government and Mustafa Barzani to grant an autonomous region to the Kurds following a ceasefire of a nine-year war with the central government.[138] The geographical location was to be determined by census even though the Kurdistan Democratic Party (KDP) sought to rely upon the 1957 census to determine the regional boundaries.[139]

There is a marked tension between the central government and the KRG over the extent to which the latter can exercise control, if at all, of the oil resources in the region. In essence, this dispute comes down to the interpretation of the relevant constitutional provisions. Since 2005 the KRG has passed its own laws for investment[140] and hydrocarbons[141] in an attempt to boost economic activity in the region from international investors. This incentive to create a prosperous economy serves to engender Kurdish independence by having a self-contained economic and political identity.

Currently the KRG is operating as a de facto independent state in relation to oil production and distribution. Although the central government has not recognised the agreements entered into by the KRG, as it considers them to be illegal, international companies are continuing to operate in the region. This is so despite the central government blacklisting and preventing these companies from obtaining contracts in the rest of Iraq. The contracts offered by the KRG differ in their terms to federal contracts and are arguably more favourable to international investors which is evidenced by the movement of operations by some majors from Iraq to the Kurdish region.[142] Undoubtedly the KRG is making every effort to compete with the central government and provide a stable framework for operations in the region through contractual terms, legislation,[143] and economic incentives.[144]

In response, Baghdad has reduced and in some cases ceased payments from the federal budget to the region. This has caused considerable inconvenience to the KRG in meeting its contractual obligations for payment to the oil companies with some companies responding through legal action.[145]

The provisions of the KRG Hydrocarbons Law 2007 contain key features for an industry framework. The material scope of the document is outlined in Article 2, Second, as being pursuant to Articles 115 and 121(1) and (2) of the Constitution with express agreement of the "relevant authority of the Region", required for petroleum operations. The federal Constitution is further cited as authority for the creation of this document in Article 3 which cites article 111 and 112 of the constitution as the basis for the KRG's title to petroleum and a share in the revenues.

The legislation stipulates that in cooperation with the Federal Oil and Gas Council (FOGC), the "KRG will agree with federal government the joint management of oil and gas extracted from current fields in the region" and "co-operate with the federal government in formulating strategic policies". Further regional revenues are to be placed in a fund for Iraq.[146] However, in a somewhat weak and odd attempt to restrict the power of the federal government, conditions are stipulated which are to be met by the federal government, before the above cooperation provisions take effect.[147] There are then provisions for the specific contract terms for PSCs.[148]

KRG hydrocarbons legislation suggests that the federal government only has a right to deal with oil fields in production in the region, which were non-existent at the time of the 2005 constitution. The main issue between Baghdad and Erbil is that the KRG believes itself to be an autonomous entity when dealing with oil contracts in the region whereas the federal government believes that it should control national oil policy throughout Iraq with the KRG having a participatory role in the allocation of contracts.

In 2009, KRG deals with IOCs fell through due to a dispute between the federal government over who should pay the foreign oil firms developing fields in the region. The government in Baghdad declared the contracts illegal and the firms would be paid out of the KRG's percentage of the annual national budget.[149] The KRG declined to go along with this interpretation. In October 2009, the KRG suspended exports and its output subsequently dropped to 20,000 b/d.[150]

Without agreeing the status of PSCs, the KRG and Baghdad eventually agreed to resume production and exports in February 2010 and production from Iraqi Kurdish oilfields was publicly announced.[151] The resumption of oil exports was claimed by Shahristani to have no connection with finding a solution to the problem of the earlier KRG contracts.[152]

To date, the federal government still considers KRG contracts to be illegal and has a policy of blacklisting IOCs that enter into agreements in the northern region. In 2012, the Iraqi government has gave Exxon time to consider its position regarding its contract for one of the supergiant oilfields in the South but the company's response was not publicised.[153] Although the consequences for Exxon's contract seemed unclear with speculation that the oil ministry has lined up other oil majors to take over the contract if necessary, it appears from more recent media reports that the Iraqi government is in negotiations with Exxon to develop further fields in the south of Iraq and looking to restructure its existing signed agreements in light of the lower oil prices. As at 2016, government withdrawal of the West Qurna contract seemed unlikely.[154]

It would appear that the KRG considers itself as independent of the constraints of the federal government and by enacting legislation ahead of the federal government and objecting to the terms of the draft legislation it is maintaining its position as an independent region in an attempt to exploit Iraq's reserves.

In 2005, the World Bank noted that the region operates autonomously[155] and the mainstream media has also commented on the situation with the central government.[156]

4.2 The Federal Draft Oil and Gas Law (DOGL) and revenue sharing

For stability in the industry, a comprehensive law is required to provide investors and stakeholders with security. This will allow the government to develop its plans for expanding foreign investment in Iraq and attract a wider range of companies to bid for future contracts thereby providing more choice for selection by MoO and greater competition which could potentially raise industry standards. Pursuant to Article 112 of the Constitution, management of oil and gas in Iraq is to be regulated by legislation.

The key issue in drafting petroleum legislation is to identify its purpose and establish the balance of power between the state and corporate entities. Often companies engaged in the industry are seeking stability for investment and a clear avenue for recourse should the relationship with the host state get into difficulties. Thus the rules for ownership, contract formation, dispute resolution, revenue distribution and the fiscal regime are fundamental issues.

Issues with management and coordination of the reserves in the north could have been prevented or resolved shortly after the implementation of the current constitution. The difficulty in passing any oil and gas law lies in the opposing political interests within Parliament. The fact that the KRG were quick to pass their own hydrocarbon legislation ahead of the federal law demonstrates a clear Kurdish agenda to undermine the government and weaken any influence from and accountability to Baghdad thereby furthering the desire for a fully decentralised state.

Currently, there are several versions of the draft FOGL with the initial draft in 2007 and subsequent revised versions in 2011 by the MoO and CoM. The later versions are more comprehensive and address key issues in an attempt to strengthen the federal government's control of a national oil policy. The 2011 version forwarded by the MoO was submitted for parliamentary review in late August 2011 but in negotiations with the federal government, the KRG still refers to the 2007 version as it provides more scope for negotiation and they have rejected the 2011 versions of the law.

For ease of analysis the 2007 and 2011[157] versions of the DOGL will be addressed by topic as follows:

1. Definitions
2. Purpose and application of the law
3. Control and management of resources
4. Contract review
5. INOC
6. Field development
7. Contract negotiation
8. Model contracts
9. Licences and obligations of licence holders

10 Unitisation of fields
11 Gas
12 Transportation
13 Protection of resources
14 Inspection
15 Petroleum returns and financial obligations
16 Conflict resolution
17 Transparency
18 Final provisions

The 2007 DOGL commences with a preamble and the ownership of resources whereas the 2011 version places definitions in Article 1.

4.2.1 Definitions

Reference to the Competent Body/Designated Authority in both versions of the DOGL refers to the Ministry of Oil, Iraq National Oil Company or Regional Body, with the latter being an authorised ministry in the Regional Government.[158] The qualification for a producing governorate changed between the two drafts with minimum continuous production in the 2007 version being 150,000 bpd reduced to a 100,000 bpd commercial rate in the 2011 document.[159]

The 2007 DOGL stipulated the formation of the "Federal Oil and Gas Council"[160] (FOGC): a Council formed by the Council of Ministers under the DOGL "to exercise the authorities designated to it according to the provisions" of the Law. The FOGC is to appoint a "Panel of Independent Advisors"[161] being experts selected according to the provisions of the Law.

Both versions cover the standard definition for petroleum operations to the point of transfer or delivery and exclude refining.[162] Iraqi companies in both DOGLs are corporate entities headquartered in Iraq with at least 50% Iraqi ownership by citizens, being public or private companies.[163] In the 2011 version, Article 2 commences by reiterating Article 111 of the Constitution[164] referring to the fair distribution of the resources to the people. Article 2 of the 2007 version expressly excluded refining petroleum in the scope of its application which was placed in Article 50 of the 2011 DOGL.

4.2.2 Purpose and application of the law

In the 2007 document, the objective of the legislation is set out in a preamble, which is not followed in the 2011 document as no preamble is provided. In essence, the preamble stipulates the aim to be the efficient coordination of oil policy between federal and regional authorities as well as between the Iraq authorities and international commercial entities.[165] The further aim is to harmonise the oil industry with the development of society and the national economy maintaining sustainable development for the economy and the environment to promote diversification in the long term so as to decrease dependence on Oil and Gas revenues. The preamble concludes that

> the conditions for regulating the Petroleum sector are of great importance to the whole nation as well as to all Investors in the sector, there is a need for a clear, fair, transparent and efficient system of governance that inspires confidence, efficiency and cooperation among all participants in the petroleum sector, including governmental authorities at Federal, Regional and Governorate level, and among national and international actors.

In essence, the 2011 document provides that the DOGL is designed to increase production, coordinate and consolidate key functions within the industry for the development and benefit of the Iraqi economy.[166] In contrast to the 2007 version, the later DOGL provides a more detailed and developed scope with the former being a superficial attempt to establish its purpose.[167] The 2011 DOGL Article 2 provides the objectives of the legislation, which follows the 2007 preamble for regulation of the industry to be in the national interest. It is clear that the objectives are protectionist in nature to preserve national control over the extraction process. Reference is made to the national interest and highest benefit to the Iraqi people as the benchmarks to be achieved in upstream petroleum operations, regulation and policy development which are all to be managed and developed by the federal government.[168] The nationalist aim is also evident in the objective to "achieve the highest level of growth in reserves and [p]roduction"[169] and to ensure technology transfer to and training and development of Iraqi staff[170] in addition to developing an "efficient, qualified and capable" Iraqi private sector to contribute to the industry.[171] A further aim is for the optimal use of resource wealth "on sound and profitable technical and economic bases"[172] and the "development of the infrastructure and protection of the environment".[173] The final provision under the Article provides an objective to "[e]nsure full professional efficiency, and technical and financial competence of licence holders and those from the private sector who deal with this field".[174]

Following the objectives, Article 3 provides the means for achievement by establishing "a new and advanced system for managing Petroleum Operations in Iraq, including setting long, medium and short term strategies, policies and plans" to be "based on the latest technologies and market economy". The Article provides for "[s]etting the bases for cooperation among the relevant ministries" and authorities and "for coordination and consultation between" the federal, regional and producing authorities. In terms of application, both versions of the draft law apply to petroleum operations within Iraqi territory on land, inland waters and territorial waters, which may be extended by international agreement and subject to Iraqi law.[175]

4.2.3 *Control and management of resources*

Both versions of the DOGL establish the FOGC. The head of CoM is to lead FOGC with members comprising the Deputy Prime Minister, Minister of Oil,

Minister of Finance, Minister of Planning and Governor of the Bank of Iraq. The FOGC further includes a regional representative, a representative of each producing governorate, heads of INOC and the Oil Marketing Company along with three experts selected by the Chairman of CoM for a five-year period.[176] There is no stipulation for the experts in the FOGC to be Iraqi which leaves open the possibility of foreign experts being placed on the panel. The role of FOGC is to propose and approve federal petroleum policies; E&D field and pipeline plans; endorse regulations on the qualification, negotiation and contracting process and model contracts; approve, decide and amend EDP contracts for licences; approve the funding entity and share allocation having regard to national participation; support INOC in operations, set the national level of production and to ensure the protection of the interests of the Iraqi people.[177] FOGC is to meet once a month and make decisions by a two-thirds majority for contracts, policies and plans and by simple majority for all other matters. It may also issue bylaws for its own functions including divisions and formations.[178] Another prescribed function of FOGC is to select experts for and to establish a "Bureau of Independent Advisers[179] to study exploration,[180] Development and Production contracts, Oil and Gas Field Development Plans, and all other matters related thereto; and provide advice and recommendations on same to the Council".[181]

Article 6 provides for the management of resources to be within the remit of the House of Representatives, CoM, FOGC, MoO, INOC and the Regional Body. There then follows the competencies of these various bodies in subsequent provisions:

- The CoR shall legislate and endorse agreements.[182]
- CoM shall submit draft laws to CoR and endorse and supervise implementation of petroleum policies submitted by FOGC in addition to supervising all petroleum operations, issuing regulations and ensuring consultation with producing governorates to achieve the objectives of the oil legislation.[183]
- MoO is to set petroleum policies and draft laws, plans and regulations and issue instructions and statements for their implementation[184]; supervise operations in coordination with authorised bodies for uniform and harmonised implementation of policies throughout Iraq; submit plans and policies for EDP to FOGC; prepare model EDP contracts in cooperation with INOC and regional bodies; verify costs and expenses of licence holders and ensure the collection of revenues; negotiate international agreements for submission to FOGC and represent the government of Iraq in regional and international fora; administer licensing rounds for EDP[185] and implement legislatively sanctioned supply and service contracts beyond the scope of EDP contracts.[186]

The regional bodies are to provide proposals to MoO for petroleum operations to be included in federal plans; attend FOGC negotiations; to assist in the implementation of federal plans, regulations and legislation; participate in relevant licensing rounds.[187]

4.2.4 Contract review provisions

The 2011 MoO DOGL provides under Article 46, second, that oil and gas contracts entered into prior to its enactment will be subject to two levels of review, first by a special committee, comprising the federal oil minister, a KRG minister and the head of the Parliamentary Oil and Energy Committee and then the FOGC.

By contrast, the 2007 DOGL at Article 40B is more general in scope and merely provides for a review of contracts to ensure and validate the maximum economic return for the people of Iraq.

4.2.5 INOC

INOC is revived in both versions of DOGL with express provisions for its operation. In some respects, the 2011 document provides a more detailed description of the company's rights and functions. However, the 2007 version contains details of formation where the later document is silent, merely stating in the definitions that INOC is to be established by a law.[188] INOC shall be the operator for the industry delegated to enter into service and management contracts directly with qualified companies "for producing Fields and adjacent undeveloped Fields"[189] and enter into contracts with IOCs for development of designated fields. INOC is also authorised to manage, operate and develop currently producing fields, discovered undeveloped areas near producing fields; participate in EDP operations on a competitive basis, conduct EDP; transport and storage operations and manage export ports and the oil and gas pipelines.[190] Further for the transport and sale of hydrocarbons and EDP contracts outside Iraq, the company may contribute as a trading partner in international contracts with CoM approval.[191] Subsidiaries or joint operating companies[192] may be established in producing governorates or outside Iraq to increase efficiency in operations with approval from CoM.[193] INOC may own assets and rights according to law, and may "sell its production of crude oil to the Oil Marketing Company at delivery price that covers costs plus a reasonable profit to enable the company to develop in the fields of exploration and Production".[194]

INOC shall be granted all development and production rights for currently producing fields along with EDP rights to adjacent undeveloped fields[195] and shall act as a partner on behalf of the government as specified by contract for other fields for EDP. Rights for the management and operation of existing main pipelines shall be granted to INOC or another specifically established specialised Iraqi company.[196] The 2007 version provides for INOC to negotiate with hydrocarbon shippers and a transitional two-year window for MoO to reorganise companies where INOC is required to operate the main pipeline network and ports based on a coordinated proposal by MoO and the company.[197]

In March 2018, the INOC law was finally passed through the Iraqi Parliament with some criticism against it.[198] It was announced in October 2018 that nine state oil companies had been transferred to INOC.[199]

4.2.6 Field development

One of the most important aspects for all parties to an upstream contract is the provision for field development. From the state's perspective having a legal framework upon which to base contracts and assist with transparency and dispute resolution between commercial entities or even neighbouring governments. For the contractors it provides a point of reference, and to some extent security, when there may be uncertainty or ambiguity in the contractual relationship on issues of development.

The 2011 DOGL provides that the EDP contract shall provide exclusive rights to the contractor for the transportation of petroleum and conduct of operations in the contract area.[200] Crucially, it sets out contractual time-scales of an initial period of four years for EDP with an extension for a maximum licence period of two years provided contractual obligations are fulfilled and a work plan is submitted by the contractor within the initial period.[201] If the contractor works on and implements the work plan, a further two-year licence may be granted. All extensions are subject to contractual provisions for state retrieval of the contract area. In the event of discovery, further extensions may be granted for the purpose of determining its commercial value,[202] for non-associated natural gas[203] and to complete the evaluation of discovered undeveloped fields within the remit of the EDP contract.[204]

The 2007 version stipulates INOC as the operator with authorisation to sign service and administrative contracts.[205] MoO is to propose best methods for development of discovered undeveloped fields to FOGC and prepare the model contracts.[206] There is reference to "speedy and efficient development" in collaboration with oil companies approved by FOGC. FOGC, MoO and regional authorities are to explore and assess resources to "compensate [p]roduction, and to add new reserves".[207]

4.2.7 Mechanisms of negotiation

Outlining the method of contract negotiation in legislation provides a level of transparency for investors and guidance for state negotiators. Following the licensing rounds, an initial EDP contract will be entered into with the selected investor to be concluded and provided to FOGC within thirty days of signature for approval.[208] Failure to adhere to this deadline will render the contract void. The process for approval by FOGC is to refer

> the contract to the Bureau of Independent Advisers to study the contract; present an opinion on conformity thereof to the model exploration, Development and Production contracts and the Development and Production contracts approved by the Council, and the instructions issued thereby regulating Petroleum Operations; and make recommendations thereon.[209]

Failure to substantially comply with the model contract requires the guidance of the Bureau of Independent Advisers and a final decision of FOGC achieved by a two-thirds majority of members present.[210] FOGC will inform the competent body of its decision within ninety days of receipt of the contract. Where FOGC raises objections to the contract, the competent body shall amend and re-submit in the same manner as before.[211]

The 2007 DOGL provided similar measures to the above save that a mandatory form of wording must be included in the E&P contracts to the effect that there has been no objection from FOGC in accordance with the legislation.[212] Different time-scales are provided in this version in that FOGC has sixty days from the date of receipt of the initial contract to inform the relevant authority of any objections. If for extraordinary reasons FOGC cannot hold a meeting within sixty days a further forty-five days is provided for a decision on the contract. Should all of these deadlines be missed by FOGC the contract is deemed valid by default:[213] note that there is no such default provision in the 2011 document.

4.2.8 Model contracts

There is a minimum criterion for mandatory contractual provisions in the 2011 DOGL. Model contracts for all petroleum operations must include terms as to

> national control; Iraq's ownership of Petroleum resources; maximum national economic return; waiver by the licence holder of unused lands within the Contract Area; appropriate return for the investor in accordance with the provisions of this law; obligations of contract parties and the consequences of breach; arrangements and conditions for the exercise of data related rights.[214]

There must also be

> reasonable incentives granted to investors to ensure the provision of optimal solutions to Iraq regarding: improved and enhanced extraction; transfer of technology; training and development of Iraqi staff working in the field of Oil; optimal use and development of the infrastructure; plans and solutions to ensure the protection of the environment.[215]

There are further specifics as to contractual terms providing exclusive rights to the contractor for EDP in the contract area and transportation.[216] The contractual period is outlined with an initial four-year term which can be extended by two years provided a work plan is submitted to the competent body in this time and a further two years for continuation and implementation of the work plan. All of these periods are subject to a term within the contract for the retrieval of the contract area by the state. If there is commercial discovery, an additional two years may be granted to determine its value which is increased to four years in the case of non-associated gas. Finally, a further two years may be granted for the evaluation of discovered undeveloped fields within the contract area.[217] INOC and licence holders may retain exclusive rights for EDP within the contract area for a maximum period of twenty years from approval of the contract by FOGC. However, CoM may extend this period for a further five years "for technical and economic considerations" only for the development and operation area as all other areas within the contract area will be relinquished. The operator will be named in the initial contract as the entity approved by the competent body based on criteria issued by FOGC.[218]

The 2007 DOGL is essentially in the same terms as the 2011 document save for an absence of criteria for contractual provisions as stipulated above.[219] Further, the incremental time-scales in the provision, although they are the same, totalling ten to twelve years, are less stringent due to the provision being prefaced with an exception for additional time to complete assessment operations which can easily be open to abuse by the contractor in delaying operations to extend the contract term. FOGC can grant a contractual period of 15–20 years from the date of initial approval based on the field development plan with a further extension of five years based on re-negotiation of the contract with all other land outside the development and production area being surrendered by the contractor.[220]

4.2.9 Licences and obligations of licence holders

The criteria for the award of licences required under the E&P contracts is set out in DOGL 2011, Article 15. Licences are based on the head EDP contract between MoO or the competent body and an eligible company in accordance with FOGC criteria, the contract and negotiation provisions of the OGL. Principles are specified for the granting of licences:

- The protection of national interests[221]
- Clearly defined competitive licensing rounds
- Providing the main provisions of the model contract in the call for contracting
- The model licence contract which "includes the characteristics and requirements for each proposed area, field, or prospect, especially data on fields in terms of being discovered or undiscovered, the potential risks and benefits, and technological and operational challenges"
- Qualification of the company in accordance with provisions of the DOGL and selected on the basis of economic benefit to Iraq and the quality and efficiency of proposed plans
- The announcement of the text of the main EDP contracts within sixty days of endorsement by FOGC[222]

Licence holders are obliged to:

- perform operations in accordance with best practices and legislative provisions[223];
- inform the competent body of discoveries within the contract area and identify and assess the same for commercial value;

- in the case of commercial discovery to prepare and amend the field development plan and submit it for approval, upon approval to implement the said plan;
- at least two years prior to expiration of planned production to submit a plan for the handover of the mandate to FOGC; and
- compensate any affected parties for loss and damage arising from operations.

MoO has the sole entitlement to receive, market and transport produced hydrocarbons "in accordance with agreed arrangements and conditions" and should provide support for research and development to Iraqi institutions which are to supply MoO with data collected free of charge.[224]

INOC and licence holders shall give preference to the purchase and use of Iraqi products and services on a competitive basis, employ and train qualified and experienced Iraqis, increase opportunities for training, development and technology transfer to Iraqis and Iraqi institutions for all phases of operations.[225] Further, there shall be observation of international standards and domestic legislation for environmental protection, provision of a report of environmental impact and mitigation; damage must be avoided to reservoirs and all land areas affected by oil and gas operations with the immediate notification to MoO of any environmental accident or emergency. In addition, there must be prevention and control of any leakage or petroleum loss incidental to operations and the submission of reports for the same, clean-up the site and comply with environmental requirements during shut-down operations, ensure worker safety, compensate affected parties. Any violation of these requirements will result in a penalty and compensation to be paid.[226]

The 2007 DOGL makes no reference to licences. However, there is reference to the obligations of rights holders under an E&P contract.[227] Under this provision the contractor as rights holder must:

- comply with the OGL, other regulations and good practices;
- report any discovery promptly to the designated authority;
- delineate and evaluate the discovery for commercial purposes;
- prepare and submit a revised field development plan for approval by the designated authority and implement the same upon approval;
- at least two years prior to planned termination of production submit a decommissioning plan to the designated authority;
- compensate for any loss or damage caused to injured parties as a consequence of operations; give access to pipelines and preference to the designated authority in acquiring petroleum from the contract area;
- support research and development by Iraqi institutions and collect and maintain useable data from operations to be provided to MoO free of charge.[228]

4.2.10 Unitisation of fields

Where hydrocarbons are discovered in a field located in more than one contract area, there shall be joint development in accordance with a unitisation agreement submitted to and approved by FOGC.[229] Failure to reach agreement by the licence/rights holders on unitisation within 180 days of notification to submit the agreement will be resolved by FOGC within the following 90 days.[230] If the area extends to non-contracted production areas, approval of FOGC is required to be considered in the interests of the Iraqi people. CoM is responsible for protecting national interests where discoveries extend beyond the Iraqi boarders.[231]

4.2.11 Gas

Although the issue of gas is not specifically covered in this book, it is necessary to briefly review the provisions contained within the DOGL as it is a key natural resource which is often a by-product of crude oil exploration. Therefore, even if oil companies are not specifically contracted to deal with gas there are provisions dealing with associated gas. Significant returns may be drawn from gas production and will be used for purposes ranging from injection in reservoirs; generating energy and electricity; petrochemical, chemical, industrial, and domestic use and export.[232] INOC shall be responsible for the optimal use of gas extraction. Costs incurred for its processing and provision to the federal government shall be recoverable.[233] Associated gas may be used in petroleum operations at no extra cost and its use and disposal must be included in the field development plan (FDP) with any and used gas provided to the MoO.[234]

The flaring of associated and non-associated[235] gas is prohibited except for crucial prescribed operations within the first year of production.[236] Signed agreements relating to the sale of gas, gas products or liquid from non-associated gas following discovery must be submitted to CoM for approval and incorporated into the FDP approved by MoO.[237]

In the 2007 version of this document similar terms to the above are used save that there is reference to the use of gas for replacement of fluid fuels for beneficial environmental reasons and to maximise revenue from fuel oil and crude export.[238] INOC and contractors should consider optimal commercial use of surplus gas and if they fail to do so it shall be given free of charge after processing to the government with the associated costs recoverable under the terms of the contract.[239]

4.2.12 Transportation

The main method of hydrocarbon transportation in Iraq is through a pipeline network owned by the federal government.[240] INOC shall be the owner of the main pipelines,[241] and may be constructed and operated by its subsidiaries subject to MoO approval.[242] The transporter, through provisions of the EDP contract, shall transport petroleum according to reasonable commercial standards provided there is capacity in the pipeline. Technical issues with the pipeline shall be resolved where possible and an alternative transportation system shall be provided by MoO where necessary.[243] Any main pipeline disputes shall be referred to MoO.

Contracts containing pipeline implementation plans incorporating the assistance of domestic or foreign companies shall include terms as to implementation and funding, operation, uses and alternatives for the new or modified pipeline.[244] Outside Iraq, MoO is responsible for the management of transportation pipelines.[245] Within Iraq, INOC is responsible for transportation to the main delivery points transferring responsibility thereafter to the relevant company.[246] All activity is to be in accordance with good pipeline practices.

Rights of access[247] to main pipelines according to reasonable commercial terms shall be granted in EDP contracts including, where necessary, the construction of field pipelines for delivery to the transfer point.[248] INOC and EDP licence holders shall: prepare and implement a FDP and with MoO approval construct subsidiary pipelines; submit to FOGC for approval an amended main pipeline development plan according to the FDP, negotiate the use of the main pipeline with the transporter; and submit a handover plan no later than two years prior to expiration of planned production.[249] The 2007 DOGL is in similar terms to the foregoing.

4.2.13 Protection of resources

Both versions of the DOGL contain several provisions for the protection of resources to prevent waste and leaks from reservoirs and pipelines, using new technology for optimal recovery and reservoir knowledge.[250] FDPs are to be presented following consideration of alternative extraction strategies for high production at low cost.[251] Relevant data is owned and controlled by MoO and shall be provided to INOC with the competent bodies collating and storing useable data and providing MoO with updated information for petroleum operations[252] and penalties shall be imposed for transfer or sale of this data without contractual authorisation.[253] Permits may be granted by the competent body for transfer or delivery of oil data where justified.[254]

The 2007 version stipulates that rights for petroleum operations are to be granted via the E&P contract between MoO and the contractor following a transparent tender process based on competitive licensing rounds and consideration of financial capability and technical competence for efficient conduct of operations.[255] Contractual terms are to be placed in model contracts taking account of specific requirements for the contract area and are to be attached to the letter of invitation.[256]

All contracts[257] shall contain terms respecting national interest, conservation, health and safety and environmental protection, but particularly as to:

- national control;
- ownership of the resources;
- optimum economic return to the country;
- an appropriate return on investment;

and reasonable incentives to the investor for ensuring solutions which are optimal to the country in the long-term related to improved and enhanced recovery, technology transfer, training and development of Iraqi personnel, optimal utilisation of the infrastructure, and environmentally friendly solutions and plans.[258] For the licensing round, only pre-qualified companies shall be short-listed and considered according to criteria specified in the invitation to bidding according to the regulation and instructions issued by FOGC.[259]

Applicant selection shall be based on the quality of the proposed work plan and likely economic return. The aim of allocation of E&P Rights in Iraq is to enhance efficiency by attracting a variety of oil companies for the purposes of performance, competition and transparency based on experience and expertise: if necessary, a consortia of companies may be used. The contract must be published within two months of approval by the designated authority and it is to be regulated by the OGL and regulations of FOGC.[260]

National participation in any phase of petroleum operations is essential for compliance with Article 111 of the Constitution. INOC is granted EP Rights for existing producing fields, fields yet to be developed and is also assigned the main pipeline network within Iraqi borders.[261]

Article 15 of the 2007 document stipulates a national aim to develop a competent and effective private sector to participate fully in the petroleum operations. Consequently, companies holding exploration rights are encouraged to cooperate with private Iraqi companies and give preference to Iraqi products and services on a competitive basis in addition to training and employing suitably qualified Iraqi citizens. Training and technology transfer opportunities should be created at all levels of operations for Iraqi nationals.

As to conservation, the 2007 version is similar to the later document providing for good oil field and pipeline practices and the use of the latest technology to avoid waste with high levels of production and low cost.[262] Likewise, reference to access to the main pipelines is closely worded to the later document. Any disputes concerning pipelines shall be resolved by the MoO.[263] Data ownership is also the same as the 2011 version. The 2007 version does however also contain a provision for restrictions on production levels which may be invoked in accordance with National policy considerations.[264]

The role of MoO is to approve petroleum regulations and submit them to the FOGC for approval.[265] Land use is regulated by other legislation and may be protected for the benefit of petroleum operations in accordance with contractual terms to assist with rights-of-way and for items such as land installations.[266] Any land damaged as a result of operations shall be compensated by the operator.[267] If any right-of-way is owned by an Iraqi the land shall be rented or purchased by INOC or its subsidiary. There is also brief mention of Maritime jurisdictions in the 2007 draft.[268]

Environmental protection is a key issue and both documents make reference to compliance with international standards for environmental management in order to prevent ecological damage and implement mitigation measures which are monitored through impact assessments, health and safety measures and clean up procedures.[269]

Once the contract has expired, ownership of all facilities is to be transferred to the relevant Authority or MoO. The 2011 version provides for the transferred facilities to be "in a state of the actual operation".[270] Any costs associated with relinquishments shall be paid by INOC in accordance with the decommissioning plan[271] an outline of which should be included in the FDP.[272]

4.2.14 Inspection

Contract areas may be inspected by the relevant authority with records kept by INOC and the contractor. Such inspections shall be regulated and may be conducted by an independent entity or commission without unreasonable interference to operations.[273] The 2011 version provides exceptions to interference on grounds of "environmental protection, occupational health, industrial safety, preserving the petroleum resource in accordance with applicable laws and regulations".[274] Council bylaws shall set out terms for inspection.[275]

4.2.15 Petroleum returns and financial obligations

In terms of national interest, the most common provision referred to relates to petroleum revenues and financial obligations. The DOGL stipulates that the revenues include income from the sale of hydrocarbons and all other bonuses from contractors are to be distributed fairly in a manner to be regulated by law with a percentage of surplus revenues to be placed in funds for future generations.[276] Contractors will be required to pay taxes, fees or other specified sums with company accounts subject to audit by the supreme audit board and investments may be made, in accordance with domestic law.[277] Once all of the required payments have been made, profits may be transferred abroad. Records shall be submitted and maintained by the MoO and the supreme audit board.[278]

The 2007 DOGL states that CoM must submit a draft schedule of the revenue law to COR in order to regulate matters of revenue distribution and the monitoring of federal revenue allocation.[279] The definition of revenues in this version of the document includes royalties, signature bonuses, production bonuses and all government revenues from hydrocarbons which must be deposited in a regulated fund to ensure fair distribution. There will be an additional future fund for which a proportion of revenues will be allocated. INOC, its subsidiary companies, and other contractors are subject to payments of royalty, property contribution, property transfer tax, municipal and local taxes and income tax as regulated by law.[280] Audits of income from petroleum operations will be conducted by the Commission of Financial Audit. Proceeds from exports may be repatriated by foreign companies.[281]

Royalties at a rate of 12.5% of gross production[282] shall be paid in cash[283] or kind by INOC and other contractors for petroleum produced in the contract area.[284] Any net profit may be transferred outside Iraq after payment of taxes and fees. Proper accounting records must be maintained in English and Arabic with accounts to be submitted annually or quarterly.[285]

4.2.16 Conflict resolution

In the event of conflict, as to the interpretation and application of the law there are provisions for resolution within the DOGL which initially involves negotiation followed by reference to the oil minister for resolution.[286] In the event that further action is required, arbitration shall be invoked according to the contractual provisions and in accordance with Iraqi law following procedures of the International Chamber of Commerce. Work may be suspended by the relevant authority pending the arbitration award.[287] Any violation of the OGL shall avoid the contract.[288]

The 2007 document is similar to the later version for the resolution of disputes save that there is reference to senior officers of the contracting parties and reference to the minister if negotiations fail. There is also provision for an independent technical expert to be referred to for recommendation of resolution.[289] Arbitration is to be conducted with the rules for proceedings at Paris, Geneva or Cairo based on Iraqi law where the dispute is between the state and foreign investors.[290] The application of other international standards to be applied must be expressly stated in the arbitration clause of the contract.[291]

4.2.17 Transparency

The issue of transparency has become important in recent years and any oil and gas law should have provisions outlining transparency initiatives to assist in complying with international industry standards. The 2011 document contains provisions for publishing significant financial information relating to activities in petroleum operations[292] including revenues[293] and in-kind payments for all receipts in excess of 1 billion Iraqi Dinar provided to any state representative or the public sector; returns from use and distribution of hydrocarbons; financially significant contracts for upstream activity and bidding on licensing process; the annual report of FOGC and any periodic reports of INOC or other head contractors.[294] Any agreement to prevent publication of the above information shall be void. Further, if anyone is to be found breaching Iraqi laws preventing corruption, the contract will be avoided and criminal penalties may ensue.[295]

The provision relating to transparency in the 2007 version is longer. There is reference to keeping secret non-financial information about royalties in accordance with provisions of domestic or international law.[296] The list of information to be disclosed is slightly more lengthy and includes profits from cartels in the industry, customs and taxes, revenue investment yields and revenues from asset sales.[297] The provisions relating to corruption are the same. There is a provision[298] for competitive public bidding whereby all oil companies must submit competitive public bids in accordance with legislation with an amount to be set by FOGC in order to offer any goods or services. Bidding must be conducted within a reasonable timeframe and results should be made public with competitors provided an opportunity to object to the decision.[299] Any contract concluded in breach of this provision (if enacted) shall be void.

4.2.18 Final provisions

The DOGL concludes with provisions for existing contracts, use of land and exclusions. Existing contracts will be subject to revision by MoO within ninety days of enforcement of the law who shall submit them to the bureau of independent advisors for recommendations to FOGC for a final decision.[300] The KRG is provided with three months from the date of enactment to review all contracts to ensure they conform with the provisions of this law which will then be assessed by the bureau of independent advisors who will make a decision on the handling of these contracts.[301]

Land used for the purposes of petroleum operations will have restricted areas according to instructions from MoO and compensation shall be provided to landowners or other rights holders who will be compensated for damages caused by the operations. Land may only be leased from Iraqi land owners.[302] The OGL will not apply to refining operations, manufacturing, storage, transport and distribution of oil products.[303] Bylaws and instructions assisting implementation of the OGL shall be issued by the Minister of oil.[304] The provisions of the OGL will prevail over any contradictory provisions elsewhere.[305]

The wording of the 2007 provisions are similar to the later version but slightly more favourable to the Kurdish region as prior to the OGL coming into effect the authority in the region is responsible for reviewing contracts to harmonise them with the general provisions of the legislation within three months of the date of enactment.[306] The overriding responsibility for the assessment of contracts rests with the panel of independent advisors.

In conclusion, many of the terms in 2011 version of the DOGL are closely aligned to the previous version with some sections being developed more than others. It is clear from an overall view of the legislation that it needs to be supported by further laws on issues such as transparency, revenue collection, bid processes and specific issues relating to petroleum operations. It is beneficial for an oil and gas law to be generalist in its formulation to allow for contractual provisions to be implemented freely and for parties to decide on how to resolve the issues on the one hand and for the government and state institutions to have the flexibility to be able to develop policies and react to economic factors accordingly. Unlike other jurisdictions, the OGL, if following the form of the drafts outlined above, will not be fully comprehensive. However, it is a starting point and given that it is now a policy in Iraq to attract foreign investment in order to develop the industry for the purposes of reconstruction and strengthening the economy, a balance needs to be drawn between nationalist preservation and the protection of resources. This is critical for the long-term development of the industry in addition to allowing for some element of contractual negotiation to provide the investor with a commercial incentive to bid for participation in petroleum operations. Whatever form the final OGL takes, it will not be the sole source of governance for the oil industry as reference will need to be made to supplemental, related legislation, regulations and instructions to understand the overall legal framework of the industry.

4.3 Tender process

The oil industry, as in other extraction sectors, is notorious for corruption and one method of assessing compliance with legislative provisions is to analyse how companies are awarded their contracts. Through the progression of bid rounds in Iraq since 2009, model contracts offered to IOCs have developed as the initial round sought to obtain the maximum protection of national control but resulted in only one contract being awarded due to all the surrounding uncertainty.

The key legislation for transparency and the procurement of oil contracts by foreign companies is CPA Order number 87 of 2004 on Public Contracts (CPA Order 87).[307] The legislation contains several sections, including details on the principles for government procurement and procedures, the financial requirements and the dispute resolution system. The applicability of CPA Order 87 to E&P contracts requires consideration. Section 1(1) of the order provides "[p]rocurement is the acquiring by contract with public funds of goods, services or construction services by and for the use of the government through purchase or lease". Section 2(2)(c) confirms the position: "This Order applies to Iraqi state-owned enterprises when awarding public contracts for the procurement of goods, services or construction services that are directly financed by government funds".

It is clear that the selected oil companies operating in Iraq are providing a service under s.1. A crucial element of application of the order is the expenditure of public funds and it is therefore necessary to consider whether awarding contracts to oil companies by MoO requires the expenditure of government funds.

In 2005, the World Bank reported that Iraq's public contract procurement policies were not sound practice due to:

> (i) inadequate requirements for registration of suppliers and contractors … may lead to lack of fairness; (ii) insufficiently transparent and fair debarment procedures; (iii) continued use of obsolete … procedures for procurement …, (iv) undue restrictions on access to bidding documents, (v) insufficiently transparent…procedures, (vi) … Kurdish language in the northern regions and Arabic language in the other parts of country; and (vii) lack of effective bid protest mechanisms and publicity on contract awards.[308]

Given that this report was published two years after the US-led invasion, there was and remains considerable room for improvement in the tender process. The consequences of such poor procedural mechanisms mean that from the perspective of governance there is a greater risk of a lack of control over the industry which may lead to exploitation against the national interest thereby failing to protect the ownership rights of citizens to their resources under Article 111 of the Constitution. However, it must also be noted that Iraq is capable of creating its own model for procurement without necessarily following the reports of international institutions and should implement the best possible procedures for its own benefit and according to Iraqi domestic requirements.

The tender process and the technical mechanisms through the four bid rounds to 2015 were different in that they were producing field technical service contracts,[309] development and production service contracts,[310] exploration and development contracts (Gas)[311] and exploration and development service contracts (gas and oil contracts).[312]

Under the first bid round, the government offered the development of known fields with existing reserves for production (brown fields). As the central government uses service contracts rather than PSCs, the oil company does not have ownership rights to the fields. The contract contains a provision that the land is to be made available for a term, usually four to six years, and if no discovery is found it is to be relinquished to the state.

The World Bank considers that oil revenue management should be open with

> readily accessible policies and procedures. Such transparency can help foster a democratic debate, increase accountability, improve macroeconomic management, and enhance access to finance. Transparency is needed both in the flow of budgetary funds and in the accounts of the national oil company.[313]

To increase transparency, it is suggested that Iraq should conduct independent audits of revenues and the downstream chain to incorporate all actors in the industry in all areas of the sector. Results of the audit would be made publicly available through independent publication. In addition, the tax administration and all institutions involved in oil revenue management, including the central bank, should have a plan for transparency.

> In the short to medium-term, it will be important to develop accounting concepts, rules, and procedures in the form of an accounting manual clearly specifying the accounting requirements, particularly those related to direct foreign investments, other bank accounts, oil assets, letters of credit, and other types of investments.[314]

4.3.1 Law currently governing tenders

The post-2004 procedure for contract procurement in the public sector was set out in CPA Order 87

> approved as part of the CPA efforts to rebuild public governance frameworks and capacities in Iraq. It suspended application of the previous 2001 Tender Instructions for State Agencies and the Social Sector and the 1988 Instructions for Implementation and Follow up of Projects and Works of National Development Plan.[315]

The Order created the Office of Government Public Contract Policy (OGPCP), within the Ministry of Planning and Development Cooperation (MPDC),[316] with responsibility for:

- coordination of government public contract policy for all ministries and public entities of the government;
- the establishment of an independent Administrative Tribunal for complaints and disputes; recommending improvements to Order 87 and related Iraqi laws;
- development and adoption of standard government public contract provisions and training of government public contracting personnel.[317]

The Order runs to fifteen sections outlining principles for government contracting through open competition and negotiation. It includes provisions for issuance of standard contact terms[318] and stipulates the right of government to terminate the contracts when "it is the government's best interest" subject to compensation.[319] In the event that an interested party to the tender process has suffered unfair treatment, there is a right of recourse to dispute resolution in the government department or unit concerned with the right to appeal through the judicial process.[320]

According to the World Bank, in 2004, anti-corruption initiatives were implemented by the Iraqi Governing Council and CPA including the creation of

> (i) an independent Inspector General's office within individual Iraqi ministries to perform a variety of functions involving both internal audit and control and the investigation of corruption-related cases; (ii) a Commission on Public Integrity; and (iii) a revitalized Supreme Audit Board.[321]

Part of the initiative was to harness a reporting and transparency system through an independent Inspector General's (IG) department reporting to the Commission on Public Integrity and the Supreme Audit Board auditing public procurement finances. This mechanism was criticised by the World Bank as

> ... In the absence of a clear legal and regulatory framework, it is questionable on what basis the Supreme Audit Board and the Commission on Public Integrity may be able to assess the regularity of the public procurement procedure. The capacity of the Inspector General departments and the Supreme Audit Board to handle procurement reviews and audits will need to be strengthened when the new regulations are enacted and enforced.[322]

The 2007 procurement regulations were issued by OGPCP to support CPA Order 87, which were subsequently replaced by the 2008 Regulation of Governmental Contracts Implementation.[323] A contracting guide was also issued by the Procurement Assistance Centre to explain the provisions.[324] The following year, procurement instructions for Government Contracts' Execution were issued based on Order 87 as an explanatory document.[325] A draft Public Procurement Law was prepared in 2008 by MPDC and sent to the Government for approval.[326]

The OECD found that the procurement regulations:

> are changing rapidly and not always in a transparent manner. The coexistence of … rules, instructions and regulations … the unclear responsibility sharing … result in confusion in the daily work of Iraqi public procurement officials, and contributes to its limited efficiency. In addition, … different ministries follow different procurement rules. [327]

The suggested solution to this by the OECD was:

> Institutionally, the issuance and implementation of government procurement regulations currently belong to the MoPDC. … it might be considered beneficial to transfer the responsibility of the supervision of the overall contracting process from a ministry level to a higher authority.[328]

Given the above comments, more needs to be done to separate supervision from the ministries, not through a 'higher authority' but possibly through an accountable audit committee independent of perceived government influence. The appointment of appropriately qualified and experienced members of this independent body should be rotated over a fixed term, which should not coincide with local or national elections. Further, salaries should be competitive to attempt to reduce the risk of corruption.

4.3.2 Bid process

4.3.2.1 Pre-selection

As with many of the procurement procedures in oil producing countries, Iraq has a pre-selection stage to qualify oil companies prior to the main bidding. This ensures that the contract awarding process is efficient and effective to enable swift commencement of the E&P process. Initially a public announcement is made through MoO inviting tenders for the relevant field or to prospect in a specific area. Quite often in practice, the major IOCs are given prior warning by those involved in the political process so that some time is available in order to prepare the best tender documents and forewarn about participation fees, signature bonuses and other up-front costs likely to be associated with the tender for the potential contract.

Due to the nature of commercial activity, to which the oil industry is no exception, governments will have a tendency to favour established companies with good reputations for effective operations and compliance with contractual obligations. It is probably of no surprise that among the initial companies in contact with the transitional and subsequent governments post-2004 were Shell, BP and Exxon.

4.3.2.2 Bid rounds

MoO officially launched the first bid round for the extraction of oil in Iraq by international companies on 30 June 2008. The tender process was for technical service contracts for six producing oil fields and although the bidding process itself was made public and televised, the pre-qualification process was not publicised.[329] The pre-qualification process took place in early 2008 where more than hundred national and international oil companies submitted financial and technical information to MoO to express their interest in the pre-qualification for bidding.[330] Thirty-five companies were selected by the Petroleum Contracts and Licensing Directorate (PCLD) of which thirty-two paid participation fees.[331]

A final tender protocol stipulated the rules to be followed by companies participating in the licensing round. A Producing Field Technical Service Contract (PFTSC) was drafted for the winning oil companies specific to each field.[332] A process timeline is provided in the document providing a level of transparency for the participants. Participation requirements include a compulsory payment by the companies for the fields for which they will submit bids. For Rumaila, Kirkuk, West Qurna, Zubair and Bai Hassan the participation fee was US$500,000 and for Missan US$350,000.[333] In relation to consortia the companies must be individually prequalified in order to participate in the bid round. Only one offer may be made for each contract area, in order to prevent new companies, whether prequalified or not by the MoO, from entering into contracts after the selection process. Section 6.2(f) of the protocol provides that where a company withdraws following the submission of a successful bid which is part of a consortium, the remaining companies within that consortium must assume the obligations of the withdrawing company.[334]

The non-disclosure provision within the protocol provides that only the bids submitted by the prequalified companies will be made publicly available with all prior documents subject to permanent confidentiality.[335] There is a disqualification provision within the protocol that clearly outlines the circumstances in which pre-qualification may be cancelled including: bankruptcy, dissolution or sale of the company, misrepresentation, illegal acts and failure to comply with the provisions of the bidding process.[336]

The Iraqi procurement process in 2005, did not contain criteria for prequalification but relied on a classification system created by MPDC.[337] The lowest bid was often selected in practice even though the selection criteria valued quality of work and timelines over price. Where the lower price was not selected, the preferential bidder was often persuaded to revise their bid downwards by a minister or government official and the bid evaluation committee could request bid clarifications.[338] Prior to 2003,

> [a] two-envelope system, consisting of using a sequential successive opening and evaluation of technical and financial bids, used to be permitted and was regularly practiced, and even considered mandatory in many procuring entities under the former regime. However, this practice appears to be diminishing, and a single-envelope process is more often used, whereby all bids (technical and financial) are opened and evaluated in one stage.[339]

This latter process is considered more efficient due to one stage being removed and arguably making the procedure less susceptible to interference and corruption.

In order to award the contract, committees[340] were formed in the ministries and state companies for bid opening and analysis; they would open, tabulate and then evaluate the bids in order to recommend a preferred bidder. The analysis and study committee would negotiate with the bidder and seek approval from management to sign the contract.[341] However, the process was slow due to the lack of clear oversight and regulation as there was no standard documentation or specialised staff.[342] It was recommended by the World Bank that the existing procurement staff could be trained according to its guidelines and procedures, subsequently leading to the creation of new procurement procedures for implementation by the Office of Government Public Contract Policy (OGPCP) for onward development.[343]

The qualification process for the first bid round9 was outlined in an announcement by the PCLD in 2009 where marks were awarded according to five criteria: technical, financial, legal, training and HSE on a points-based system. IOCs were assessed on their submitted pre-qualification documents and deemed qualified if they attained the minimum level of marks following which, they were sent a letter of invitation to participate in the licensing round.[344] The points-based system was as follows[345]:

Criterion	*Min (mark)*	*Max (mark)*
Technical	7.0	22.5
Financial	50%	100%
Legal	4 (yes)	4 (yes)
Training	4	10
HSE	8	13

4.3.2.3 Development of the bid rounds

The first round was generally considered to be unsuccessful due to only one contract being awarded which resulted in the MoO gradually amending the bid process and contracts to make the tenders more attractive to international companies.[346] In the first round the signature bonus was a loan by the company against the initial production and therefore a production cost. This changed in the second round to a non-recoverable sum dependent on the field.[347]

The procedure for the first round was such that bids were offered in a unique sealed official envelope and bid form, which were then publicly opened with the result announced prior to the offering of the next contract area.[348] Consortia did not need to disclose the composition of their consortium ahead of the bidding process.[349] Bidding parameters and evaluation criteria were provided in the protocol[350] and points awarded to each of the prospective companies according to a formula.[351] Calculations were provided for the remuneration fee bid and the plateau production target[352] with the highest scoring formula being the minimum accepted bid.

The winning bidder's obligation to sign the contract for the relevant field was secured by way of a bid bond in the sum of US$5 million exclusive to each contract area.[353] The bonds take the form of a letter of credit by 'A' rated financial institutions. Unsuccessful bidders would have their bonds returned within a week of the bid round. The bid bond would be drawn upon where the company does not sign the contract by the specified date; the performance guarantee is not provided in accordance with the section four of the protocol; the signature bonus is not paid and where the conditions in Annex F to the contract are not complied with. The bid bond would to be returned to the presenting company if none of the stipulated circumstances arise.[354]

A proposed development approach was required to be submitted to MoO within two weeks of the bidding which should contain a proposed overview of the development approach in support of the winning bid.[355] Contracts were to be signed with the relevant Iraqi oil company within a month of the bid announcement, following ratification of the agreement by the CoM.[356] The only contract awarded in the first round was the Rumaila field to BP and CNPC.

By the fourth bid round, the criteria was amended providing more clarity to participants, for example, the front of the envelope for bidding contained company details, acceptance of bidding conditions, percentage interests, names of the authorised representatives of the company or consortia and bid bond information.[357] The envelope was then checked for compliance with the bid requirements and any corrections were sought by PCLD following which there was an announcement of the participating companies who were invited to officially place the sealed envelopes, for security and anti-corruption purposes, in the bid box. Upon receipt of the bids the chairman of the bid committee opened all of the envelopes in turn for examination and announcement of their contents.[358] In accordance with the aforementioned formula, points were allocated to the companies and the highest scoring bid "equal to or below a pre-defined maximum" was announced as the winning participant.[359]

4.4 Transparency of the law

Having reviewed the legal framework, the next issue to consider is the level of transparency within the system and steps that could be taken in order to place Iraq's oil industry at a competitive advantage for the future. Efforts have been made to tackle the issues of transparency and corruption in the oil industry since 2004. As of 12 December 2012, Iraq was awarded compliant status to the Extractive Industries Transparency Initiative (EITI). Earlier the same year the government commenced payments in kind to IOCs that could sustain a 90-day threshold of commercial activity.[360] The Iraq EITI report[361] does not provide information about the cost recovery and remuneration fees claimed by state partners from the oil-in-kind payments to the IOCs which is criticised by Jiyad[362] as:

> … disaggregation is a prerequisite legally and contractually because remuneration fee is the base for calculating the State Partners share … and … the corporate income tax on IOCs (after deducting the State Partners share) …

> … Surely the accounting and auditing capacities at Regional Oil Companies – ROCs and MoO levels have to be enhanced to perform this mission for the protection of the national interests and the proper relation with working IOCs.

The International Advisory and Monetary Board of Iraq (IAMB) was created by the UN as an auditory body to oversee the Development Fund for Iraq (DFI). Its principal role

> is to help ensure that [t]he DFI is used in a transparent manner for the benefit of the people of Iraq, and [e]xport sales of petroleum, petroleum products, and natural gas from Iraq are made consistent with prevailing international market best practices.[363]

The IAMB is an organisation designed to promote UN objectives and its terms of reference are to ensure DFI transparency

> through the Iraqi budget including to satisfy outstanding obligations against the DFI and that all proceeds of export sales of petroleum, petroleum products and natural gas from Iraq are deposited into the DFI in accordance with the provisions of resolutions 1483, 1546, 1637, 1723, 1790, 1859, 1905 and 1956.[364]

Revenue Watch International published a report in 2013[365] placing Iraq 29/58 overall, 24th for reporting practices and 35th for institutional and legal setting.

At national level, once the legal framework has been amended to maximise the interests of the national economy, Iraq can position itself to become a leader in transparency and compliance for the global hydrocarbon industry. This opportunity is not afforded to many major oil producing countries whereby to an extent the regulation of the industry and commercial transactions can be revised from scratch. With the right level of expertise and vision, a model could be created for the future benefit of the industry as a whole.

4.5 Conclusion

Since its creation, Iraq has seen many variations of oil agreements ranging from the original concession agreements with the IPC companies through to the current service contracts. The balance of power between the relevant government and the oil companies has evolved over time with the original agreements heavily in favour of the foreign oil companies through to the legislative changes which made it possible for Iraq to complete its nationalisation process in 1972. Since 2003, there has been a gradual reversion to private agreements leading to the bid round processes which commenced in 2009.

Even during the nationalisation process, Iraq entered into agreements with countries deemed to be friendly. Since 1972, contracts were signed with countries such as the USSR, Bulgaria, Romania, Brazil and France for services and technological equipment and expertise to assist the oil industry. Until 2003, every oil agreement was ratified by an announcement in the Iraqi Gazette.

Although amendments have been made to the draft legislation, more needs to be done for a comprehensive framework to be implemented. Quite often the lack of a legal regime does not prevent companies from entering into locations where the prospects of production are commercially viable. The primary reason is that most of the uncertainty created by a defective regulatory system can be accommodated and resolved during the negotiation of the agreement between the host government and the IOC. For this reason, the terms of the contracts in place are vital to understanding the parties' position and the degree of control that the state has over its resources. There can easily be a situation where, even if there is legislation in place protecting the public right to ownership of natural resources, this can be diminished or even extinguished through the terms of whatever form of contract signed by the government and the oil company. When considering sovereignty and revenues it is necessary to address the provisions relating to the duration of the contract, title to assets, work obligations and targets, taxes, participation, assignment, termination and relinquishment.

Notes

1 2005 Constitution, Article 2, Islam is a foundation source of law.
2 This will not be considered further in this book. All legislation has to pass through the Shura council for conformity with the Constitution and Islamic principles.
3 This is evidenced by the initial reluctance of any of the oil majors to invest in the Kurdish region due to a policy endorsed by the US government to support the authority of the federal government in Baghdad.
4 Oil companies tend to be less risk averse than their counterparts in other industries.
5 Article 130, 2005 Constitution.
6 The contracts awarded post-2003 were signed under the terms of the Transitional Administrative Law (TAL). Article 25(E) and CPA Order 84.
7 See previous chapter.
8 BP Statistical Review of World Energy 2018, 12.
9 I.e. the organically produced laws authorised since the appointment of Parliament in 1921. See previous chapter.
10 Further details are provided in Chapter 4.
11 As previously mentioned, Iraq had a mixture of Ottoman, British and tribal influences with different laws in Baghdad and Basra.
12 Munir al-Qadi.
13 Zuhair E. Jwaideh, 'The New Civil Code of Iraq', *The George Washington Law Review*, 176,178, 1953–1954.
14 The former code regulated the Mixed Courts whereas the latter regulated the National Courts.
15 Jwaideh 178–179.
16 Ibid., 180. Al-Sanhuri also assisted in the drafting of the Egyptian and Syrian Civil Codes, both enacted in 1949, two years prior to the Iraqi Code.
17 as amended.
18 Law 40/1951.
19 Law 83/1969.
20 The first National Development Plan was drafted in 1951. See Alnasrawi, *The Economy of Iraq*, 37.
21 Law 101 of 1964.

22 Law 101 of 1964, Article 1, although not explicitly in reference to the oil industry it would be affected.
23 By Law 5 of 1965 (with retrospective effect).
24 Article 1.
25 Law 97/1967.
26 Article 7.
27 Law 97 – "In this case the conclusion of a Contract in this respect shall not be effected except by law".
28 Comprising directorates of administration and personnel, accounts and a legal department.
29 1970 Interim Constitution Article 43.
30 Law 49/1970 which repealed Law 13/1961 and Law 125/1964; minor amendments were made by Regulation 45/1971. Offices included the Board of Directors of Oil Administration, the Administrations of Oil Refineries, Distribution of Oil Products, Oil Planning and Construction and the Inspection Department of Oil Administration with all administration departments containing an inspection division for auditing and supervising the functions of the administration. Article 3 1970 Constitution.
31 Law 49/1970 Article 24.
32 Law 33 of 1970 makes minor amendments to the Law for Organising Oil Affairs and Law 49 of 1970 which is the oil administration law for the Ministry of Oil and Minerals.
33 Iraq Gazette 1970, Vol. 49.
34 Iraq Gazette 1971, Vol. 37.
35 Law 229/1970.
36 Articles 3 & 4.
37 Including daily well operational reports.
38 Article 16.
39 Articles 53 & 54.
40 Article 51.
41 Law 97/1971.
42 Permitted in Law 97 under Article 3.
43 Replacing the Oil Planning and Construction Administration established under Law 49 of 1970.
44 Article 3(2). Under Article 3, the company is responsible for the research, supervision, execution and inspection of the projects and provides "engineering and consulting services" to Government departments.
45 Law 13/1972, Articles 6–7.
46 With authority to draw up programmes and plans, approve budgets, conclude contracts and prepare draft regulations relating to employees and foreign experts (the Company being exempt from the Civil Service Law). Article 8.
47 Law 13/1972, Article 8.
48 See previous chapter.
49 Law 69/1972, Article 1.
50 Law 69/1972, Article 7.
51 Compensation was to be provided for the seizure by the State to the IPC group.
52 Law 69/1972, Articles 9 & 10.
53 Law 101/1976, Article 1. This law was amended by Decree No. 649/1983.
54 It also cancelled Law 229 of 1970 which deals with national hydrocarbons.
55 Law 101/1976, Article 11.
56 Ibid., Article 3.
57 Ibid., Article 9(e).
58 Iraq Ministry of Justice, *Legal System Reform Law* 1977, 7.

59 Ibid., 10.
60 Ibid., 21.
61 Ibid., 26–27.
62 Explanatory Memorandum to Iraq Ministry of Justice, *Legal System Reform Law* 1977.
63 Iraq Ministry of Justice, *Legal System Reform Law* 1977, 37.
64 Iraq Ministry of Justice, *Legal System Reform Law* 1977, 48.
65 Ibid.
66 Law 30/1984.
67 Resolution 272/1987.
68 A further environmental law was passed in 2009 as Law 27.
69 Amended in 2004.
70 Article 2: This law is aimed at organizing state companies, with regard to their establishment, management and liquidation, under unified financial and administrative bases and rules so as to enable them to attain a high level of growth in their work and production and to adopt the principle of proper economic accounting, competent investment of public funds, and efficiency in achieving state aims and improving the performance of the national economy.
71 Any excess profit is to be provided to the Ministry of Finance.
72 As defined in Article 11.
73 45%.
74 32%.
75 5%.
76 5%.
77 Any remaining profits from the 30%.
78 Article 14.
79 Article 15.
80 Article 20.
81 Article 35.
82 s.3. SOMO did not control imports by the CPA.
83 CPA Order 39.
84 In July 2017 at an Iraqi Embassy conference in London, the Oil Minister confirmed that the draft INOC law has been ratified by the Cabinet and is currently with the Council of Representatives for approval.
85 Article 3(2) of Law 97/1967; the precise terminology of the act is "effected by law".
86 Although prior to this from 21 April 2003–6 May 2003 Jay Garner was the chief administrator.
87 Discussed in the previous Chapter 3 at Section 3.5.2.
88 Saad Jawad, 'The Iraqi Constitution: Structural Flaws and Political Implications', *LSE Middle East Centre Paper Series/01*, 8, 2013.
89 Ibid.
90 Even if the drafters had taken a look at the US constitution and previous Iraqi constitutional documents this would be evident. Some positive provisions of the TAL include Article 11 which recognised the Kurdish language and declared Iraq to be a bilingual state, Article 27b which prohibited militias and Article 30 which required female representatives to make up 30% of the Iraqi parliament (Jawad).
91 Formed by Bremer.
92 Jawad 8.
93 Ibid., 8.
94 Ibid., 10.
95 See Article 52 of the TAL and Article 115 of the constitution.
96 According to Jawad, the "TAL was written by US nationals assisted by two expatriate Iraqis holding US and British nationalities, and who had not lived in Iraq

since they were young children. The document itself was written in English and was poorly translated into Arabic". Saad Jawad, 'The Iraqi Constitution: Structural Flaws and Political Implications', *LSE Middle East Centre Paper Series/01*, 2013. Jonathan Morrow observes, 'the TAL process … was notoriously, if unintentionally, hasty and secretive, and was heavily influenced by US political interests' 'Iraq's Constitutional Process II: An Opportunity Lost' (November 2005) United States Institute of Peace Special Report 5.

97 Jawad:

> There was considerable pressure within Iraq for Iraqi involvement in the process. Most notable …was a fatwa issued by Ayatollah Ali Sistani in June 2003, … 'Those forces … had no authority to write a constitution for Iraq. … The CPA's plan to use US advisors… was foiled by Iraqi opposition and Bremer … wanted to make the TAL look as if it was an interim constitution written by Iraqis and approved by them.

98 TAL Article 10.

99 Article 54(B) strengthened the Kurdish position by permitting them to "amend the application" of federal laws in the Kurdistan region where matters are not within the exclusive competence of the federal government.

100 Article 25.

101 Pursuant to Article 144 of the 2005 constitution, the effective date of the Constitution is the first sitting of Parliament following publication in the official gazette.

102 Nathan Brown, 'Iraq's Constitutional Process Plunges Ahead', Carnegie Endowment for International Peace, (July 2005) 2. Congressional Record, Congress, 29 June 2005. Within eight months of it being elected, the National Assembly was expected to have a complete draft constitution by 15 August 2005 with a referendum on that draft to be held by 15 October 2005. Following a successful referendum, parliamentary elections were to be held by 15 December 2005.

> But if the referendum fails – or if the National Assembly does not approve a draft in time – then a new National Assembly is to be elected to start the process over again. Should the current National Assembly decide by August 1 that it needs more time, it may be granted up to six additional months.

103 Ibid.

104 Ibid., 2.

105 Ibid.

106 Ibid.

107 There have only been two Constitutions since the formation of Iraq – 1925 and 2005. All interim constitutions reacted to the current political situation. Given the limited space, the interim constitutions will not be addressed here.

108 Zaid Al-Ali, 'Constitutional Legitimacy in Iraq What Role Local Context', in Grote & Roder (Eds.), *Constitutionalism in Islamic Countries: Between Upheaval and Continuity*, Oxford, Oxford University Press, 2012, 642.

109 Due to external geopolitical events where progress in Iraq were fundamental to foreign policy programmes particularly in the United States and the United Kingdom.

110 Deeks and Burton 54.

111 Nathan Brown, 'Iraq's Constitutional Process Plunges Ahead', Carnegie Endowment for International Peace, Policy Outlook, Democracy and the Rule of Law, July 2005, 2, http://carnegieendowment.org/files/PO19Brown.pdf, accessed 10 January 2015.

112 Deeks and Burton 54.

113 Elkins and Ginsberg, 'The Iraqi Draft Constitution in Comparative Perspective', Center for the Study of Democratic Governance, University of Illinois, http://

comparativeconstitutionsproject.org/reports-and-other-publications/, accessed 17 January 2015.
114 Deeks and Burton 66.
115 Ibid.
116 Ibid.
117 Article 141.
118 Deeks and Burton supra n944.
119 Ibid.
120 Deeks and Burton 84.
121 The distribution is governed by Article 121, Third.
122 2014.
123 Roula Khalaf, 'Baghdad and Kurds Reach Budget Deal', *Financial Times* (London, 13 November 2014), www.ft.com/content/ecfe1e42-698c-11e4-9f65-00144feabdc0, accessed 12 January 2018.
124 Article 110.
125 Ibid.
126 Crawford, Katzman et al.
127 Article 120.
128 KRG Website, 'Dr Hawrami: Just and Fair Oil Management Ensures Iraq's unity' (7 February 2008), http://cabinet.gov.krd/a/d.aspx?s=02010100&l=12&asnr=&a=22663&r=223&s=010000, accessed 8 March 2011.
129 Article 141.
130 Translated version of the Final Report of the CRC dated 7 July 2008.
131 Ibid.
132 Ibid.
133 Ibid.
134 Quote from Jonathan Morrow, by Toby Dodge, Iraq from War to a New Authoritarianism, 45 fn60.
135 Jawad 8.
136 Ibid.
137 Ibid. Kirkuk's centre is predominantly Turkoman, to the north are the Kurds and Arabs to the south. Although the dominant population of Kirkuk is Turkoman, since 1964 Iraqi governments have attempted to alter the province's demographics through the settlement of Arab tribes.
138 MERIP, 'Iraq and Kurdish Autonomy, MERIP Reports No. 27', 30 *Middle East Research and Information Project (MERIP)*, 26–27, April 1974, www.jstor.org/stable/3011338, accessed 18 July 2013.
139 Ibid., 27.
140 Law No. 4 of 2006.
141 Law No. 22 of 2007.
142 E.g. Exxon and Total.
143 Oil and Gas Law, Investment Law, Law 5 of 2013.
144 The recent pipeline construction in the region connecting to the main Ceyhan pipeline has caused considerable tension with MoO particularly given that it is now on stream with oil from the region being stored in Turkish tanks for export.
145 Pearl Petroleum Company Ltd & Ors v The Kurdistan Regional Government of Iraq [2015] EWHC 3361 (Comm).
146 KRG Hydrocarbons Law 2007 Article 18.
147 Article 19. Article 20 provides that until the conditions in Article 19 are met the KRG shall proceed with its rights on the basis of Article 112, 115, 121(3) of the federal constitution with revenues to be received by the Kurdish Oil Trust Organization (KOTO).
148 Article 37.

149 Michael Gunter, 'Economic Opportunities in Iraqi Kurdistan', XVIII (2) *Middle East Policy Council*, Summer 2011, www.mepc.org/journal/middle-east-policy-archives/economic-opportunities-iraqi-kurdistan?print, accessed 20 December 2011.
150 Ibid.
151 Ibid.
152 Ibid.
153 Reuters, 'Iraq has Set a Deadline of the Next Few Days for Exxon Mobil' (6 March 2012). Reuters, 'Exxon Mulls Baghdad Offer, CEO Meets Kurdish Leader – Sources' (23 January 2013), www.reuters.com/article/exxon-iraq-idUSL6N0AS0G520130123, accessed 23 January 2013.
154 Reuters, 'Exxon in Talks with Iraq over Oil Agreements: CEO' (4 March 2015), www.reuters.com/article/us-exxon-mobil-outlook-iraq-idUSKBN0M023M20150304, accessed 1 September 2016. Bloomberg, 'Iraq Seeks Exxon, Petrochina Help to Develop Two Oil Fields' (27 July 2016), www.bloomberg.com/news/articles/2016-07-27/iraq-seeks-exxon-petrochina-help-to-develop-two-oil-fields, accessed 1 September 2016. Reuters, 'Iraq's New Oil Minister Sticks by Demand to Review Foreign Contracts' (22 August 2016), www.reuters.com/article/us-iraq-oil-energy-bp-idUSKCN10X1J4 accessed 1 September 2016.
155 World Bank Iraq Operation Procurement Review 2005 at 15:

> the Erbil Region and the Sulaymaniyah Region have created central procurement agencies to handle procurement on behalf of their different ministries ... A similar unit ... was established in June 2004 within the Erbil governorate ... These centralized procurement agencies report directly to their respective regional Council of Ministers and Prime Ministers.
>
> ... The agency uses the Kurdish language as its official language and English as a second language.

156 The Economist, 'Iraq, Kurds, Turks and Oil A Tortuous Triangle', 22 December 2012:

> Iraq's central government seems bent on wrecking the Kurds' thriving oil industry, saying that their regional government has no legal authority to export oil independently or sign contracts with developers. The government in Baghdad has delayed payments to Iraqi Kurdistan's oil producers, who say they are owed about $1.5 billion ... the Kurds ... oil policy ... threatens to tear Iraq's fragile federation apart by fostering similar aspirations in its oil-producing provinces in the south.

157 Only the 2011 draft compiled by MoO will be considered given that it was approved by the CoR on 28 August 2011. There is another version compiled by the Parliamentary Oil and Energy Committee in 2011 that was rejected by Parliament on 22 April 2012.
158 Which at the time of writing refers to the KRG due to Basra not falling within the constitutional definition of a region although this might change in the near future.
159 2011 DOGL, Article 1(12) 2007 DOGL Article 4(24).
160 Article 4(37).
161 Article 4 (38).
162 2011 DOGL, Article 1(13) 2007 DOGL Article 4(19).
163 2011 DOGL Article 1(18), 2007 DOGL Article 4(17).
164 This was done in Article 1 of the 2007 version.
165 Referred to as "players" in the document.
166 Found at the end of the document.
167 2007 DOGL: Article 3: Purpose.

> (a) This law establishes the regime for the management of Petroleum Operations in the Republic of Iraq, taking into account the existing international treaties between the Republic of Iraq and other countries on Crude Oil transportation.

(b) The law aims to build upon existing co-operation between the relevant Ministries in the Federal Government administration, in addition to building a base for coordination and discussions among the Federal, Regional and Producing Governorates' authorities.

168 2011 DOGL, Article 2.
169 Ibid., Article 2(5).
170 Ibid., Article 2(7).
171 Ibid., Article 2(9).
172 Ibid., Article 2(6).
173 Ibid., Article 2(8).
174 Ibid., Article 2(10).
175 2011 Article 4, 2007 Article 2.
176 2011 Article 5.
177 2011 Article 9.
178 2011 Article 9, the 2007 version provides for the creation of entities to assist FOGC.
179 Previously the panel of independent advisers (2007).
180 The 2007 version has more specific qualification criteria: Article 5(6)

They should be qualified and have a good reputation and long practical experience in Exploration and Production operations and in Petroleum contracts, and they should be chosen by a unanimous decision of the Council and contracted for a year, which can be extended.

181 2011 Article 10.
182 2011 Article 7 effectively the same as 2007 Article 5.
183 2011 Article 8.
184 2011 Article 11.
185 2011 Article 11.
186 2011 Article 12.
187 2011 Article 14.
188 2007 Article 6A – "The Iraq National Oil Company (INOC) is a holding company fully owned by the Iraqi Government and based in Baghdad. INOC is financially and administratively independent and runs on commercial bases."
189 2011 Article 13(1).
190 The 2007 version includes marketing and sales to delivery point – Article 5.
191 2011 Article 13(3).
192 Also provided for in the 2007 document, Article 5.
193 Ibid., 2007, Article 6 provides for the subsidiaries to be represented on the INOC Board "and will be paid for the cost they incur in addition to a specific reasonable profit in order that they can develop and enhance their operations." Other members of the board include "members from the Federal Government, the Regions, and the Producing Governorates".
194 Wording similar to 2007, Article 5(E).
195 2011 Article 19(1st).
196 2011 Article 19, 2007, Articles 5 & 6.
197 2007 Article 6(4th).
198 The 2018 law has not been considered in this book. For commentary see Ahmed Jiyad, 'INOC Law: Dysfunctional, Unconstitutional and Disintegrative', *Iraq Business News* 12 March 2018, www.iraq-businessnews.com/2018/03/12/inoc-law-dysfunctional-unconstitutional-and-disintegrative/, accessed 30 April 2018.
199 Ahmed Aboulenein, 'Iraq Transfers Ownership of Nine State Oil Companies to New National Oil Company', *Reuters* (Erbil, 18 October 2018), www.reuters.com/article/us-iraq-oil/iraq-transfers-ownership-of-nine-state-oil-companies-to-new-national-oil-company-idUSKCN1MS27E, accessed 12 December 2018.
200 2011 Article 21(1st).

201 2011 Article 21(2nd).
202 Two years.
203 Four years.
204 Two years.
205 2007, Article 8.
206 Ibid.
207 Ibid.
208 2011 Article 18.
209 Ibid.
210 Ibid.
211 Ibid.
212 2007 Article 10 provides:

> the contract is valid with no objection from the Federal Oil and Gas Council according to the provisions of the Oil and Gas Law No. ____ of 2007 including the contractual guidelines on negotiations and model contracts and any amendments to these that might be issued by the Federal Oil and Gas Council.

213 2007 Article 10.
214 2011 Article 16.
215 Ibid.
216 2011 Article 21.
217 Ibid.
218 Article 21.
219 2007 Article 13.
220 Ibid.
221 "in issues such as defence, the right of Iraq to sail its national waters, research, development, health and safety, and a high level of environment protection".
222 2011 Article 15.
223 2011 Article 22.
224 2011 Article 22.
225 2011 Article 23.
226 2011 Article 24.
227 2007 Article 14.
228 Ibid.
229 2011 Article 25, 2007, Article 16.
230 The 2007 version stipulates 6 months for its decision if parties fail to agree. Article 16.
231 Articles 25 and 16 for 2011 and 2007, respectively.
232 2011 Article 26.
233 Ibid.
234 2011 Article 27.
235 2011 Article 29.
236 2011 Article 28.
237 2011 Article 29.
238 2007 Article 23.
239 Ibid.
240 2011 Article 30.
241 2011 Article 31.
242 Ibid.
243 2011 Article 30.
244 2011 Article 31.
245 INOC is responsible for the subsequent follow-up upon instructions from MoO.
246 2011 Article 31.
247 The 2007 expressly stipulates this as a non-exclusive right.

248 2011 Article 32.
249 Ibid.
250 2011 Article 33.
251 2011 Article 34.
252 2011 Article 35.
253 2011 Article 36.
254 2011 Article 37.
255 2007 Article 9.
256 Ibid.
257 In order to meet objectives and criteria, model contracts may be based upon service, field development and production, or risk exploration contracts.
258 2007 Article 9.
259 Ibid.
260 Ibid.
261 2007 Article 12.
262 2007 Article 17.
263 2007 Article 18.
264 2007 Article 20.
265 2007 Article 27.
266 2007 Article 28.
267 2007 Article 28.
268 2007 Article 29.
269 2007 Article 31.
270 2011 Article 39.
271 The 2011 version is less specific as to who pays the costs on completion and there is no reference to a decommissioning plan.
272 2007 Article 32.
273 2007 Article 30.
274 2011 Article 38.
275 Ibid.
276 2011, Article 40.
277 2011 Article 41.
278 2011 Article 42.
279 2007 Article 11.
280 2007 Article 33.
281 Ibid.
282 2007 Article 34 – Measured at the entry flange of the main pipeline.
283 At the prevailing market price.
284 2007 Article 34.
285 2007 Article 35.
286 2011 Article 45.
287 Ibid.
288 2011 Article 46.
289 2007 Article 39.
290 Ibid.
291 Ibid.
292 2011 Article 43.
293 Including from the sale crude oil and derivatives, signature and production bonuses, property rights, revenues of assets, taxes and fees, shares in consortia, commercial activities from oil and gas contracts, return of investors and any further payments from production of hydrocarbons.
294 2011 Article 43.
295 2011 Article 44.

296 2007 Article 36.
297 Ibid.
298 2007 Article 38.
299 Ibid.
300 2011 Article 47.
301 Ibid.
302 2011 Article 48.
303 2011 Article 50.
304 2011 Article 51.
305 2011 Article 52.
306 2007 Article 40.
307 Later supported by the 2007 Procurement Regulations subsequently replaced by Regulation No. 1 of 2008.
308 World Bank, Iraq: Operation Procurement Review, June 2005, vi.
309 BR1.
310 BR2.
311 BR3.
312 BR4.
313 World Bank Report 'Iraq' Chapter 5, 96, http://siteresources.worldbank.org/IRFFI/Resources/Iraqch5-final.pdf, accessed 23 January 2013.
314 Ibid.
315 OECD Benchmark Report 2009 17. CPA Order 87 s.13(1).
316 CPA Order 87 s.2.
317 CPA Order 87 s.2.
318 CPA Order 87 s.6.
319 s.11.
320 s.12.
321 World Bank Report 'Iraq: Operation Procurement Review' (June 2005) 16.
322 Ibid., 17.
323 Regulation No. 1 of 2008.
324 OECD Benchmark Report 2009 18.
325 OECD Benchmark Report 2009 18.
326 Ibid.
327 Ibid.
328 Ibid.
329 Peter Cameron, 'Managing the Politics of Oil Reforms: Lessons from Iraq: Keynote Address at the Oil and Gas in Federal Systems Conference, March 4, 2010, Washington DC', International Energy Law and Policy Research Paper Series No: 2010/07 CEPMLP 15.
330 Ministry of Oil PCLD, 'Final Tender Protocol for the Award of Service Contracts: Iraq's First Petroleum Licensing Round' (23 April 2009) 1.
331 Ibid.
332 The key terms of which are discussed in the next section.
333 Supra n1150, 7.
334 Ibid., 8.
335 Ibid.
336 Ibid.
337 World Bank Report Iraq: Operation Procurement Review 12.
338 Ibid.
339 Ibid.
340 Usually standing committees of six-month appointment durations.
341 Supra (n1161) 15.
342 Ibid.
343 Ibid.

344 Iraq Oil Forum, 'Pre-qualification', www.iraqoilforum.com, accessed 17 April 2013.
345 Ibid., The pre-qualification took place in 2008 with the results announced on 30 June 2009.
346 For example, the fourth bid round saw the removal of requirement for signature bonuses.
347 Model contracts.
348 Iraq Oil Forum, '1st Licencing Round Factbox – Bidding1', www.iraqoilforum.com/?cat=802, accessed 17 April 2013.
349 Iraq Oil Forum, '1st Licencing Round Factbox – Consortia1', www.iraqoilforum.com/?cat=802, accessed 17 April 2013.
350 Ministry of Oil PCLD, Baghdad, *Final Tender Protocol for the Award of Service Contracts: Iraq's First Petroleum Licensing Round*, 23 April 2009.
351 Producing Field Technical Service Contract (PFTSC): Bid Score = (PPT – IPR) * (100 – RFB). "The bids were scored by "multiplying the Plateau Production Target ("PPT") bid less the Initial Production Rate ("IPR") by an amount equal to one hundred (100) less the Remuneration Fee Bid ("RFB")". Final Tender Protocol, supra.
352 "Bids will comprise two parameters:

(a) The Remuneration Fee Bid, expressed in US$, to the nearest ten (10) cents, per Barrel of Crude Oil of Incremental Production delivered to the Transfer Point, (US$x.x0/bbl).
(b) The Plateau Production Target, expressed in Barrel of Crude Oil per day to be delivered, at or to the nearest increment above the minimum, as specified in Section 3."

Supra.
353 supra n1174.
354 Ibid.
355 Remaining Process Timeline, Ministry of Oil PCLD, Baghdad, *Final Tender Protocol for the Award of Service Contracts: Iraq's First Petroleum Licensing Round*, 23 April 2009.
356 Ibid.
357 Iraq Oil Forum, Oil Ministry document 'Bid Round Four – The Process, www.iraqoilforum.com, accessed 13 June 2013.
358 Ibid.
359 Ibid.
360 IEITI, 'Iraqi Oil Revenues 2012: Oil Export, Local Consumption and Field Development' (2013), http://ieiti.org.iq/ArticleShow.aspx?ID=96, accessed 8 July 2013.
See also Ahmed Jiyad, 'IEITI 4th Annual Report 2012 – Pros and Cons' (5 January 2015), www.iraq-businessnews.com/2015/01/06/ieiti-4th-annual-report-pros-and-cons/, accessed 10 January 2015.
361 Ibid.
362 Ahmed Jiyad, 'IEITI 4th Annual Report 2012 – Pros and Cons 3'.
363 IAMB Website, 'Purpose', www.iamb.info, accessed 13 January 2015.
364 IAMB terms of reference available at http://www.iamb.info.
365 Resource Governance Index 2013, www.resourcegovernance.org/sites/default/files/country_pdfs/iraqRGI2013.pdf, accessed 10 January 2015.

5 The contractual framework for Iraq's oil industry

5.1 Introduction

This chapter seeks to analyse the contractual terms in Iraq. In general, upstream contracts should incorporate key issues such as flaring and accommodate provisions used in the hydrocarbon industry for capturing byproducts of production for processing which could provide additional sources of government revenue. By placing obligations on the parties to maximise the efficiency of the exploitation process in retaining energy for downstream use, the oil companies could benefit from increased profit and the government would have the option to refine the byproduct for domestic use, thereby reducing dependence on energy from external sources. Such contractual provisions turn environmental irresponsibility into commercial and economic benefit. An example of such a provision would be that once commercial production has commenced, the lead contractor is obliged to make provisions on-site, through the use of a sub-contractor if necessary, to build gas (or other byproduct) processing facilities in addition to the standard drilling facilities to extract the crude.

After oil nationalisation in 1961, due to a lack of industrial resources, technology, skilled workers and knowledge, partnerships were formed with foreign entities in order to buy in the required know-how to develop the production process in Iraq. Following the creation of INOC,[1] a call for negotiations was made[2] by the government leading to an agreement with the Soviet Union through the Iraq-Soviet Protocol in 1967.[3] Thereafter, agreements typically contained provisions for the IOC involved to provide funds to enable the operations to proceed.[4] In 1968, a "technical, financial and commercial" service contract was entered into with Entreprise de Recherches et d'Activités Pétrolières (ERAP) "to be remunerated through the guaranteed sales at an agreed price of 30% of the quantities discovered and produced and not set aside as National Reserves".[5] This was followed by a significant economic and technical cooperation agreement with the Soviet government in 1969.[6] This agreement provided for the Soviet establishment to operate the North Rumaila oil field[7] to produce 5–18 million/ton of oil.[8] Technical aid was to be provided by the Soviet Union for the Ratawi field[9] and to survey and develop four fields in Southern Iraq along with technical assistance for Halfayah.[10] The agreement also included a loan for 60,000,000 roubles (ID 25 million) at an interest rate of 2.5% to be used to finance the surveys, and the development and planning operations in North Rumaila and Ratawi in addition to the construction of the Rumaila to al-Faw pipeline.[11] Payment of the loan was to be through delivery of oil to the Soviet Union assessed at market price.[12] In the event of a dispute, the contract was subject to mediation.[13] INOC had previously entered into an agreement with the Soviet establishment in a contract known as 'Machinoexport' ratified under Law 167/1969.[14]

A further agreement for another joint public-private identity 'Technoexport' was signed with Russia.[15] This agreement was for installation of pumping and degassing stations and to support pipeline construction between oilfields and terminals.[16] Later agreements included a technical cooperation agreement with a Hungarian company[17] for drilling operations and the provision of equipment for five wells in North Rumaila, to assist the Soviet company engaged in the region, and provide a loan of US$15 million at an interest rate of 3% p.a.[18]

From the early days of nationalisation, the Iraqi government realised that foreign companies could assist in developing the oil sector by providing technology, expertise and know-how. Without these agreements the industry would have been slow, some say impossible,[19] to develop and acquire the necessary facilities for oil export. 1972 saw the first commercial export of oil from Iraq. Thereafter, previously unexplored fields were surveyed by INOC. In order to develop prospective fields, six exploration service contracts were entered into between INOC and "oil companies from the Soviet Union, East Germany, Bulgaria, Czechoslovakia, Hungary and Romania, whereby these companies were given authority to carry out any activities related to surveys and drilling of exploratory wells".[20] Through these contracts the government was able to develop the oil sector and acquire the necessary expertise and technology to make a significant contribution to global oil production.

5.2 Contracts typically used in the industry and common terms

The original industry contract, originating from mining operations, is the concession agreement. Today, there are currently three main forms of contract in the oil industry, production sharing contracts (PSCs), service contracts (SCs) and licences. The key difference between them is one of ownership as under the PSCs and SCs the state retains ownership of the resource but not under a licence. Generally, under a PSC the IOC is exempt from the wider tax system and therefore this is a key consideration for IOCs when entering into such a contract. As will be seen, the fiscal regime is at the heart of oil agreements for both parties through the division of profits and revenues in the event of commercial discovery.

5.2.1 Concession agreements

Some advocates of the concession agreement suggest that they are a tried and tested system with inherent flexibility to incorporate new terms and develop with the industry.[21] Concession agreements are the original form of contract used in much of the oil producing world and given their history tend to be prominent in industrialised countries, as developing nations generally opt for alternative forms of agreement such as service contracts or PSCs.[22] Certainly in the majority of cases where colonial powers exploited hydrocarbon resources, in the Middle East and South America, this was the agreement of choice. Many of these agreements entitled the foreign party to access the territory and underlying reserves with impunity, merely providing the host state with a token income from revenues. The design of these agreements traditionally created a significant imbalance between the oil companies and the state which was highly exploitative and ultimately led to numerous nationalisations and renegotiations of contracts[23] usually in the form of the agreements outlined below.

Under traditional concession agreements[24] exclusive rights are offered to the IOC for E&P over land with ownership of hydrocarbons usually being transferred to the IOC at the wellhead.[25] The whole production process is also owned by the company. The government take is from royalty payments[26] and taxes based on net profits of the IOC. Due to the historic political inferences attached to a concession,[27] the modern reference to this type of agreement is that of a licence.[28] Historically, the duration of concession agreements averaged seventy-five years. These agreements benefit the oil company, as the associated conditions are the payment of royalties and surface rents with some contracts providing for the IOC to supply the domestic market. At the end of the term the host state will normally be entitled to retain the equipment and installations on-site at no additional cost.[29]

More recent concession agreements vary in length with the Norwegian licence containing nine articles and the Danish licence containing forty clauses.[30] The gradual move to modern agreements was a consequence of the limited control given to the state and has led to the gentle erosion of IOC dominance over a national economy. Clauses such as minimum work obligations and the state retaining ownership of oil in situ along with the requirement for the IOC to relinquish unused land at stipulated stages of the operations have gone some way to redressing the balance for the host state and are still used to date in many developed nations.[31] Smaller exploration areas, shorter durations of around 20–30 years, the employment of nationals and returns based on a percentage of the value of production in addition to tax on the IOC's net revenue has led to a mixture of concession and other forms of agreement in countries including Algeria, Angola, Khazakstan, Russia and Nigeria.[32] Since the 1970s windfall profit tax has been added to royalties and more recently, rate of return (ROR)[33] and R-factor[34] fiscal systems and calculations have found their way into agreements.[35]

5.2.2 Production sharing contracts

PSCs are common agreements in today's oil industry. They typically provide the investor with title to oil in exchange for revenues and other social development provisions in the agreement. In the 1950s, Bolivia introduced the PSC which was subsequently popularised by Indonesia in the 1960s and used in many countries including Iraq.[36] The main features of the contract were that the IOC was appointed as the exclusive contractor by the host state for a specified area and timeframe. The IOC operates at its own risk and expense under the control of the NOC. Production belongs to the host state except for cost and profit oil. Unlike concessions where the IOC owned the production, this passed control to the state. Once the IOC has taken its cost oil, which is usually paid in kind, the profit oil is then split according to a formula between the company and the state on a percentage share basis,[37] pre-determined in the contract. The profits of the IOC arising from the contract are usually taxable thereby providing the state with an additional source of revenue from the hydrocarbons. The technology and installations brought into the operations by the IOC become the property of the state at the end of the contract.[38]

In the same year as the establishment of OPEC, the PSC debuted as an alternative to the concession agreement in Indonesia[39] which was signed with an independent US oil company in Denver in 1966[40] followed by another hundred US independent oil companies.[41] Initially these contracts offered a revenue split of profit oil of 65/35 in favour of the state along with state management of operations which caused concern for the IOCs given their dominance over operations and understanding of the associated capital risk.[42] Once Indonesia provided an alternative form of contract in the industry, other countries followed suit in revising their agreements including those in the Middle East. As a result of these new contractual terms, OPEC managed to increase production from 9 mbpd in 1961 to 30 mbpd in 1973.[43]

In 1969, following a coup,[44] Libya made demands to increase the posted price of crude in order to alter the dominance of IOCs and increase state revenues.[45] Following pressure placed on the operators in the country by the government, Occidental entered into settlement negotiations thereby boosting the confidence of Gaddafi who gave the remaining IOCs the ultimatum of settling their debts within a week or face nationalisation.[46] Two years later Iran sought similar terms in its agreements marking a shift of bargaining power from the IOC to the state. The Tehran agreement of 1971 provided for a 55% tax rate in addition to royalty payments.[47] OPEC made an agreement with the IOCs in 1972[48] which provided for an incremental increase in state participation of 25% to 51% in 1982. The 1970s nationalisations contained 100% state participation[49] where all states entered technical service agreements (TSAs) with the former concessionaires.[50]

Under a PSC, a share of production is taken by the IOC for services rendered. Some contracts are signed by the IOC with the state and the NOC or solely the NOC. Duval et al argue that the clause on royalties within a PSC is unnecessary as royalties are usually associated with ownership of production and as the IOC does not own production, and takes its share of profit oil as compensation for its services, it is difficult to see from that perspective where the royalty payments slot into the agreement.[51] An alternative analysis is that the royalty is applied as an additional tax or fee imposed by the state for the IOC to benefit from operations.[52] The IOC is usually entitled to the oil when it becomes available for export or at a mutually agreed delivery point, whereas the transfer of ownership of oil was passed to the IOC at the wellhead under the concession agreements.[53]

In addition to the change in ownership for IOCs, there is also the problem with bookable reserves[54] under a PSC. Only a percentage of total field production and reserves corresponding to the IOC's share of production can be booked.[55] Concessions permitted the total amount of reserves and production to be booked by the IOC due to the ownership rights under the contract so it is clear to see how the financial incentive of the IOC, in terms of company accounts, diminished in the transition to PSCs. Due to profit and cost oil being based on a per barrel basis under the PSC, it will be oil price dependent and booked on that basis by the IOC.[56] Cost oil is calculated on the basis of the number of barrels at a set market price against the cost of production which can be capped in the terms of the PSC.[57] Generally, 30–50% is allocated for costs of production calculated according to a formula usually annexed to the PSC under 'allowable costs'.[58] Profit split is generally calculated as a percentage of production[59] or on a progressive split based on average daily production, cumulative production or profitability of the project.[60]

To prevent the IOC from taking windfall profits when oil prices are excessively high, a price cap excess fee can be applied by the host state as a form of tax based on specified volumes produced over a period of time, usually a daily basis.[61] Profitability is commonly calculated on a ROR or R-factor basis.[62] Usually, the IOC prefers tax to be calculated prior to the profit sharing distribution as it would leave them with the net oil to use for onward sale so that the tax payment can be made to the state in cash, whereas the state prefers to apply the tax post profit split allocation as an additional source of revenue.[63]

The operations under a PSC are generally controlled by the IOC save for where the contract has integrated work programmes and there is a joint control of operations. Usually the host state will become involved in the operations following commercial discovery, particularly where participation clauses are incorporated.

5.2.3 Service contracts

Iraq's central government uses service contracts, with the KRG preferring PSCs considered illegal by Baghdad for reasons set out above.[64] By comparison, Venezuela uses a joint venture (JV) contract and Mexico has recently opened up its industry offering a form of PSC.[65] Mexican contracts with third parties are under a restricted form of service contract.[66]

In Mexico, no royalties or bonus payments are made by the investor under the service contracts. Payment is made by the government on a fee per barrel plus cost recovery basis which can be either 75% or 100% depending on the bid round and is subject to available cash flow.[67] Payment will only be made for extractions delivered to the metering point and there is expressly no guarantee that PEMEX will pay expenses or that the contract will be profitable.[68]

5.2.3.1 Risk service contracts

Risk service contracts (RSCs) were designed to avoid passing ownership of reserves from the state to the IOC, originating in Latin America in the 1950s and expanding to the Middle East in the 1960s.[69] Argentina, Bolivia, Brazil, Iraq and Iran were among the first to use these agreements. Venezuela developed an operations contract in the 1990s for its mature fields and Iran created buy-back agreements to redevelop existing fields.[70] In Venezuela, Article 5 of the 1975 Reserving Law allowed contracts to be granted to private companies through operating service agreements and strategic associations, usually for a twenty-year term with income tax at 34% and a 30% royalty.[71] A model JV contract was introduced in 2006 and approved by the National Assembly with further amendment in 2009, resulting in PDVSA taking control of more than 50% of the JV contracts through CVP.[72]

No mineral rights or transfer of production are given to the IOC unless there is a buy-back clause in the agreement.[73] The IOCs are hired for their technical and financial capabilities and, upon commercial production, the IOC will be reimbursed for its costs and entitled to a pre-determined service fee which is generally paid in cash. However, at no stage during the contractual period is the IOC entitled to a share of production as ownership remains with the state/NOC at the wellhead all the way through to the point of export. The transfer of control of operations to the NOC usually takes place prior to expiration of the contractual period.[74]

There are some similarities to the terms found in PSCs, for example, all of the IOCs' financial risk is reimbursed on commercial production but profit oil is substituted for a service fee.[75] Payment is usually made in cash and not in kind.[76] Where reimbursement and fees are paid in cash, the IOC cannot book the reserves but if payment is made in kind the IOC is granted an economic interest in the reserves equal to a share of projected reimbursement for the duration of the RSC. However, some contracts incorporate specific express terms to exclude the contractor's right to production to prevent any of the reserves being booked.[77] Given the more stringent restrictions on the commercial freedom of IOCs, it was only in the 1960s when the industry came under pressure from producers and there appeared to be a clear shift in the balance of power, that RSCs were accepted. The first agreement was between NIOC and ERAP in 1966 followed by INOC and ERAP in 1968 and INOC and Petrobras in 1972.[78] The first Brazilian RSC followed the development of the Garoupa offshore field,[79] Petrobras offered larger remuneration for IOCs at cost reimbursement which, given the increase in crude price in the 1970s, was attractive to the IOCs.[80] The 1998 amendment to Brazilian oil policy ended the E&P monopoly of Petrobras[81] allowing IOCs to compete for concession agreements with ANP for exploration and JVs for production thereby ending RSCs in the country.[82]

Iran and Iraq's agreements with ERAP, contain terms requiring the general contractor (IOC) to supply NIOC with finance for the E&P operations which are considered to be interest-free loans repayable upon commercial discovery and production.[83] In addition, ERAP was to act as NIOC's broker for onward export of crude. Reimbursement to ERAP, as consideration under the agreement, was for NIOC to guarantee the sale of crude to the IOC at an agreed price for the duration of production under the contract. NIOC was financially responsible for the operations[84] "until the cashflow accruing to NIOC as a result of operations ... shall be sufficient to enable NIOC to provide the financing of appraisal and development operations".[85] Title to petroleum was owned by NIOC at the wellhead which also owns all assets created and used in the operations.[86] For the period of twenty-five years from the date of commercial production NIOC was to sell to ERAP f.o.b.[87] 35–45% of developed/corrected production capacity of each field at a defined price stipulated in the contract.[88]

In Venezuela in 1968, the minimum conditions for the RSC were set up by Corporación Venezolana del Petróleo (CVP)[89] for the area south of Lake Maracaibo.[90] The contractor assumed financial risk and received up to 90% of production for cost recovery, profit and tax payments. The market price was agreed between CVP and the IOC with CVP participating in the exploration and development through its committee. In 1970, agreements were signed with Shell and Occidental but ended with the nationalisation of the industry five years later.[91] La apertura[92] bid rounds were organised in 1992, 1993 and 1997 in addition to a direct negotiation for the Boscan field project.[93] Operation/association contracts were permitted due to the 1975 nationalisation law,[94] resulting in an increase in production of 500,000 bpd in 2005. The IOCs received service fees in US$ per barrel produced within the contract area for capex, risk fee, profit tax[95] and other taxes. In 2005, the contracts changed to JVs.

In Brazil, the RSCs in 1975 were limited to financial and technical assistance as Petrobras was the sole owner of production.[96] The IOC took the financial risk and Petrobras was to take over production upon commercial discovery.[97] IOCs were reimbursed without interest for exploration activities, subject to commercial discovery, and development costs were reimbursed with interest at the US prime rate + 1%. IOCs received quarterly cash payments equal to a percentage of market value for each commercial field for around fifteen years of production, paid in proportion to oil prices which amounted to profit oil subject to a dividend tax of 25%.[98] The IOC could purchase and export limited amounts of crude against the value of payments from Petrobras.

5.2.3.2 Technical service contracts

Technical service contracts (TSCs) are used to buy in the expertise of IOCs and former concessionaires.[99] Usually, the IOC will advise on the preparation of technical studies for existing/future fields for the NOC. Under a pure service agreement the IOC is paid a fee for its services. These contracts were brought in after nationalisation[100] but generally are no longer used in the industry.

5.2.4 JVs and joint operating agreements

Given the significant amount of investment required in E&P operations, joint operating agreements (JOAs) developed as a form of consortium agreement to pool resources and share the geological, commercial, political and financial risk of operations. Although there can be a number of parties to a JOA, usually only one,[101] is the nominated operator on behalf of all members.[102] Historically dominated by IOCs, the JOA now has significant NOCs involved due to the prominence of participation clauses in the head agreement.[103]

The American Association of Petroleum Landmen (AAPL) devised a model JOA in 1956 to assist in the development of the US oil industry by creating a vehicle for companies to share the risks and financial burden of operations.[104] The idea was a success which spread to Canada and then international territories ultimately creating a common form of agreement in the industry; now standardised.[105] Due to the allocation of risks and responsibilities between the parties the contract can, at times, seem lengthy.[106] The Association of Petroleum Negotiators (AIPN) created a model JOA in 1998 which was later released in 1990.[107] As an ancillary document, the JOA by its nature is dependant on the main international petroleum agreement between the state and the IOC operator, thus the legal context of the location and nature of the operations will usually dominate its terms. Typically the JOA will stipulate and confine the contractual and geographical location of the operations usually specifying upstream activities and excluding downstream operations.[108] There may be some reference to downstream activity under a separate agreement to be referred to at a later date.[109]

The participating interests of the companies are usually expressed as a percentage of their contribution to the venture. The NOC has a 'carried' right in the agreement corresponding to its option to become involved in the venture upon commercial discovery and/or production.[110] Typically with only one of the companies holding the role of the operator, the others in the consortium will form a committee to manage operations. The main operator will usually be entitled to reimbursement of its expenses but will not be entitled to profit from its position.[111] The operator will have an option to resign or may be removed by a vote of the committee. In the event of financial insolvency there is usually an express provision in a JOA that the operator would then give up its position. In the event of a breach of contract, the operator would be given a time period in which to remedy the breach, but failure to rectify the position is likely to result in the termination of the company's position as operator.[112] Any replacement operator would usually require the approval of the host state. In general, the rights and duties of an operator include the following:[113]

- To conduct operations in a proper manner in accordance with good industry practice; comply with the law and exercise due diligence
- To prepare and implement work programmes, budgets and anticipated financial costs (AFCs)

- To plan and provide reports, data and information to the operating committee
- To plan for and obtain all relevant materials and services, provide technical advisory services for the efficient performance of operations
- To prepare and submit a development plan and decommissioning programme
- To establish and maintain appropriate business standards, insurance and HSE[114] plans

The operating committee can have a significant influence over the operator due to its position of overall supervision and control of all aspects of the JOA. Policies, procedures and methods of operation consistent with good industry practice along with the determination of E&P strategies and procedures for the contract are all part of the committee's decision-making powers.[115] The voting rights of committee members will usually be proportionate to their percentage interest in the venture which will lead to an aggregate minimum percentage interest known in the industry as a 'passmark' which can amount to a bare majority.[116]

Operator liability is usually restricted to wilful/reckless misconduct, but varies between contracts.[117] Under the 2002 AIPN model JOA, parties elect to hold the operator liable for gross negligence, while the mere negligent conduct of an operator is shared between the parties to the JOA according to their share of the participating interest.[118] Liability may solely be that of the operator, proportionately distributed in the case of gross negligence. The rationale behind this is that given the operator should not profit from its role within the JOA, it should also not suffer a loss. This is particularly important given its likelihood of incurring liability in risky locations which may be hostile environments.

Funding is released to the operator by the other parties when considering an AFE (authorisation for expenditure) specifying the activity for which the funds are required.[119] There is usually a slippage margin of about 10% of expenditure in the JOA which may be exceeded by the operator.[120] Where a member of the committee is outvoted, some JOAs provide an opt out provision so that party does not need to participate in that aspect of the operations.[121] The party will then have carried interest, often termed a sole risk/exclusive operation where certain prescribed criteria stipulated in the contract need to be met or specified from a list of options. Minimum work obligations in the underlying E&P contract cannot usually be opted out of[122] as opting out amounts to a relinquishment of rights for that specific task. Some contracts stipulate a premium to be paid where consent is withheld and the party wants to opt back into the project. In Norway, a non-consent premium of 1,000% was stipulated in the eleventh round concession model JOA.[123]

When one of the parties opts out or there is a sole risk operation, issues that arise include the distribution of profit and cost oil; the allocation of production bonuses from the lead contract; and the allocation, compensation and use of joint property.[124] All of these should be provided for in the terms of the JOA where there is an option for exclusive/sole risk operations.

Often the parties to JOA have independent rights to dispose of their share of production but lifting/off-take agreements are usually used to assist in allocation and logistic coordination or downstream activity to avoid disputes relating to, inter alia, transportation and quantity allocation.[125] There is also a right of transfer available to the parties which is usually restricted to the transferee taking over the obligations of the transferring party. Such transfer would be subject to pre-emptive rights[126] and right of first registration. Other parties may withhold consent where there are concerns as to the transferee's financial and technical capabilities and subject to all relevant permissions from the host state being obtained by the transferee.[127] Withdrawal occurs upon giving notice once obligations have been fulfilled under the agreement (usually minimum work obligations). The withdrawing party will remain liable for costs of approved operations it had agreed to participate in. If all parties withdraw it is considered an abandonment and the JOA will be wound up according to its governing law and any obligations arising from the abandonment or decommissioning fund in the underlying lead contract will take effect. A security agreement is usually required by the host state to bind parties to operations relevant to the development plan prior to production. This allows for funds to be set aside for the costs of decommissioning at the end of the project.[128]

Guarantees, standby letters of credit, on-demand bonds, and corporate guarantees may be required as security by the host state.[129] Even though assets are usually transferred to the host state, the IOCs involved in operations are likely to be liable for future decommissioning costs, which is another useful benefit of the fund. IP rights are joint in the operations, all acquired data and information is confidential save for specified individuals or entities necessary to the operations.[130] In the event that IP is vested in the operator only, other parties to the JOA usually have an irrevocable perpetual royalty-free licence for the use of those rights. IP can also be granted to the HC. As to choice of law, the parties are free to choose which law governs the JOA, but usually the law of Texas, New York or England is chosen due to a well-developed body of commercial law and understanding of the oil and gas industry.[131] Arbitration is usually the main method of dispute resolution.

5.2.5 Licences

In the United Kingdom, there are two types of licence, landward and seaward, which are granted for a limited period and confined to a specified area to 'search and bore for and get' hydrocarbons.[132] Under English law, a licence is a deed binding the parties regardless of whether it is being used.[133] The Fallow Initiative was created by PILOT[134] to ensure that the United Kingdom continental shelf licences exploit the resources effectively.[135]

There is an annual charge for licences (rentals) and the licence administrator[136] will be invoiced by Oil & Gas Authority (OGA) who will make the required payments. Each licence is valid for a specified duration to coordinate with the usual stages of production and life cycle of the field. Each term of the licence will therefore correlate to the exploration, appraisal, development and production of the field which can range from four to twenty years. The licence may be surrendered in whole or in part at any time.[137] Unworked areas may be relinquished and partial surrenders subject to restrictions by the OGA. Multi-block licences may be issued. The issuing and processing of the licence is done electronically[138] thereby avoiding the need for paper documents and applications.[139]

Under the Petroleum Act 1998, model clauses are required to be published in secondary legislation which, since the nineteenth licensing round has been incorporated into the licence in full.[140] The Hydrocarbons Licensing Directive Regulations 1995 set out main requirements for decisions on whether to issue a licence. Typically a production licence will have three successive terms; the initial term which expires once the agreed work programme has been completed and a minimum amount of acreage has been relinquished. The second term which commences upon approval of the development plan and acreage outside of the development plan has been relinquished, and the third term is an extended period to allow for production.[141] Traditional licences in the United Kingdom are typically seaward and last twenty-six years. Under the initial term there is a mandatory relinquishment requirement of 50%. There is a third type of licence, the promote licence, which is designed to assist small and start-up companies to obtain a production licence in order to attract the necessary operating and financial capacity.[142] The annual rental rate under these licences is reduced by 90% in two years. If the financial technical environmental capacity required to fulfil the licence is not in place by the end of the second year, the licence will expire.[143] Finally, there are two determinative licences, one for six years and one for nine years.[144] The former has an initial and second term of six years with the third term being eighteen years. The latter follows the same format save that the initial term is nine years.[145] For both of these licences there is a mandatory relinquishment of 75% after three years of the initial term and then 50% for the remaining term of the licence.[146]

The petroleum, exploration and development licence (PEDL) is a thirty year landward licence with the mandatory relinquishment of 50% after the initial term.[147] Exploration licences granted for seismic activity or non-exclusive rights to drill can be used for production outside of existing production licence fields.[148] Permission from the licence holder for producing fields would need to be sought to explore acreage within the area.[149] Flaring and venting requires permission from the Secretary of State to dispose of natural gas.[150]

Licensing rounds take place every year with out-of-round invitations being offered in exceptional circumstances. Seaward exploration licences can be applied for at any time. In order to sign the licence or effect a change of control of the licencee, consent is required from the Secretary of State otherwise the action would be prohibited leading to immediate revocation of the licence.[151] An extension may be granted to producing fields for the production life of the field. If there is no production within twelve months, OGA may terminate the licence.[152] As production licences confer exclusive rights to the licencee, the licencee must establish a tax base in the United Kingdom through company incorporation.[153] Where there is more than one party to a licence, liability is joint and several and JOAs may require the consent of the Secretary of State, depending on its purpose.[154]

Since 2003, no royalties or bonuses are payable in the United Kingdom.[155] Annual rent was paid under each licence and there is no special participation.[156] Corporate tax is ring fenced on profit from oil and gas extraction activities and separated from the trading activities charged at a rate of 30%[157] based on book profits which are adjusted to account for taxable deductions.[158] Since 2011, there has been a supplementary charge of 32% on ring fenced activity[159] which will reduce to 20% if the oil price falls below £45 per barrel.[160] For licences before March 1993, a revenue tax of 50% applies in addition to the ring fenced corporation tax and supplementary charge. Some tax reliefs are given for brown-field investments and small or technically challenging fields.[161]

In Norway, the licensing system is considered to be a step-by-step process as once the licence is granted, further approvals are needed from the government for production to take place, for example, separate approval for the plan for development and operation.[162] Shares in licences are provided to groups of companies to enter JOAs based on the government terms and conditions.[163] State participation, through Petoro, is also a requirement under the licence. All activity is offshore, and since 2003, a new policy has simplified the licensing procedure for mature blocks in providing a tax incentive allowing companies with no taxable income to claim a refund for exploration costs which would otherwise be deductible if the company were taxed.[164]

All resources are owned by the state.[165] The King in Council awards production licences for E&P[166] which provides exclusive rights in the licence area subject to approval of the development and operation plan of the IOC by the government.[167] Exploration licences are not exclusive[168] and the concessionaire under the licence acquires ownership to production.[169] Terms and conditions of the licence are subject to negotiation post-award and there is a requirement for equal state participation.[170] It is usually a condition of the licence that the concessionaires enter into a JOA drafted by the Ministry of Petroleum (MoP) with the special part of the JOA governing terms between the parties with the general part generic to all licences.[171]

Licensing areas must be announced in a Norwegian official publication and the official Journal of the European Union, provides a minimum of ninety days for applications to be submitted.[172] The award must be based on criteria specified in the invitation applications.[173] Technical and financial capability are the main criteria.[174] Similar to the United Kingdom, it is a condition of the licence that the companies are registered and incorporated in Norway. Production licences have a duration of up to ten years and an extension may be granted following successful performance and commitment by the licencee.[175] Extensions can be granted usually for thirty years but up to fifty years in exceptional circumstances.[176] Any application must be made at least five years before expiry of the licence.[177] Another similarity to the UK system is that assignments or changes in control require the consent of the MoP. Only Petoro is granted pre-emption rights. Subject to permission from the MoP, licences may be mortgaged for collateral for the purposes of financing operations and any mortgagee is registered on the petroleum register.[178]

There is a requirement that activities are conducted prudently and in compliance with relevant regulations for HSE.[179] The Licence and all activities based on it are subject to Norwegian law.[180] The government take comprises an area fee and petroleum tax. The area fee is charged per square kilometre after the expiry of the initial licence period and designed to encourage the relinquishment of unused areas. The fee is Nkr 30,000 per square kilometre in the first year rising to Nkr 120,000 per square kilometre for the third year and beyond.[181] State participation takes the form of direct interest in licences through Petoro for an equal and proportionate share of production.[182] Statoil is responsible for the sale and distribution of petroleum under a 'marketing instruction' from Petoro.[183] Although Statoil was privatised in 2001, the state remains its major shareholder and receives an annual dividend which is administered by the Ministry of Trade and Industry. The petroleum tax is 50% on net income from production and pipeline transportation which is paid in addition to 28% corporation tax. The valuation of production is based on market price to reflect arms-length transactions. Costs are deductible on taxable income, usually set-off against the petroleum tax exploration costs, when incurred and investments are usually depreciated over six years.[184]

5.2.6 Farm-out agreements

This is where an owner of a right in an existing lead contract transfers part of its participating interest to a new company for a performance benefit, usually for economic or geological purposes.[185] The farmee is an assignee for the farmors work. Often the agreements are used for an opinion on geology such as seismic information on the general area. Historically, IOCs would farm-out shortly after winning a contract but host states limit or prohibit this prior to completion of minimum work obligations.[186] Farm-outs are usually offered by bid process and invitations are made on a strictly confidential basis to prevent bidders revealing information about the operation to competitors.[187]

AIPN drafted a model farm-out agreement in 2004.[188] The farmee will usually acquire a direct continuing participation in the exploration/development of the contract area and become a co-contractor under the underlying lead contract in consideration for its specified work obligation. Non-participating interests may instead be granted where the farmor sells an overriding royalty interest to the farmee, if permitted by the law of the host state, which provides the farmee with receipt of a cost-free percentage share of production.[189] Alternatively a net profit interest may be sold to a third party which is a percentage share of net operating profits of the project.[190] In the agreements, profits are usually specifically defined to avoid confusion.[191] The latter is dependent upon revenue exceeding costs where the former provides for payment of the royalty upon production regardless of profitability. These two options mean that the third party does not have a participating interest in the JOA or underlying contract.

Supporting agreements are similar in nature but the third party will provide finance for the task or interest in other acreage.[192] The farm-out is not a separate agreement as it is appended to the original underlying contract and subordinate to it. The host state will need to approve any transfer of interest which may lead to the renegotiation of the existing underlying contract.[193]

The farmee can pay cash for the assignment or perform and pay costs for the work, known as drill to earn clause. A typical clause stipulates that if the farmee does not complete the work by a specified time he will be in default and bear the cost of completion by the farmor.[194] A participating interest can be subject to a condition precedent that the party completes the work successfully, pursuant to the assignment exhibited to the agreement. The model farm-out agreements provide that during interim periods where the condition precedents have to be satisfied, then the requirement for host state approval is waived.[195] As in most contracts, failure to satisfy conditions precedent give a right of termination by either party.

5.2.7 Common clauses

The modern-day oil agreement tends to incorporate a combination of terms taken from the various contract types discussed above. The terms will usually depend on the political history of the state involved and the formulation will be dependent on domestic factors. However, the most common term is for the host state to participate in the production process through the NOC or designated government entity taking a share of the production process.

5.2.7.1 Participation agreements

These are clauses contained in any of the contracts referred to in this chapter where the state or NOC holds a participating interest and finances its own share of the operation proportionate to its interest and costs.[196] The clause will usually provide the host state or NOC with a right or option proportionate to their interest in the operations which can be exercised at any stipulated stage of the process. Essentially it converts the contract, of whatever format, into a joint venture where the NOC rights become similar to those of the IOC. The different forms of participation clauses/contract are progressive,[197] fixed,[198] optional[199] or carried interest.[200] Through these clauses the state can acquire knowledge and skills from the IOCs which can then be carried forward and used in future projects.

These provisions were developed in the 1960s and 1970s and inserted into existing concessions by states demanding a greater input into the upstream process prior to nationalisation in many instances in the Middle East,[201] Africa, Asia and South America. In the Netherlands a 40% participation was imposed for the Groningen gas field. Norway, Denmark and the United Kingdom required state participation in North Sea operations in the 1970s. Norway created Statoil in 1972 to hold participation rights in contracts.[202] AGIP signed a contract with NIOC on a 50/50 basis establishing SIRIP where NIOC took 75% of the profit oil.[203]

5.2.7.2 Buy-back agreements

In 1995, Iran introduced buy-back agreements as a form of RSC. Subsequently, 20 agreements were entered into for development rather than exploration operations. The contractor has a right to payment in kind for a share of the production. The IOC provides funding for the development operations and technical expertise in accordance with the master development plan. Therefore the contract usually incorporates the development period, and production phase (usually ten years) for cost recovery and predetermined remuneration.[204] Upon commencement of production, control of the operation is transferred to the NIOC and the IOCs petroleum costs are recovered in US$ with an interest rate pegged to LIBOR plus a remuneration fee and a premium paid in monthly instalments.[205] The costs and fees are paid in kind by providing the IOC access to a given quantity of oil produced from the relevant field and sold at international market prices up to a maximum percentage of field production and it is this feature which forms the buy-back clause in the contract.[206] In recent years the contracts have expanded to incorporate exploration as well as development.[207]

At the time of writing, sanctions are due to be lifted in Iran.[208] There has been a flurry of activity for Iran's oil sector as IOCs jockey for position to obtain potentially lucrative contracts. Interest has been intense enough for the Iranian government to redraft the contracts to be offered and Iran has looked to Iraq to learn from its experience as part of that process. The new contractual terms were revealed at a conference in Tehran in November 2015, and rather than the buy-back agreements used to date, going forward the contracts will be RSCs where the parties will 'bear the risks of the operation' and remuneration is likely to be on a fee per barrel basis with an entitlement 'to an increase in profits in face of dramatic oil price fluctuations'.[209]

5.3 Oil agreement structures in Iraq

In Iraq, all of the oil agreements are awarded through the Ministry of Oil (MoO). As stated in Chapter 3, there have been four types of contract since 2007. These model contracts were drafted and used in the bid rounds since 2009 with the terms of the agreements progressively amended to adapt to the needs of the industry and to satisfy the demands of the IOCs. The move by some IOCs from the centralised government-controlled oil fields to those in the KRG region is perhaps an indication of the commercial benefit of what is perceived to be more favourable terms offered by the KRG PSCs when compared with Iraqi central government TSCs. Although the important question remains whether in fact the terms of the KRG PSCs really are more favourable to the IOCs. The next few sections will seek to assess three agreements[210] to find out the true position.

Since June 2009, there have been four bid rounds with twelve oil companies awarded service contracts in BR1[211] and BR2.[212] BR3[213] was designated a non-associated gas round where three TSCs were awarded.[214] Producing Field Technical Service Contracts (PFTSCs) were awarded for three giant fields to the Korea Gas Corp at Akkas, Kuwait Energy at Siba and Turkish Petroleum International at Mansouriya.[215] Development and Production Technical Service Contracts (DPTSCs) were awarded for a further nine oil fields.[216]

The PFTSC for the Rumaila field[217] near Basra was awarded in 2009, in the first bid round to a consortium of BP,[218] CNPC[219] and SOMO.[220] The infamous[221] bid remuneration fee was $2 per barrel and production plateau suggested to be 2.85 mbpd. The contract term is for twenty years with an option to extend for a further five years.

Since 2009 all of the contracts awarded by the central government are TSCs. The bid rounds commenced with producing fields given that the fields awarded[222] were already in production. On 13 October 2009, Eni in a consortium with Occidental and Korea Gas Corp was awarded the Zubair oil field.[223] Less than a month later, West Qurna 1 field was awarded to ExxonMobil and Shell.[224] The second round saw the use of the DPTSC contract, the third bid round was for a gas development contract and the fourth bid round was based on the model EDSC. For the purposes of analysis, the key provisions of the model contract and the Rumaila agreement are outlined below, with reference, where appropriate, to more recent agreements in order to compare relevant provisions to provide perspective on any development of the contractual terms.

5.3.1 Technical service contracts

Iraq is known as an attractive proposition for IOCs from a geological perspective given that the oil is plentiful[225] and relatively close to the surface thereby lowering extraction costs.[226] However, after 2003 it quickly became apparent to the companies seeking to add Iraqi reserves to their books and commercial portfolios, that other risks and circumstances made entry into the industry more burdensome than expected. This was mainly due to the security situation and uncertain political environment. Also, contractual terms were considered unfavourable to the IOC as they sought to protect the state's position when maximising government take. Likewise, the influx of companies expected to engage in a bidding war that would result in paving the way to rebuilding Iraq's economy was not as easy as the government or MoO anticipated.

Under the service contracts in Iraq, the investor pays a one-off signature bonus that provides ready capital to the state. Initially, this bonus was considered to be a form of repayable loan but with the development of the bid round process it has decreased in value and became non-refundable.[227] The state holds a 25%

share in the contracts awarded to date and corporate income tax is payable at a rate of 15–35%. The Iraqi government receives all of the oil revenues for redistribution, which has led the IMF to suggest the use of a sovereign wealth fund to manage revenues effectively.[228]

5.3.2 Development and production technical service contracts

Some of the key agreements in place have recently been amended[229] to reduce the production levels and plateaus.[230] For example, the contract for Rumaila has provided an increased share to CNPC[231] and BP[232] while significantly reducing state participation through SOMO.[233] Production levels for the giant field have been reduced from 2.85 mbpd to 2.1 mbpd.[234]

The primary concern for investors in the energy industry is one of stability, particularly given the historical performance of host states unilaterally withdrawing the rights of foreign companies through acts of expropriation. Although the risk of expropriation does still exist, the key issue is the consequence of legislative actions by the host state affecting the economic position of the investor, in essence reducing this to whether damages are payable or specific performance invoked through whatever form of stabilisation clause in the contract.[235]

5.4 Key contractual provisions

The fourth bid round in 2012 saw contracts awarded entitled exploration development and production service contracts (EDPSC). One marked difference appears to be that of remuneration for the IOC given that the Rumaila contract was agreed on a $2 per barrel return, whereas the block 10 award following the fourth bid round provided for $5.99 per barrel to the IOCs in the event of commercial production.[236] Arguably the latter is justified given that there is an exploration and development phase required, whereas Rumaila was already producing albeit inefficiently due to outdated equipment.

5.4.1 Fundamental provisions

5.4.1.1 Term and participation

The Rumaila contract has a twenty-year term with an option to extend for five years if South Oil Company (SOC) is notified a year prior to the expiry date.[237] For the later contracts, given that exploration is involved in the operations, the duration is longer, for example, INPEX and Lukoil were awarded a thirty-year contract with a five-year exploration period for exploration block 10 in the south of Iraq.[238] Events such as force majeure may also give rise to an extension of the contractual term.[239] The scope of the contract is for the rehabilitation of the Rumaila oil field to improve production and enhance recovery of the petroleum. The improved production target rate is a net production rate of 10% above the initial production rate with a plateau production target of 2.85 mbpd.

Under the contract there is an exclusive right for the contractor to negotiate a separate agreement for the E&P of undiscovered potential reservoirs for a period of six years from the effective date of the contract.

Preference is to be given to local goods and services offered on a competitive basis[240] in an attempt to assist the local economy. Associated gas is not to be flared unless permitted by law, and any gas not used in operations is to be delivered to the SOC.[241] The SOC will hold the contractor harmless for its non-performance or breach including liabilities incurred by third parties operating in the contract area under SOC's permission.[242]

Through the Shell gas agreement in the south of Iraq, the government has attempted to significantly increase the capture and storage of gas.[243] A suggested environmental and economic improvement to current contracts would be to oblige the IOCs to ensure that processing and storage facilities are in place at all producing fields to capture associated gas which could be connected to a central distribution network and transported through an integrated infrastructure for domestic use and export. The network could be developed through competitive bidding.

Participation is a fundamental provision of the contract as it demonstrates how the parties allocate responsibility and associated benefits. For the Rumaila contract, the state holds a 25% participation share, BP holds 38% and PetroChina holds 37%.[244] The state is entitled to a 25% share of the remuneration fee paid to the contractor and the companies are to pay all of the state's share of the costs.[245] For the Block 10 contract, Lukoil holds a 60% share and INPEX a 40% share.[246]

5.4.1.2 Minimum work obligations

Within thirty-six months of approval of the rehabilitation plan the operator is to provide to SOC enhanced redevelopment and revisions, 3-D seismic surveys, geological and reservoir engineering studies, drilling appraisal and/or development wells and to achieve planned production according to the rehabilitation plan.[247] Upgrading necessary service installations is required according to the rehabilitation plan and initiating engineering work in the enhanced redevelopment plan.[248] A minimum of $300 million dollars is to be spent by the operator in implementing the minimum work obligations.[249] Performance of the minimum work obligations is to be generated by commercial affiliates of the contractor specified in the contract.[250] MoO is to provide guarantees to the companies, the state entities and partners and failure of the contractor to perform in a timely manner shall lead to contract termination.[251]

To assist, Article 7 provides the obligations of SOC, for example, provision of technical data, de-mining of contract area, security within the contract area and political assistance, if required, along with access to contract area, water and petroleum for use in operations. For block 10 under the Lukoil/INPEX EDPSC the minimum work obligations include a 2D seismic survey of 1,375 kilometre and the drilling of one exploratory well.[252] These obligations are designed to ensure that the production targets are met and provide a method for MoO to monitor the progress of IOCs' work in the fields.

5.4.1.3 Phases

No work can be conducted unless approved by the Field Operating Division (FOD).[253] Within six months of the effective date, the rehabilitation plan is to be submitted for approval to the joint management committee containing a detailed work programme and budget for the remainder of the calendar year.[254] Overall targets and phases of redevelopment are to be included in the plan. A remedial programme to "halt any non-optimal operations, to arrest production decline, and to achieve a sustainable and improved production rate" is essential to the rehabilitation plan in addition to an appraisal programme for producing undeveloped and existing reservoirs requiring further appraisal. After completion of the additional appraisal programme and/or within three years of the effective date, the enhanced redevelopment plan is to be submitted by the contractor for approval.[255]

By 1 October in each calendar year the contractor is to provide annual work programmes and budgets including a four-year forecast.[256] An improved production target should be achieved no later than the end of the rehabilitation period and plateau production target no later than six years from the effective date.[257] All plans are to be based on best industry practice and sound principles.[258]

5.4.1.4 Production targets and relinquishment

In the Rumaila contract, the improved production target is the NPR (Net Production Rate) of 10% above IPR (Initial Production Rate) which is to be achieved as soon as possible after approval of the rehabilitation plan.[259] The PPT (Plateau Production Target) is a NPR of 2.85 mbpd for the plateau production period of seven years.[260] This is to be implemented within three years of the ERP (Enhanced Redevelopment Plan) approval date when PPT has been achieved for a minimum continuous period of thirty days.[261] The contractor is to relinquish discovered but undeveloped reservoirs not forming part of development operations within six years of the approval date of the ERP.[262]

5.4.2 Assignment and subcontracting

There is no right to assign the contract or any part thereof without prior written consent of the other parties except for the case of assignments to affiliates or successors of the contractor, provided SOC has one month's notice.[263] In the event of anticipated assignment to a third-party, SOC will within three months have the option to assign the contract to an Iraqi entity on the same terms.[264]

5.4.3 Signature bonuses and exclusivity clauses

Article 4 of the model contract provides for a signature bonus and the value of these bonuses varied between the contracts and bidding rounds. There has been much debate about the relevance of the value of the bonuses demanded by the Iraqi government with some commentators claiming that the sums should have been much higher than achieved. Signature bonuses are often seen as a form of "soft loan" to the government.

The signature bonus is payable within thirty days of the effective date and in the Rumaila contract this was in the sum of US$500 million.[265] This is recoverable as a supplementary cost by the contractor and the participating interest share is calculated on a pro rata basis.[266] To put it in context, there was a signature bonus awarded in Brazil for the seventh bid round in 2005 for $425 million.[267] For block 10 in the south of Iraq which was awarded following the fourth bid round the signature bonus was US $25 million.[268]

5.4.4 Measurement policies (SOMO and MoO)

The contract stipulates in clear terms how the crude is to be measured and transported. The PMP (Production Measurement Point) is immediately upstream of the TP (Transfer Point). The SOC transporter is to deliver crude oil, which may be mixed with oil from other fields, from the TP to the DP (Delivery Point).[269] The price of export oil "shall reflect prevailing export market price f.o.b. delivery point".[270] SOMO's official selling price shall apply in any lifting quarter and any different pricing mechanism shall be notified to the contractor by SOMO.[271] The contractor shall cooperate with SOMO at its own cost for the assessment of global export qualities of crude oil, market studies and forecasts along with any other information about market conditions for export oil.[272]

5.4.5 Taxation

The commercial parties are to pay corporate income tax up to a maximum of 35% of taxable profit, that is, the remuneration fee during the tax year. No additional taxes are to be paid by the contractor and SOC is not liable for any taxes paid outside Iraq.[273]

There is no restriction on the use of foreign currency or bank accounts by the contracting parties operating in Iraq.[274] Further, imports and exports for petroleum operations are exempt from customs duties.[275]

5.4.6 Investor returns – cost recovery and remuneration

Payment of petroleum costs is found under clause 19 of the agreement.[276] Contractors have forty-five days after the last month of the quarter to send an invoice to the Regional Oil Company (ROC) outlining petroleum, remuneration and supplementary costs based on their operating accounts.

Clause 10[277] provides for the non-recoverable costs under the agreement, namely, those incurred as a result of gross or wilful misconduct, costs arising from failure to obtain adequate insurance, incidental costs to the raising of finance for petroleum operations, PR, costs relating to activities post-delivery point, signature bonus, corporate income tax, the Training, Technology and Scholarship Fund (TTSF) and any other costs stated in the agreement as non-recoverable.

Under Article 19,[278] supplementary fees and costs are reimbursed to the operator and include signature bonus, de-mining costs, access to water, gas transportation to SOC, downstream transportation facilities and costs for remediating environmental conditions. Service and supplementary fees at expiry or termination of the contract are immediately due and payable within thirty days. Export oil payments are delivered by SOMO to the delivery point estimated in advance and payable in the lifting quarter.[279]

In an attempt to promote transparency and efficient operating procedures, there is a proscribed format for accounting procedures and auditing in the contract and accounts must be made available to the government for inspection.[280]

5.4.7 *Title to and use of assets*

One of the most sensitive clauses for both the state and IOC is title to assets. For the state it is often an issue of sovereignty and national protection of resources to attempt to ensure that control is retained by the relevant ministry. For IOCs, there is a commercial impact in that the question of title to resources can often determine whether or not reserves are bookable and therefore incorporated into the balance sheet of the company and reported to shareholders.

In terms of the equipment used[281] by the contractor during operations, save for those acquired by lease,[282] the state has incorporated into the contract a condition that these assets will pass to the NOC upon contract expiry. Consideration for this lies in the contractor being able to recover the costs as part of its entitlement to 'cost oil'.[283]

During the term of the contract both parties are entitled to the 'full and free' use of the assets and assignment; sale or disposal is only permitted through joint agreement.[284] Save for leased or sub-contractor assets, all assets acquired by the contractor and subject to cost recovery become the property of SOC upon "landing in Iraq".[285] The contractor and operator are entitled to the full and free use of the assets.[286]

5.4.8 *Force majeure*

Any delay in performance due to force majeure, as defined in the contract, shall be notified in writing by the parties to SOC within fourteen days.[287] In the event of operations being delayed for more than ninety consecutive days, the contract term will be extended accordingly. Any disagreement between the parties is to be referred to arbitration.[288] Security conditions in the contract area along with general political and security conditions prevailing in Iraq at the time of signing the contract shall not constitute force majeure at the contract date unless they prevent implementation of operations.[289]

5.4.9 *Stabilisation*

In the event of the contractors financial interest being "adversely and substantially affected by a change to the Law that was in force on the Effective Date" the parties shall agree on adjustments within ninety days.[290] If the parties are unable to agree then the matter will be referred to arbitration.[291]

5.4.10 Technology transfer

A key term for Iraq's contracts is that of technology transfer (TT) given that there is a significant amount of development required for the industry to meet its production targets. One of the most valuable, if not *the* most valuable, benefits for governments engaging with IOCs to exploit their natural resources, is the ability to buy in the know-how and technology that comes with the experience of the IOCs engaged in global production. Given the competitive nature of the business models adopted by oil majors and the amount of investment in technology to find more efficient and effective methods to exploit, produce and distribute hydrocarbons, the IOCs are strategically placed to assist developing states' oil industries in maximising commercial efficiency using 'good industry practice' by introducing modern technology, equipment and know-how to often outdated practices to effectively exploit domestic reserves going forward. The state is then able to learn and adopt the technologies and equipment used for ongoing production and development of their fields beyond the lifetime of the contracts. It is therefore essential to improve the workings of the domestic industry which should, in turn, assist economic development.

Article 26 of the TSC provides for employment, training and TT. There is a requirement for the IOC to employ Iraqi nationals with the relevant qualifications and experience 'to the maximum extent possible'[292] and, within twelve months of the contract date, to establish and maintain training programmes for Iraqi national staff positions at 'each phase and level of petroleum operations including skilled, technical and management positions'.[293] This latter provision is to ensure continuity of field production beyond the lifespan of the contract and ensure development of domestic knowledge of the industry to reduce reliance upon external assistance to maintain and develop national petroleum operations in the future. This is a step towards self-sufficiency to boost the economy through domestic job creation with a view to reducing the number of IOC employees over the period of the contract as a hand-over strategy. The DPSC contains an amended term for the training programme providing a definitive period six months from the contract date for the contractor to establish a training programme for Iraqi nationals.[294]

A training and scholarship fund[295] is to be established between the parties to allow for on-the job training of Iraqi nationals and to support the research and development of technology in hydrocarbons which includes 'the establishment or upgrading of research institutes inside the Republic of Iraq'.[296] The maintenance of the relationship between the state and the IOC is assured through the option for independent agreements to be entered into between the parties for ongoing technical assistance.[297]

In an attempt to conform with industry standards, there is a provision for general business ethics whereby the parties undertake to implement anti-corruption, anti-bribery and anti-money laundering policies with the right to terminate sub-contracts. This is to minimise the risk of contractors feeding into the existing corruption at all levels of society and explicitly in the political sphere.[298]

5.4.11 Dispute resolution

There is an aim to settle disputes amicably through negotiation within thirty days of notification by one party to the other.[299] If this cannot be resolved then the matter is referred to senior management to be resolved within a further thirty days.[300] Failure of the senior management to find a solution can lead to referral to an independent expert or by one of the parties providing the other with sixty days' notice to refer the matter to arbitration.[301] In the event of independent expert determination, this is to be provided within one month of the expert accepting the appointment.[302]

In the event of arbitration, the governing rules are ICC with the seat in Paris; the applicable law is that of Iraq and the arbitration is to be conducted in English.[303] Operations are to continue pending the arbitral award unless otherwise agreed by the parties.[304] The arbitration is to be initiated within two years of the date of notification of the dispute by one of the parties to the other.[305] There is a general long-stop of three years from the date of expiry or termination of the contract to commence arbitral proceedings.[306]

In order to prevent the subversion of dispute resolution in the contract by the use of third parties there is a further protection mechanism. In addition to the above provisions, the contractor and operator are to include a provision in their sub-contracts that the sub-contractor shall undertake to "abide by and comply with the Law".[307]

The difference between the main agreement and the sub-contracts is that the procedure for dispute resolution is more extensive with arbitration being the last resort. As seen above, there are various stages to resolve issues arising under the main contract which are fairly comprehensive and it is this mechanism that distinguishes the oil agreements from purely private law commercial contracts where the dispute resolution provision is arbitration, mediation or litigation. The governing law, conciliation and arbitration provision under Article 37 of the DPSC provides for internal dispute resolution prior to arbitration:

> The Parties shall endeavour to settle amicably any dispute … Where no such settlement is reached within thirty (30) days of the date when one Party notifies the other Party of the Dispute, then the matter may, as appropriate, be referred for resolution by the senior management of the Parties to the Dispute. Where no such settlement is reached within thirty (30) days of such referral to management, any party to the Dispute may refer the matter, as appropriate, to an independent expert or, by giving sixty (60) days notice to the other Parties, refer the matter to arbitration as stipulated hereunder.

It is clear that the contract offers a good selection of dispute resolution processes.

5.4.12 *Termination*

In the case of Rumaila, SOC may terminate in the event of contractor bankruptcy or upon three months' written notice where the contractor commits a material breach of an obligation if not remedied within the three-month notice period.[308] If operations are suspended or seriously jeopardised for more than twelve months due to force majeure, either party may terminate the contract by giving two months' notice.[309] Clearly implemented as a consequence of the former sanctions in Iraq, if the contractor suspends obligations due to order/decree of the home country, SOC can assume full responsibility of operations however it deems appropriate provided that it gives the contractor one-month written notice.[310] The contractor may give three months' written notice with reasons to terminate before the end of the term and in the event of termination the contractor warrants not to obstruct operations.[311]

5.5 The KRG PSCs

In the Kurdish region, PSCs have been in place prior to the promulgation of the Iraqi Constitution in 2005, and are protected under Article 141.[312] Since 2005 the KRG has considered it to be its constitutional right to enter into oil agreements independently of the central government, hence the use of PSCs in the region.

To assure the public that the contracts signed are legitimate and that the region has an effective and transparent oil industry, the KRG website contains some but not all of the contracts.[313] Crucially, the most controversial agreements have not been published.[314] For consistency three contracts have been selected from those published for comparative analysis within the PSCs, the first being for the Shaikan block as it is an early contract,[315] the second is Ain Sifni and the third is for the Topkhana field being one of the latest available. However, the date of the contracts has no relevance to the passing of the regional OGL given that all of the contracts since 2007 are subject to English law.

Given the clear lack of legitimacy in the KRG exporting oil independently of the central government, some countries are treating the issue with caution in order not to encroach upon a domestic sovereign issue. A Texas court was recently confronted with a dispute between the central government and the KRG about the KRG's conversion and refusal to return a tanker of oil[316] seized off the coast of Galveston in July 2014. The court refused to recognise Kurdistan as a foreign state as it is only "a political subdivision of Iraq"[317] and "undisputedly is a region within Iraq".[318] On 7 January 2015, Judge Miller determined that the plausibility of MoO's pleadings could be "interpreted to give the MoO title to the oil as opposed to the KRG" and the motion to dismiss the action by the KRG was denied.[319] Ultimately the ownership of the oil is a constitutional issue to be determined in the Iraqi courts.

5.5.1 *Legitimacy*

As discussed in previous chapters, there has been an ongoing dispute between the KRG and central government in relation to the oil agreements in the Kurdish region and the so-called disputed territories. The central government has on several occasions refused to pay the IOCs for the oil exported from the north of the country on the basis that the contracts entered into with the KRG are not recognised as they have not been approved by MoO. Consequently, the KRG has halted exports from the region or restricted the flow of oil through the pipeline to a fraction of the daily production. There are occasionally reports of deals between Baghdad and the KRG which become strained as they are subject to the political whim of the governments, which although is not of significant effect to the Iraqi economy given that the Kurdish region holds a small proportion of Iraq's oil, it does cause instability for investors. From the perspective of the central government this is not an issue as the KRG contracts are considered illegal in any event.

5.5.2 Governing law and dispute resolution

It is worthy of note that despite the efforts of the KRG to exert their authority over the natural resources within the region, primarily through the passing of a regional OGL, there is no reference to the OGL in the contracts. From the PSCs assessed,[320] English law has been the governing law[321] with LCIA mediation initially selected as the dispute forum, to be followed by LCIA arbitration in the event that mediation proves unsuccessful.[322]

Mediation is to be entered into by the parties where direct negotiation has failed. The process commences with a notice of dispute sent to the other party for resolution by senior representatives of the party to meet within thirty days of receipt of the notice.[323] If there is no resolution then within a further thirty days, the matter is to be referred to LCIA mediation.[324] The parties then have sixty days from the date of mediator appointment to resolve the matter otherwise it is referred to arbitration of a tribunal of three arbitrators.[325] Disputes may alternatively be submitted for expert determination. If the parties cannot agree on the expert it will be referred to the President of the Energy Institute in London for referral.[326] Terms of reference are to be prepared by the management committee and the expert is to be appointed within thirty days thereafter.[327] Parties are to make submissions with forty-five days of expert appointment with a right of reply within a further thirty days from date of receipt of the information and expert determination within forty-five days following their appointment and receipt of the information.[328]

All contractual obligations are to continue pending resolution of the dispute.[329] As an assurance to IOCs engaging with the KRG, all of the PSCs contain a waiver from sovereign immunity for the purposes of dispute resolution.[330]

5.5.3 Key terms

The key provisions to consider in the PSCs are similar to those under the TSCs and include; participating interest, term of the contract, minimum work obligations, participation, phases, production targets, relinquishment, discovery and development, title to and use of assets, signature and other bonuses, royalties, taxation, cost recovery, profit division, assignment and subcontracting, measurement policies and decommissioning.

The PSC provides for the operator to have exclusive rights to petroleum operations for the duration of the contract.[331] The PSCs duration is five years extendable to seven years for exploration, twenty years for development from the effective date with an automatic right to extend for a further five years.[332] Termination of the agreement by the contractor requires ninety days' notice from the operator.[333] Title to the assets during E&D remains with the contractor save that upon completion, title passes to the Kurdish government.[334] Use of assets resides with the contractor exclusively for operations by it or its affiliates in "Kurdistan".[335] Assets cannot be transferred or disposed of without contractor approval.[336]

5.5.3.1 Bonuses

None of the bonuses are considered a petroleum cost.[337] There is a signature bonus payable by the contractor within thirty days of the effective date.[338] In addition, a capacity building bonus is to be payable within the same time frame.[339] Production bonuses are to be paid within thirty days of first production of crude,[340] when cumulative production from the contract area reaches 10 mb,[341] when it then reaches 25 mb[342] and again when it reaches 50 mb.[343]

5.5.3.2 Participating interest

All of the assessed PSCs contain an optional participating interest of up to 25% for the government through a public company.[344] To exercise its option to participate which must be no less than 5%, the public company needs to notify the contractor in the period between the effective date and 180 days following the first commercial discovery. If no notification is provided by the public company to exercise its option then it will be deemed to have been waived.[345] Government participation commences from the date of the notice or first commercial decision date if earlier.[346]

5.5.3.3 Government revenues

The royalty payable for produced and saved petroleum and exported non-associated natural gas is 10% which is payable in cash or kind by the contractor to the KRG.[347] By default the payment is to be made in cash and only payable by the contractor in kind if stipulated by the KRG by giving ninety days' notice.[348] International market price of crude at the delivery point is the valuation measure for cash payments.[349] Provided that the royalties are paid quarterly, the contractor is free to export the level of crude corresponding to the royalty payment.[350]

Profit oil is the produced oil available after cost recovery and the contractor is entitled to a pre-calculated percentage share from first production.[351]

The calculation is based on the R-factor which is the amount of cumulative revenues[352] received, divided by the cumulative costs incurred by the contractor from the date of entering into the contract.[353] Where the R-factor is less or equal to 1 the contractor's share of profit oil is 30%, where the R-factor is between 1 and 2 there is a specific calculation and where the R-factor is greater than 2 the share of profit oil is 15%.[354] In the event of a miscalculation of the R-factor there is a rebalancing clause where adjustments are made from the quarter that the error was recognised but not to exceed 25% of the share of profit petroleum surrendered by the party that benefitted from the error.[355]

Profit oil is provided to the contractor at the delivery point where title and risk passes from the government.[356] The government share of the profit oil includes corporate income tax payable directly and profit oil is to be provided to the government at the delivery point. In order to keep a record of quantities of crude oil and gas provided to each party to the PSC, an annual production report is required by the government from the contractor.[357] Any costs incurred by the contractor in lifting the government's share of crude is to be reimbursed.[358]

The PSC's financial provisions stipulate that payments are to be made in dollars by the contractor to the KRG within thirty days of becoming due. The specific payments which may be requested are royalties, proceeds from sale of KRG oil and production bonuses.[359] The payments are to be placed into a revenue sharing fund established through central government legislation.[360] Government payments due to the contractor are offset against future payments or paid in cash[361] within thirty days of the invoice date.[362]

The contractor and its affiliates are exempt from income tax and other taxes relating to its assets and activities under the PSC with any tax liabilities indemnified by the KRG.[363] However, the contractor is solely subject to payment of corporate income tax at 40%[364] on operations payable directly to the KRG tax authorities. Within sixty days of the end of the tax year, the contractor shall provide the tax authority with a statement of profits subject to corporate income tax with the relevant calculations.[365] This is a beneficial payment in that it is initially paid by the KRG from its share of profit petroleum for the account of each contractor and provides the contractor within ninety days of the end of the tax year with statements of payment confirming that the contractor has met its tax obligations.[366]

There is reference to an exemption of the contractors from the surface or successor tax referred to in the KRG laws.[367] Double tax treaties have effect to prevent "an additional burden of taxation" and any VAT is considered a petroleum cost.[368]

5.5.3.4 Cost recovery

The contractor is fully entitled to recover all costs according to the PSC but this is capped up to the value of 40% of annual production with unrecovered costs carried over to the following year indefinitely until all costs are recovered by the contractor.[369] Recoverable costs include those for production, exploration, gas marketing, development and decommissioning.[370]

The petroleum provided for cost recovery is transferred to the contractor at the delivery point where title passes from the KRG for export.[371] Upon ninety days' notice by the government, the contractor is to provide reasonable assistance to sell the government's share of the oil in accordance with "prudent international petroleum practice".[372]

The valuation of crude is based on the international market price weighted average on an arm's length sale to be obtained by the contractor at the delivery point.[373] An accounting statement is to be produced between the government and contractor, evidencing the sales and storage of crude and gas.[374] Metering equipment is installed by the contractor in accordance with industry practice, with government having a right to inspect.[375] Disputes as to the valuation of crude are to be settled by expert determination.[376]

There are no restrictions on the flow or repatriation of the contractor's share of proceeds from operations including the transfer of oil or cash abroad.[377] Further, subcontractors and expatriate personnel may be paid in any foreign currency and repatriate proceeds of sale of their belongings.[378] Operations may be financed externally from third parties or affiliates on an arms-length basis.[379] Any imports for the purposes of operations and personal belongings are exempt and free from all taxes on import and have the right of re-export save for where title has passed to the government where approval by the management committee is required.[380]

5.5.3.5 *Assignment and subcontracting*

Priority is to be given to subcontractors in the Kurdish region and other parts of Iraq. The contractor is to ensure that all of the subcontractors have "the requisite experience and qualifications".[381] Subcontractors are to be selected on the basis of procedures submitted by the contractor to the management committee who shall approve the same.[382] The KRG is to be provided with copies of the subcontract agreements where the management committee's limits have been exceeded.[383]

The PSC may be assigned freely to a company affiliated to the contractor or where the KRG has provided prior consent which shall not be unreasonably withheld.[384] In all other circumstances the assignment or disposal, whether wholly or partially, of assets must be approved by the KRG upon reasonable evidence of the technical and financial capabilities of the third party.[385] Assignment, transfer or disposal is only effective upon the conclusion of an "enforceable instrument of assignment and novation" incorporating an undertaking that the third party will fulfil all contractual obligations.[386]

5.5.3.6 *Relinquishment and decommissioning*

Parts of the contract area are to be surrendered by the contractor at the end of the initial exploration period which amounts to 25% of the net area with a further 25% to be relinquished at the end of the first extension period of the exploration phase.[387] Thereafter all remaining areas which are not part of the production area are to be surrendered.[388]

The contractor may create a decommissioning reserve fund, with payments made in USD, within the final ten years of the production term but may be established earlier with the consent of the KRG.[389] Contributions to the fund are considered petroleum costs and therefore recoverable. Any shortfall in the fund to cover the decommissioning costs will be payable by the contractor unless the KRG decides to take over operations in the production area whereby the KRG will become liable for the future decommissioning costs.[390] The contractor is to submit a decommissioning plan for approval by the management committee twenty-four months before the end of commercial production.[391] Any remaining balance in the fund following the payment of decommissioning costs is to be transferred to the KRG.[392]

5.5.3.7 Termination

The KRG may terminate the contract if the contractor fails to meet financial obligations; interrupts production for more than ninety consecutive days without acceptable justification; does not conduct drilling and seismic acquisition during the first sub-period of the contract; intentionally extracts or produces minerals not covered under the contract; if the contractor as a sole entity is declared bankrupt or wilfully refuses to adhere to any dispute resolution process.[393] In the event of the KRG terminating the contract it shall notify the contractor providing it with an opportunity to remedy any default within three months of the notice or propose to pay acceptable compensation.[394]

The contractor may terminate the contract at any time before the development period and may surrender all production areas during the development phase provided obligations have been satisfied under the PSC.[395]

5.6 Differences between the PSCs and the TSCs

According to the International Energy Agency (IEA), aside from the fact that a comparison between PSCs and TSCs can be complicated by the variety of terms and the impact of key variables, notably the oil price and the size of field, the main difference is that a TSC usually provides for contractor remuneration on a fee per barrel basis where a PSC calculates remuneration on the basis of the value of oil produced which is usually linked to market prices and susceptible to fluctuation and risk.[396] Both contracts share the feature that the financing of the exploration and production operation is borne by the contracting investor often until the point of commercial production where remuneration and cost recovery commence. In countries such as Iraq where the geological risk of non-discovery is low, it is more appropriate to use the service contract model whereas PSCs should be reserved for higher risk exploration.

The differences between the key provisions in the contracts are as follows:

- Bonus payments – for the PSC none of these payments are cost recoverable, the signature bonus in the contracts reviewed ranges from \$2–12.4 million, capacity bonus \$2–50 million and production bonus \$2.5–20 million. In addition, there is a bonus payment payable for the use of non-associated natural gas. Under the model TSC and Rumaila contract, the signature bonuses are recoverable by the IOC as a supplemental cost, the signature bonuses for these agreements have ranged from \$25–500 million.
- Participation – Under the PSC the state has an option to participate in up to 25% of the operation through a public company. The TSC has a 25% state participation.
- Taxes – Under the PSCs, IOCs pay 10% royalty payments and 40% corporate income tax. The corporation tax is the sole taxation under the TSC at 35% on profit.
- Cost recovery – Under the PSC the contractor may recover all costs capped at 40% of annual production and the valuation of crude oil is based on international market prices at arms length. This makes repayment susceptible to fluctuations based on global market activity. Given this position, IOCs with a PSC would have suffered recently given the drop in oil prices from over \$100 pb in June 2015 to under \$40 pb in December 2015. Under the TSC for Rumaila the original remuneration provided cost recovery fixed at \$2 pb for the INPEX contract in a later award the remuneration was fixed at \$5.99 pb.
- Title to and use of assets – The PSCs and TSCs provide for assets to become the property of the regional oil company in the contract. Parties are entitled to full and free use of the assets for the duration of operations.
- The PSCs are subject to English law whereas the TSC is governed by Iraqi law with an ICC arbitration clause and the seat in Paris.

Another issue with the KRG PSCs is the lack of certainty in legitimacy even though IOCs operating in the area would describe the situation as 'fact' on the ground.[397] The legal position on the validity of the contracts is far from clear and is a matter to be determined by the Iraqi constitutional court despite attempts to refer the matter to courts outside the jurisdiction.[398] By entering into PSCs in the hope that at some point during the term of the agreement the contract will be legitimised is a short-sighted and high-risk strategy. IOCs currently in the region have suffered financially as a result, with the central government refusing for some time to advance payment to the KRG for production. This action is unsurprising given that the central government deems the PSCs to be illegal and against the constitution. As for the advocates of the PSC, it is not clear that in a stable environment the terms of the contract would be beneficial to the IOCs.[399] In terms of taxation, as seen above, the PSC has a higher tax rate plus royalty and bonus payments, which are non-recoverable as a cost. There is also the uncertainty of cost recovery being dependent upon oil prices rather than receiving a fixed remuneration with a price tied to barrels produced. The TSCs provide more certainty for the IOCs and are perhaps less advantageous in terms of government payments but all parties know where they stand in relation to remuneration, taxes and cost recovery.

5.7 Conclusion

In order for Iraq to progress, current agreements in place require review and where necessary, renegotiation of terms. To strengthen governance of the oil industry and have MoO approved operations in the Kurdish region, the difference in approach between the KRG and central government should be bridged through formulating a coherent comprehensive contractual approach, for example, using a form of TSCs. The different experiences between the Kurdish region and the rest of Iraq should be collated and assessed to produce the most appropriate and effective contractual terms that would benefit development of the hydrocarbon sector and economy as a whole. It is clear from this chapter that there are many contractual options available and the best solution could in fact be to create a hybrid agreement to advance the interests of all parties in the near and long term.

Notes

1 Law 11/1964.
2 1964.
3 'Iraq-USSR Oil Agreement', 7 (2) *International Legal Materials*, 307–311, March 1968.
4 The ERAP, Machinoexport and Iraqi-Soviet agreements all contained provisions for financing of the operations by the party entering into the agreements with their Iraqi counterpart.
5 As stated as the object of the contract (Article 2) with Entreprise de Recherches et d'Activités Petrolières. Contract dated 3 February 1968 – Ratified under Law 5/1968 and published in the Iraqi Gazette Vol. 7, 1968.
6 Announcement dated 29 July 1969, 'Iraqi-Soviet Oil Cooperation Agreement', BP Archives 164307 D, ME.3139/E/1.
7 A super-giant field located 50 kilometre west of Basra with over 17 bnb estimated reserves.
8 On an incremental basis. Equating to approximately 37–133 million barrels based on 7.39 billion/ton ratio – OPEC 'Conversion factors', www.opec.org/library/Annual%20Statistical%20Bulletin/interactive/current/FileZ/cfpage.htm, accessed 12 January 2016.
9 A super-giant field in Basra Governorate with over 10 bnb estimated reserves.
10 Nahr Umar, Hayyith, Raji and Dujaylah.
11 Announcement dated 29 July 1969, 'Iraqi-Soviet Oil Cooperation Agreement', BP Archives 164307 D, ME.3139/E/1.
12 Ibid.
13 Ibid.
14 Iraqi Gazette 1970, Vol. 10.
15 4 July 1969.

16 Harit Intakanok, 'The Emergence of Private Authority in the Oil Industry: The Case of Oil Concession Agreements', *Thesis*, 230–233, 2010.
17 The Chemokomplex agreement was signed on 21 October 1969.
18 P. Tristiani, 'Iraq and the Oil Cold War: A Superpower Struggle and the End of the Iraq Petroleum Company', in Biagini and Motta (Eds.), *Empires and Nations from the Eighteenth to the Twentieth Century*, Vol. 2, 107.
19 Supra n1230.
20 Ibid.
21 Duval et al. 68.
22 Ibid., 57.
23 As discussed in previous chapters.
24 A distinction is made between pre and post WWII to reflect the developments in the industry.
25 Duval et al. 57.
26 Which can be in kind or for value.
27 Which equates to IOC dominance over resources leading to an element of economic political power.
28 Duval 63. Countries such as the UK and Norway use petroleum production licences (PPL).
29 Duval et al. 58.
30 Ibid.
31 Australia, Canada, Brazil, Denmark, France, Morocco, Namibia, Netherlands, Norway, Peru, Thailand the UK and US – Duval et al. 63.
32 Ibid.
33 ROR,'The Profit on an Investment, Normally Expressed as an Annual Percentage. This is Typically the Ratio of the Income from the Investment over the Cost of the Investment' *Financial Times Lexicon,* http://lexicon.ft.com/Term?term=rate-of-return, accessed 25 January 2016.
34 R-factor – Ratio of Cumulative Receipts to Cumulative Expenditure: R-Factor = Cumulative Receipts/Cumulative Expenditure.
35 Duval et al. 68.
36 Duval et al. 69.
37 Usually in favour of the host state.
38 Unless asked to be removed by the state/NOC. Duval et al. 70.
39 Law No. 44, 1960.
40 18 August, with IIAPCO due to conclude in 2017.
41 Duval et al. 70.
42 Ibid., 47.
43 Ibid., 48.
44 Ibid.
45 Ibid.
46 Ibid.
47 Ibid., 49.
48 Known as the New York agreement.
49 1974 – UAE & Kuwait, 1975 – Qatar, 1976 – Venezuela, 1980 – S.A. & Oman.
50 Duval et al. 54.
51 Ibid., 72.
52 Ibid.
53 Ibid., 74.
54 In accordance with the guidelines of the US Securities & Exchange Commission and the Society of Petroleum Engineers.
55 I.e. entered onto the balance sheet of the IOC.
56 Duval et al. 74.

57 E.g. in Peru and Indonesia where it is capped at 60%–80%.
58 Which comprises capex and operating costs.
59 E.g. Indonesia 85/15 in favour of the state, Duval et al. 77.
60 Duval et al. 78.
61 Ibid.
62 Ibid., 79.
63 Ibid., 80.
64 See Chapter 4. Contracts have only been considered to the end of 2017.
65 In September 2015, two PSCs were awarded in the first tender round – A. Barrera, Reuters, 'UPDATE 3-Mexico Gets Stronger Demand in Second Oil Auction, Eni among Winners', 30 September 2015, http://uk.reuters.com/article/mexico-oil-idUKL1N1201UZ20151001, accessed 2 December 2015.
66 As at 2016 only shallow water fields have a production sharing agreement. Onshore and deepwater fields are subject to licence agreements where the national content requirement in the production phase is a maximum of 35% and 10%, respectively.
67 Duval et al. 99.
68 Ibid.
69 Duval et al. 85.
70 Ibid.
71 Cuervo 651.
72 Ibid., 644. CVP is the Corporacion Venezolana del Petroleo.
73 Ibid., 97.
74 Supra 87.
75 Calculated at the time of contract.
76 A buy-back clause would be the exception (such as in Iran) - where payment is made based on market price at the time of payment.
77 Duval et al. 87.
78 NIOC's agreement dated 27 August 1966, INOC's agreement dated 3 February 1968, Petrobras agreement dated 6 August 1972. Duval et al. 88.
79 Ibid.
80 Ibid.
81 Ibid.
82 EIA Country Analysis Brief, Brazil, 29 December 2014.
83 NIOC/ERAP contract, Article 3, Duval et al. 89.
84 Using the loan from ERAP.
85 NIOC/ERAP contract Article 5, Duval et al. 89.
86 NIOC/ERAP contract Article 6.
87 Free on board.
88 Supra n1271 Article 29.
89 Predecessor to PDVSA.
90 Duval et al. 90.
91 See chapter 3.
92 The policy to open up E&P to foreign IOCs.
93 Duval et al. 97.
94 Article 5.
95 Of 34%.
96 Duval et al. 91.
97 Ibid., 92.
98 Ibid., 93.
99 Ibid., 85–86.
100 E.g. in Venezuela and Saudi Arabia.
101 Normally the major shareholder in the consortium.
102 Duval et al. 285.

103 Ibid., 286.
104 Ibid.
105 With 2015 being the latest version of form 610, www.landman.org/docs/default-source/forms/2015-joa-(final).pdf, accessed 25 January 2015.
106 With some agreements over 100 pages. Oil & Gas UK JOA for offshore operations. Duval et al. 286.
107 Followed by subsequent versions in 1995 and 2002.
108 Duval et al. 287.
109 For example, the UK Oil and Gas model agreement.
110 Duval et al. 288.
111 Ibid.
112 Ibid.
113 Duval et al. 290. See UK model JOA.
114 Health, safety and environmental.
115 Which will include details of issues such as budgets, work programmes, cessation of operations and decommissioning. Clause 9 of the UK model JOA. Duval et al. 292.
116 For example, in Norway, two or more parties represent more than 50% of participating interests.
117 Duval 293.
118 Ibid., 294.
119 Ibid., 298.
120 Ibid.
121 Ibid.
122 Duval et al. 295.
123 Ibid., 296.
124 Ibid., 297.
125 Ibid., 300.
126 Where are the parties to the JOA are offered the option first – essentially the right of first refusal.
127 Duval et al. 301.
128 Which can be billions of dollars for offshore operations such as North Sea.
129 Duval et al. 301.
130 E.g. Lawyers and government agencies.
131 Duval et al. 301.
132 www.gov.uk, oil and gas: petroleum licensing guidance, www.gov.uk/guidance/oil-and-gas-petroleum-licensing-guidance, accessed 15 September 2015.
133 A master deed was developed by UKOOA (UK offshore operator Association) which is used today. The relevant regulations include:

Petroleum (Current Model Clauses) Order 1999.
Petroleum Licensing (E&P) (Seaward and Landward) Regulations 2004.
Petroleum Licensing (Production) (Seaward Areas) Regulations 2008.

134 The oil and gas task force.
135 Supra 1317.
136 Through its own arrangements with the other parties.
137 Supra n1317.
138 Through PEARS.
139 www.gov.uk, oil and gas: petroleum licensing guidance
140 Prior to this a short paragraph incorporated the statutory instrument into the licence.
141 Supra n1324.
142 Ibid.
143 Ibid.

144 Ibid.
145 With an option for a drill/drop work programme with a decision to be made by the end of year six. www.gov.uk, oil and gas: petroleum licensing guidance.
146 Ibid.
147 5/5/20 years.
148 Supra n1324.
149 Licence rent is £2,000 per annum for exploration.
150 Energy Act 1976 and Gas Act 1986.
151 Energy Act 2008 s.76.
152 Oil & Gas Petroleum Licensing Guidance, www.gov.uk/guidance/oil-and-gas-petroleum-licensing-guidance, accessed 15 September 2015.
153 Ibid.
154 Upstream Oil and Gas 423.
155 Ibid., 424.
156 Ibid.
157 Cf. 24% Standard Corporation tax.
158 Which include, R&D, decommissioning, etc.
159 Prior to this it was 10% rising to 20%.
160 Upstream Oil and Gas 424–425.
161 Ibid.
162 Ibid., 368.
163 Ibid.
164 Ibid.
165 Petroleum Act s.1.
166 Petroleum Act s.3(3).
167 Upstream Oil and Gas 371.
168 Petroleum Act s.2(1).
169 Petroleum Act s.3(3).
170 Upstream Oil and Gas 372.
171 E.g. Management, Cost division, risks etc.
172 Upstream Oil and Gas 372.
173 Ibid., 373.
174 Ibid.
175 Ibid.
176 Ibid.
177 Ibid.
178 Petroleum Act s.6(2). Upstream Oil and Gas 375.
179 Health, safety and the environment.
180 Upstream Oil and Gas 376
181 Upstream Oil and Gas 378.
182 Ibid.
183 Upstream Oil and Gas 379.
184 Upstream Oil and Gas 380.
185 Duval et al. 305.
186 Ibid.
187 Duval et al. 306.
188 Ibid.
189 Duval et al. 307
190 Ibid.
191 Ibid.
192 Which can be dry-hole or bottom-hole. Duval et al. 308.
193 Ibid.
194 Duval et al. 310.
195 Ibid., 313.

196 Duval et al. 101.
197 Supra 104, varying during the term the contract based on trigger criteria such as production level.
198 Ibid., from the date of award throughout the contract.
199 Ibid., exercised by HC election or specification in the contract.
200 Ibid., allows NOC participation during exploration.
201 OPEC countries demanded participation clauses in their contracts prior to the nationalisation of most of its member countries. Abu Dhabi demanded 60% participation in its agreements since the 1970s. Duval et al. 109.
202 See Chapter 3.
203 Duval et al. 101.
204 Ibid., 98.
205 Ibid.
206 Duval et al. 99.
207 Ibid.
208 Geoff Dyer and Najmeh Bozorgmehr, 'Iran Sanctions Lifted' *Financial Times* (16 January 2016), www.ft.com/cms/s/0/7ca5b856-bc62-11e5-9fdb-87b8d15baec2.html#axzz41NvTZN1Z, accessed 16 January 2016.
209 N. Bozogmehr, 'Iran Offers Flexible Oil Contracts to Attract Foreign Investors' *The Financial Times* (28 November 2015), www.ft.com/cms/s/0/b2f6bf58-95b2-11e5-95c7-d47aa298f769.html, accessed 7 December 2015.
210 TSC, PSC and DPTSC.
211 The award was announced on 30 June 2009.
212 The award was announced on 12 December 2009. The model contract was a DPTSC.
213 The award was announced on 20 October 2010.
214 The agreement with Shell and Diamond is drafted as the Basra Gas Development Agreement (Final initialling draft 12 July 2011).
215 Abbas Ghandi and Cynthia Lin, 'An Analysis of the Economic Efficiency of Iraq's Oil Service Contracts' 7.
216 Ibid.
217 Upon reaching its estimated plateau target Rumaila is likely to be the second largest oil producing field globally after the Ghawar field in Saudi Arabia. See Ghandi and Lin 8.
218 38%.
219 37%.
220 25%.
221 Due to its wide reporting in the general media at the time.
222 Rumaila, Zubair and West Qurna 1.
223 Eni, 'Eni Awarded the Licence for the Zubair Giant Field in Iraq' (13 October 2009), www.eni.com/en_IT/media/press-releases/2009/10/2009-10-13-zubair-field.shtml, accessed 22 October 2015.
224 Gina Chon, 'Iraq Awards West Qurna-1 Oil Field to Exxon, Shell', *Wall Street Journal* (5 November 2009), www.wsj.com/articles/SB125741092983330293, accessed 12 November 2013.
225 According to OPEC at the end of 2014 Iraq held 11.9% of its market share, 143.07 bnb, which is significant given that OPEC members collectively hold over 80% of global oil reserves. See OPEC share of world crude oil reserves 2014, www.opec.org/opec_web/en/data_graphs/330.htm, accessed 22 October 2015.
226 There are 3 supergiant (over 10 bn barrels) fields in Iraq, Rumaila, West Qurna 2 and Majnoon.
227 See below.
228 Press Release No. 05/307, December 23, 2005, IMF Executive Board Approves First Ever Stand-By Arrangement for Iraq, www.imf.org/external/np/sec/pr/2005/

pr05307.htm, accessed 3 May 2013. On 30 June 2011, the UNSC issued a statement on the Development Fund for Iraq welcoming the Iraqi government's assumption of full authority over the proceeds of the fund from 1 July 2011. SC/10307-IK/636.

229 Most of the negotiations and amendments took place in August & September 2014.

230 N. Shirkhani, *Upstream* vol 19 week 37 12 September 2014, 44.

231 Increase from 37% to 46.4%.

232 Increase from 38% to 47.6%.

233 Reduction from 25% to 6%.

234 As of September 2014.

235 For a comprehensive discussion on stabilisation clauses see Peter Cameron 'Reflections on sovereignty over natural resources and the enforcement of stabilization clauses'. (2013) in KP Sauvant (ed.), Yearbook on International Investment Law & Policy 2011–2012. Oxford University Press, New York, 311–344. Peter Cameron, 'Stabilisation in Investment Contracts and Changes of Rules in Host Countries: Tools for Oil & Gas Investors' (5 July 2006) AIPN, www.rmmlf.org/Istanbul/4-Stabilisation-Paper.pdf, accessed 10 March 2016.

236 INPEX, Press Release, 8 November 2012 'INPEX signed a Service Contract for Onshore Exploration Block 10, Iraq', www.inpex.co.jp/english/news/pdf/2012/e20121108.pdf, accessed 2 November 2015.

237 Rumaila contract Article 3.

238 supra n1421.

239 Rumaila contract Article 31.

240 Article 30.

241 Article 10.

242 Article 9.

243 Shell Gas Agreement

244 Rumaila contract, Article 27.

245 Ibid.

246 supra n1418.

247 Rumaila contract, Art 6.

248 Ibid.

249 If in excess then the contractors to pay to ensure that the minimum work obligations are met.

250 Rumaila contract, Article 6.

251 Ibid.

252 supra n1421.

253 Rumaila contract, Article 12.

254 Rumaila contract, Article 11.

255 Rumaila contract, Article 11.

256 Ibid.

257 Ibid.

258 Ibid.

259 Rumaila contract, Article 2.

260 Ibid.

261 Ibid.

262 Rumaila contract, Article 5.

263 Ruaila contract, Article 28

264 Rumaila contract, Article 28.

265 Rumaila contract, Article 4.

266 Ibid.

267 J. Mariano and E. Rovere, "Oil and gas exploration and production activities in Brazil: The consideration of environmental issues in the bidding rounds promoted by the National Petroleum Agency", *Energy Policy* 35 (2007) 2899–2911, 2900.

268 "Lukoil Overseas Enters a New Project in Iraq", 1 June 2012, *Oil & Gas Online*, www.oilandgasonline.com/doc/lukoil-overseas-enters-a-new-project-in-iraq-0001, accessed 10 August 2012. Block 10 is Muthanna, 10 kilometre south west of Nasriya, awarded in the fourth bid round in 2012.
269 Rumaila contract, Article 17.
270 Rumaila contract, Article 18.
271 Ibid.
272 Ibid.
273 Rumaila contract, Article 23.
274 Rumaila contract, Article 21.
275 Rumaila contract, Article 25.
276 Rumaila contract.
277 Rumaila contract, Article 10.
278 Rumaila contract.
279 Rumaila contract, Article 19.
280 Rumaila contract, Article 20.
281 'acquired and/or provided by the contractor' Article 22.1 DPTSC.
282 DPTSC Article 22.3.
283 DPTSC, Article 22.1.
284 DPTSC, Article 22.2.
285 Rumaila contract, Article 22.
286 Ibid.
287 Rumaila contract, Article 31.
288 Ibid
289 Ibid.
290 Rumaila contract, Article 29.
291 Ibid.
292 TSC, Article 26.1.
293 TSC, Article 26.4.
294 DPSC, Article 26.4.
295 Into which the contractor is obliged to pay $5 million under Article 26.3.
296 TSC, Article 26.2.
297 TSC, Article 26.5.
298 Rumaila contract, Article 43.
299 Rumaila contract, Article 37.
300 Ibid.
301 Ibid.
302 Ibid.
303 Ibid.
304 Ibid.
305 Ibid.
306 Ibid.
307 Rumaila contract, Article 29.3.
308 Rumaila contract, Article 8.
309 Ibid.
310 Ibid.
311 Ibid.
312 Iraqi Constitution 2005.
313 The most recent contracts published are dated 2011, with the last signed document dated 7/9/2011 being the first amendment agreement and completion certificate for the termination of a refinery agreement (dated 27/7/2011) at Barda Rash, http://cabinet.gov.krd/p/p.aspx?l=12&r=296&p=1, accessed 7 November 2015. ExxonMobil acquired 6 contracts in October 2011, http://corporate.exxonmobil.com/en/company/worldwide-operations/locations/iraq/about/overview, accessed 7 November 2015.

314 The ExxonMobil contracts in particular are unavailable in the list of agreements. See http://cabinet.gov.krd/p/p.aspx?l=12&r=296&p=1, accessed 7 November 2015. As at October 2014 ExxonMobil has signed contracts in the region for Al Qush, Baeshiqa, Betwata, Arbat East [the largest at 2,102 sq. km], Pirmam and Qara Hanjeer – see Appendix 2 maps. Further no mention is made on the corporate website of the fields in which the company is operating – see http://corporate.exxonmobil.com/en/company/worldwide-operations/locations/iraq/about/overview, accessed 7 November 2015. Unlike the Chevron acquisitions, there appears to have been a censorship of the contracts in the press, given that the information is not readily available.

Chevron also operates in the region but announced its acquisition in the Rovi and Sarta blocks on its website – see www.chevron.com/chevron/pressreleases/article/07192012_chevronacquiresinterestinkurdistanconcessions.news, accessed 7 November 2015. The award of the Qara Dagh in 2013 was announced in the industry press www.ogj.com/articles/2013/02/iraq--krg-awards-qara-dagh-block-to-chevron.html, accessed 7 November 2015.

315 Although the Taq Taq agreement entered into in 2002 is available, as it pre-dates the current constitution it has been excluded from consideration. Instead, the selected contract is the Shaikhan PSC dated 6/11/2007, as it was signed after the KRG implemented its own Oil & Gas Law 3 months earlier [6/8/2007].

316 1.032,212 barrels.

317 Infra at 20.

318 Infra at 21.

319 *Ministry of Oil for the Republic of Iraq v Kurdistan Region of Iraq*, US CA 5th, Case: 15-40062/USDC No. 3:14-CV-249.

320 The contracts assessed include the Hunt Oil PSC for Ain Sifni block dated 8/9/2007, Gulf Keystone PSC Shaikan block dated 6/11/2007, the Talisman PSC for Topkhana dated 19/8/2011 & Genel Enerji PSC for Taq Taq dated 26/2/2008. Hereinafter all references to "All PSCs" indicates that the terms of the contract are identical.

321 All PSCs Article 43.

322 All PSCs Article 42.

323 All PSCs Article 42.

324 Ibid.

325 Ibid.

326 Ibid.

327 Ibid.

328 Ibid.

329 Ibid.

330 All PSCs Article 41.

331 All PSCs Article 2.

332 All PSCs Article 6.

333 Ibid.

334 All PSCs, Article 20.

335 All PSCs, Article 21.

336 Ibid.

337 All PSCs Art.32.

338 For the Ain Sifni contract it is $2 m, Shaikan $10 m, Topkhana $2 m, Taq $12.4 m.

339 The Ain Sifni contract is $2 m, Shaikan $15 m, Topkhana $18 m, Taq $50 m.

340 Ain Sifni is $2.5 m, Shaikan $2.5 m, Topkhana $2.5 m.

341 Ain Sifni is $5 m, Shaikan $5 m, Topkhana $5 m.

342 Ain Sifni is $10 m, Shaikan $10 m, Topkhana $10 m.

343 Ain Sifni is $20 m, Shaikan $20 m, Topkhana $20 m. All PSCs Article 32. Non-associated natural gas discoveries also carry bonus payments which will not be covered here.

344 All PSCs, Article 4.
345 Ibid.
346 Ibid.
347 All PSCs, Article 24.
348 Ibid.
349 Ibid.
350 Ibid.
351 All PSCs, Article 26.
352 total revenues received at the end of the relevant semester, that is, the actual amount received by the contractor for the recovery of petroleum costs and share of profit petroleum in the contract area.
353 All PSCs, Article 26.
354 All PSCs, Article 26.5: 30 – (30 – 15)*(R – 1)/(2 – 1).
355 All PSCs, Article 26.8.
356 All PSCs, Article 26.
357 Ibid.
358 Ibid.
359 All PSCs, Article 29.
360 Ibid.
361 USD.
362 Late payments incur interest at a rate of LIBOR + 2%. Any currency conversions are at the exchange rate set by the Central Bank of Iraq. All PSCs, Article 29.
363 All PSCs Article 31.
364 Article 31 stipulates that this amount will not be exceeded for the duration of the contract.
365 Ibid.
366 Ibid.
367 All PSCs, Article 31.
368 Ibid.
369 All PSCs, Article 25.
370 Ibid.
371 Ibid.
372 All PSCs, Article 28.
373 All PSCs, Article 27.
374 Ibid.
375 Ibid.
376 Ibid.
377 All PSCs, Article 29.
378 Ibid.
379 Ibid.
380 All PSCs, Article 30.
381 All PSCs, Article 22.
382 Ibid.
383 Ibid.
384 All PSCs, Article 39.
385 Ibid.
386 Ibid.
387 All PSCs, Article 7.
388 Ibid.
389 All PSCs, Article 38.
390 Ibid.
391 Ibid.
392 Ibid.
393 All PSCs, Article 45.

394 Ibid.
395 Ibid
396 IEA 'Iraq Energy Outlook' (9 October 2012) 36.
397 King's College event held under Chatham House rules, 30 November 2015.
398 Ministry of Oil of the Republic of Iraq v Kurdistan Region of Iraq, US Court of Appeal, No. 15-40062.
399 Which was a justification put forward by those operating in the region for entering into these agreements.

6 Conclusion

This book considered the current legal framework in Iraq governing the oil industry. The analysis commenced in Part I, with the issue of sovereignty over natural resources. Part II addressed Iraq's history along with the development of the present legislative and contractual position in its oil industry.

In considering the issue of sovereignty of natural resources, the mechanisms for the distribution of revenue from oil and gas in Alaska and Norway are often highlighted as potential models for other resource-rich countries. However, a clear difference between these countries is that Norway and Alaska are developed, democratic states with established infrastructures and political settlement. Iraq is at the opposite end of the spectrum with weak infrastructure, political instability and corruption. The need to establish revenue distribution funds may assist Iraq but to benefit the economy, the country requires a transparent and efficient infrastructure with checks and balances independent of political influence through external institutions auditing the collection and distribution of revenues. Alongside this, the allocation of funds should be assessed according to key areas for redevelopment and reviewed periodically.

In Iraq, it is still difficult for the people to hold the government to account and particularly in light of the political instability, unemployment, lack of infrastructure and numerous complexities. It will take time for the issue of accountability to be established. Despite the passage of time since 2003, the country is still at a very early stage of democracy and developing through a process to which it is unaccustomed, therefore the questioning of authority by its citizens is a mechanism yet to be fully developed.

This issue raises the next logical question of what is to be done in the interim period while Iraq is in its development phase. It cannot be justified to allow the country to develop organically whilst those in power are in a position to exploit and corrupt the resource wealth that is required for economic development. Protectionist measures should be put in place to facilitate hydrocarbon revenue distribution to the most urgent areas requiring development, particularly in light of the significant political turmoil. An overarching framework comprising several institutions with a specified and targeted remit, each receiving an allocated budget, with accountability and oversight independent of political influence could assist in effective revenue distribution until the economy has reached the necessary stage, with the appropriate foundations, to implement a system suited to its economy, for example, as has been achieved in Norway.

Although reference has been made to other jurisdictions, the Iraqi context is unique. Oil producing countries with small populations find it easier to manage their resources and revenue distribution. The examples of Norway and Alaska show that clearly drafted legislation when combined with a strong institutional framework, economic policy and a fund for revenue allocation and distribution can provide the basis for effective stakeholder interest in maintaining a transparent and accountable system to ensure development of their hydrocarbon sectors. It is important to note that the reason for success in these countries is due to a pre-existing stable political infrastructure, which allowed for the development and implementation of regulations that are supported by accountability and transparency, which would not otherwise exist in a situation of corruption or political turmoil.

In Iraq, contracts are governed by domestic law and arbitration clauses may be agreed. With the increase in the internationalisation of contracts, it is now common to find arbitration clauses providing for determination of disputes in a neutral international forum, and often hand in hand with a choice of law clause providing for the applicable law to be a jurisdiction independent of the contracting state party. Arguably this is to prevent any prejudice from the legal jurisdiction of the host state which may threaten the IOC's investment. A balance is required between state sovereignty and objective determinations of disputes for breach of contract.

The Kurdish interests heavily swayed the elections and the adoption of the Iraqi Constitution in 2005. More Kurds and Shi'a voters than Sunni voters went to the ballot box resulting in a lower number of Sunni representatives being elected. The benefits to the wider international community of dividing Iraq through the federal or regional form of government are all too obvious and yet there is a distinct lack of commentary on the negative effects of federalism in academic discussion. By weakening the state, access to oil wealth by IOCs is increased along with the additional benefit of gaining economic influence over regional governments thereby ensuring that the balance of power lies with individual regional politicians and international companies rather than a strong centralised government.

Even at this stage, it is difficult to see how Iraq would ever become a truly federal state.[1] The best case that the Kurds could hope for would be to declare independence but this would add to the present political turmoil. In 2017 the Kurdish government held a referendum for independence which, despite over 90% of voters in favour of secession, resulted in considerable opposition from Baghdad, Turkey, Syria, Iran, the United States and the United Nations.[2] Although this defeat is likely to suspend the Kurdish independence movement for now, it is possible that there may be another attempt to gain independence in the future which is why the political dynamics of the central government should change in order for the country to move forward. As for the rest of the country, it is highly unlikely that Iraqis will want their country to be divided, as there is no substantive basis for such division. Due to the power associated with the regulation of oil, it is likely that there will be continual argument until the balance of power within the central Iraqi government is proportionate to the population and oil reserve location. The power to control oil resources must rest with the central government, as any alternative is likely to cause ongoing tension as it inhibits the decision-making capabilities of the oil ministry, which could have an unnecessarily negative effect on economic development.

A disjointed government in the decision-making process creates inefficiency and slow development. Due to the various stages of the hydrocarbon extraction process the regulation, control and monitoring of the industry by the state must be cohesive, centralised and comprehensive in order to avoid complication and the risk of private companies finding alternative methods of operation outside the control of the relevant authorised government agencies thereby creating a detrimental effect on revenues and economic development.

Since its creation, Iraq has seen many variations of oil agreements ranging from the original concessions with the IPC companies through to the current service contracts. The balance of power between the relevant government and the oil companies has evolved over time with the original agreements heavily in favour of the foreign oil companies through to the legislative changes which made it possible for Iraq to complete its nationalisation process in 1972. Since 2003, there has been a gradual reversion to private agreements leading to the bid round processes which commenced in 2009.

Although amendments have been made to the draft legislation, more needs to be done for a comprehensive framework to be implemented. As discussed in Chapter 4, the enactment of legislation is somewhat distant. Quite often the lack of a legal regime will not prevent companies from entering into locations where the prospects of production are commercially viable. The primary reason is that most of the uncertainty created by a defective regulatory system can be accommodated and resolved during the negotiation of the agreement between the host government and the IOC.

As seen in Chapter 5, the difference between PSCs and TSCs is not as significant as may first seem. However, where there are differences, these are in fundamental areas of concern for the parties. The TSCs provide for fixed remuneration on a per barrel basis whereas the PSC allows IOCs to benefit from complete cost recovery capped at 40% of annual production so the financial risk appears minimal. However, the cost recovery is tied to international market prices on an arms-length basis and therefore hostage to price fluctuation in the valuation of crude. Under the PSCs tax can be 35–50% for royalties and corporate tax whereas a TSC only requires 35% tax on profit.

It is now accepted practice to incorporate arbitration clauses into hydrocarbon agreements. This removes the requirement for the parties to engage with domestic court systems at first instance and provides a level of control over an individual or tribunal to determine any disputes. It also allows for the parties to agree and specify the venue for the arbitration which may be and quite often is a jurisdiction independent of the location of the E&P activities or home countries of the parties. In addition, the forum provides confidentiality to the parties. Arbitration clauses are to be found in the TSC and PSC although the Iraqi government is yet to sign up to the New York convention for enforcement but is a party to the ICSID Washington Convention.[3]

Title to and use of assets is the same under both contracts but the choice of law clause differs with Iraqi law governing the TSCs and English law the PSCs. In reality, for many breaches this makes little difference, given that both contracts benefit from ICC arbitration clauses, it may however become significant for more fundamental legal arguments.

Given that oil is the heart of the Iraqi economy, further issues need to be considered alongside the legal framework. Despite all of the immediate concerns with the industry, there needs to be further research on revenue distribution, political cohesion, engagement and will to create a long-term framework of the Iraqi oil industry to meet future, global as well as national challenges in order for it to be the benchmark in the region. The context of the country is unique due to its current political situation and urgency to address the most basic needs of society. Not enough practical research has been done to date to assist the state in implementing mechanisms that will last beyond the current political structure. Without a strong central government, good governance and oversight of every stage of the extraction process, both upstream and downstream, the country will continue to be open to abuse whether it is political, legal or economic. Society needs to have confidence that the state is acting in its interests to assist in creating a stable environment that will facilitate competition for the most favourable terms for the state and investor. The country cannot operate in a vacuum and needs to take the lead in setting industry benchmarks and encouraging the most suitable IOCs to develop fields in order to benefit from peripheral contractual obligations, such as local education and training in addition to technology transfer, as well as the core benefit of oil revenue. Obtaining the revenues from the upstream process is relatively straightforward, the retention of those funds and onward use to maximise economic benefit to different industries (to diversify the economy) and sectors of society is an issue requiring further research, analysis and recommendation.

Recommendation

There are various measures to be taken in order to have a framework capable of engendering confidence in Iraq's oil industry. Diversification of the economy in the long term would benefit the state. However, given that the focus must be on the oil sector (although other sectors should also be developed) for the foreseeable future as a ready stream of revenue, the most pressing requirements for the government are:

1 Enacting unambiguous legislation which is forward-looking and attractive to investors while safeguarding state sovereignty over resources for future development in the interest of citizens in accordance with Article 111 of the Constitution.
2 Clarifying the Kurdish position in relation to the PSCs through the Constitutional Court and if necessary to amend the Constitution to rectify any perceived ambiguity.
3 Reviewing existing contractual terms with all IOCs throughout Iraq (including the Kurdish region). Where necessary renegotiate terms in the best interests of the parties on a case by case basis.
4 Revising and making publicly available a model contract in light of the review and renegotiations.
5 Drafting clear criteria for bid process and awarding of contracts. Review the current political system in an attempt to implement a system with supportive institutions that are independently audited to act in the long-term benefit of the economy and prioritise redevelopment of essential infrastructure, education and training. This will include cooperation with the KRG to ensure that any measures are also implemented in the region. The contractual process should be centralised and overseen by MoO in Baghdad with a regional representative to consult exclusively on oil within the KRG governed area in addition to a representative from Basra.
6 Establishing, implement and support independent institutional auditors to report periodically and regulate the day-to-day activities in the industry in order to support MoO.

The above recommendations are not exhaustive but transparency and accountability should be the overriding objectives. The need for reform of the sector is so wide that each segment of it requires a thorough review and analysis of the realities on the ground for each and every existing field that is being explored and developed to ascertain individual issues. This would provide an informed basis upon which to consider the necessary legislative provisions in addition to practical economic, developmental and logistical policies to expedite stability in the industry and target any necessary expenditure. For state investment, it may be that terms can be drafted into contracts to ensure that the investor/IOC contributes proportionately to local redevelopment. If this is combined with visible, responsible and transparent revenue distribution it should allow citizens to feel that they are stakeholders in their resources and to some extent stabilise the security situation particularly where they are in direct receipt the benefits of production on an individual and collective level.

Notes

1 The author is not considering the current implications for Iraq's recent turmoil with Da'ash.
2 *Al Jazeera*, 'Iraqi Kurds Vote in Controversial Referendum' (25 September 2017), www.aljazeera.com/news/2017/09/iraqi-kurds-vote-independence-referendum-170925032733525.html, accessed 31 January 2019.
3 Signature and ratification occurred on 17 November 2015 with the entry into force on 17 December 2015.

Appendix 1

Covenant of the League of Nations Articles I and XXII

A.1 Article I

"The original Members of the League of Nations shall be those of the Signatories which are named in the Annex to this Covenant and also such of those other States named in the Annex as shall accede without reservation to this Covenant. Such accession shall be effected by a Declaration deposited with the Secretariat within two months of the coming into force of the Covenant. Notice thereof shall be sent to all other Members of the League.

Any fully self-governing State, Dominion or Colony not named in the Annex may become a Member of the League if its admission is agreed to by two-thirds of the Assembly, provided that it shall give effective guarantees of its sincere intention to observe its international obligations, and shall accept such regulations as may be prescribed by the League in regard to its military, naval and air forces and armaments.

Any Member of the League may, after two years' notice of its intention so to do, withdraw from the League, provided that all its international obligations and all its obligations under this Covenant shall have been fulfilled at the time of its withdrawal".

A.2 Article XXII

"To those colonies and territories which as a consequence of the late war have ceased to be under the sovereignty of the States which formerly governed them and which are inhabited by peoples not yet able to stand by themselves under the strenuous conditions of the modern world, there should be applied the principle that the well-being and development of such peoples form a sacred trust of civilisation and that securities for the performance of this trust should be embodied in this Covenant.

The best method of giving practical effect to this principle is that the tutelage of such peoples should be entrusted to advanced nations who by reason of their resources, their experience or their geographical position can best undertake this responsibility, and who are willing to accept it, and that this tutelage should be exercised by them as Mandatories on behalf of the League.

The character of the mandate must differ according to the stage of the development of the people, the geographical situation of the territory, its economic conditions and other similar circumstances.

Certain communities formerly belonging to the Turkish Empire have reached a stage of development where their existence as independent nations can be provisionally recognised subject to the rendering of administrative advice and assistance by a Mandatory until such time as they are able to stand alone. The wishes of these communities must be a principal consideration in the selection of the Mandatory.

Other peoples, especially those of Central Africa, are at such a stage that the Mandatory must be responsible for the administration of the territory under conditions which will guarantee freedom of conscience and religion, subject only to the maintenance of public order and morals, the prohibition of abuses such as the slave trade, the arms traffic and the liquor traffic, and the prevention of the establishment of fortifications or military and naval bases and of military training of the natives for other than police purposes and the defence of territory, and will also secure equal opportunities for the trade and commerce of other Members of the League.

There are territories, such as South-West Africa and certain of the South Pacific Islands, which, owing to the sparseness of their population, or their small size, or their remoteness from the centres of civilisation, or their geographical contiguity to the territory of the Mandatory, and other circumstances, can be best administered under the laws of the Mandatory as integral portions of its territory, subject to the safeguards above mentioned in the interests of the indigenous population.

In every case of mandate, the Mandatory shall render to the Council an annual report in reference to the territory committed to its charge.

The degree of authority, control, or administration to be exercised by the Mandatory shall, if not previously agreed upon by the Members of the League, be explicitly defined in each case by the Council.

A permanent Commission shall be constituted to receive and examine the annual reports of the Mandatories and to advise the Council on all matters relating to the observance of the mandates".[1]

Note

1 The Covenant of the League of Nations, including amendments of December 1924, http://avalon.law.yale.edu/20th_century/leagcov.asp#art22, accessed 29 August 2011.

Appendix 2
Maps of Iraq

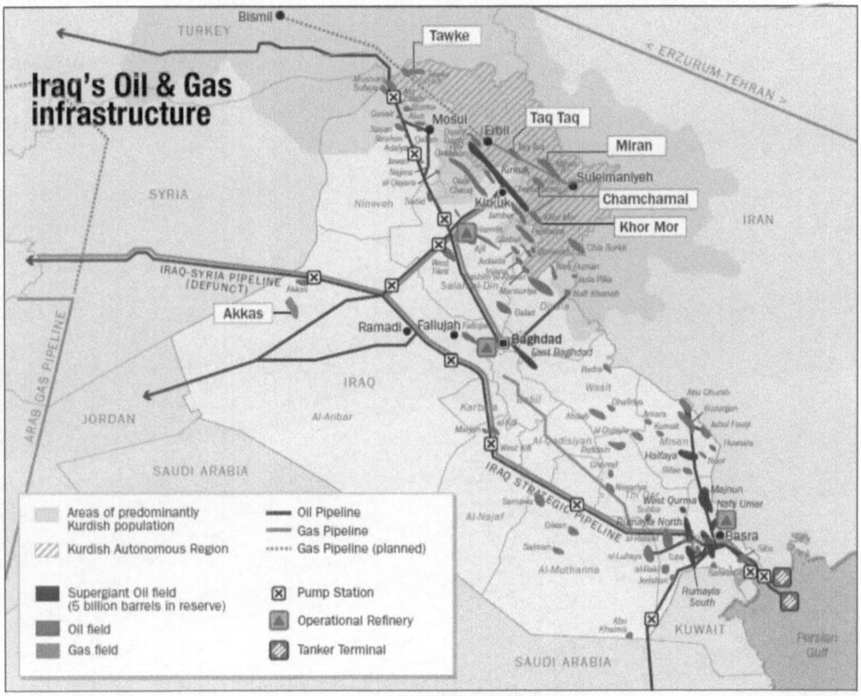

Iraq, Map No. 3835 Rev. 6, July 2014, UNITED NATIONS. The United Nations.

Appendix 3

Table of oil fields and companies in Iraq 2016

Field	Size	Location	Contract Type	Contractor	Bid Round Offered
Rumaila	18 bnb	South	PFTSC	BP – CNPC	1
Zubair	4 bnb	South	PFTSC	Eni, Occidental, Misan Oil, Kogas	1
West Qurna 1	8 bnb	South	PFTSC	ExxonMobilRoyal Dutch	1
West Qurna 2	13 bnb	South	DPTSC	Lukoil, Statoil, Oil Exploration Co	2
Bai Hassan	2 bnb	Kirkuk	n/a	North Oil Company	1
Akkas	5.6 tcf	West (Anbar)	DPTSC	Kogas	1 & 3
Mansuriya	TBC	North east of Baghdad	TSC	TPAO, Kuwait Energy and Kogas	1 & 3
Majnoon	12.6 bnb	South (Basra)	DPTSC	Royal Dutch Shell, Petronas, Misan Oil	2
Kirkuk	8.7 bnb	North (Baba Gurgur)	n/a	North Oil Company	
Halfaya	4.1 bnb	South east	DPTSC	CNPC, Total, Petronas	2
Garraf	860 mb -1bnb	South	DPTSC	Petronas, Japex	2
Badra	3bnb	East	DPTSC	Gazprom, TPAO, Kogas, Petronas	2
Qaiyarah	807 mb	North	DPTSC	Sonangol	2
Najmah	combined with Qaiyarah above	North	DPTSC	Sonangol	2
Al Ahdab	1 bnb	South east Baghdad	TSC	CNPC	Originally offered by Saddam Hussein in 1996 and signed in 2008

(*Continued*)

Field	Size	Location	Contract Type	Contractor	Bid Round Offered
East Baghdad	8 bnb	East Baghdad	no bids	state	2
Middle Furat	600 mb	Karbela	no bids	state	2
Eastern Fields	TBC	North east	no bids		2
Siba	1.1 tcf	South	TSC	TPAO, Maysan Oil Co	3
Atrush	TBC	North (noth west Erbil)	PSC	Marathon/GEP	
Al-Fakkah	2.5 bnb	South (Iran border)	n/a	state	
Hamrin	3 bnb	South (Basra)	PSC	Iraq Drilling Co	
Nahr Umr	6.6 bnb	South	n/a	state	
Ratawi	10 bnb	South (Basra)	TSC	Crescent Petroleum/state	

Field	Contract Type	Contractor
Ain Sifni	PSC	Hunt Oil
Akri Bijeel	PSC	Kalegran Ltd
Arbat	PSC	Shamaran Petroleum BV
Baranan	PSC	Talisman
Barda Rash	PSC	Komet
Bazian	PSC	KNOC
Ber Bahr	PSC	Genel Enerji
Bina Bawi	PSC	Oil Search/A&T
Central Dohuk	PSC	Murphy/Petroquest
Chia Surkh	PSC	Longford/Petoil/Genel Enerji
Dinarta	PSC	HESS
Duhok	PSC	DNO
Garmian	PSC	Western Zagros
Harir	PSC	Marathon
Hawler	PSC	Norbest
Kurdamir	PSC	Western Zagros
Mala Omar	PSC	OMV
Miran	PSC	Hertage
Piramagrun	PSC	Repsol
Pulkhana	PSC	Petoil
Qala Dze	PSC	Repsol
Qara Dagh	PSC	Niko/ Vast/ Groundstar
Qush Tapa	PSC	KNOC
Rovi	PSC	Reliance
Safen	PSC	Marathon

Field	Contract Type	Contractor
Sarsang	PSC	Hillwood
Shaikan	PSC	GKP/ MOL
Shakrok	PSC	Hess/Petroceltic
Sangaw North	PSC	Sterling
Sangaw South	PSC	KNOC
Sarta	PSC	Reliance
Sheikh Adi	PSC	GKP
Shorish	PSC	OMV
Sindi Amedi	PSC	Parenco
Sulevani	PSC	Petroquest
Shakal	PSC	Petoil
Taq	PSC	Genel Enerji
Taza	PSC	Oil Search/Shaman
Topkhana	PSC	Talisman
Tawke	PSC	DNO

 Sources: Iraq Oil Ministry https://oil.gov.iq/index.php and KRG website http://cabinet.gov.krd/p/p.aspx?l=12&r=296&p=1.

Bibliography

Constitutions

Arabic Version of the Constitutional Committee's Report, www.parliament.iq/dirrasd/des.pdf, accessed 15 February 2012.

Constitution of Iran 1979, www.constituteproject.org/constitution/Iran_1989.pdf, accessed 16 May 2019.

Constitution of Iraq 2005, www.uniraq.org/documents/iraqi_Constitution.pdf, accessed 2 April 2012. Now Available at www.iraqinationality.gov.iq/attach/iraqi_constitution.pdf, accessed 5 January 2016.

Constitution of the Kingdom of Iraq 1925, www.gjpi.org/wp-content/uploads/iraqi const19250321.htm, accessed 8 March 2011.

Egyptian Government Website, *Constitution of Egypt 2011*, www.egypt.gov.eg/english/laws/Constitution/default.aspx, accessed 11 April 2012.

Iraq Constitution 2005 (Arabic), www.niqash.org/uploaded/documents/15.10.2005.htm, accessed 3 April 2011.

Iraq Interim Constitution 1958 (Arabic), www.iraq-ild.org/LoadLawBook.aspx?SP=REF&SC=060520065141757&Year=1958&PageNum=1, accessed 8 March 2011.

Iraq Interim Constitution 1970, www.gjpi.org/library/primary/iraqi-constitution/, accessed 8 March 2011.

Iraq Interim Constitution of Iraq 1990, http://confinder.richmond.edu/admin/docs/local_iraq1990.pdf, accessed 7 March 2011.

Iraqi Parliament Website, *Iraqi Constitution* (page undated), www.parliament.iq/manshurat/dastoreng.pdf, accessed 15 October 2010 or www.gjpi.org/library/primary/iraqi-constitution/, accessed 5 March 2011.

National Revolutionary Command Council Law 1964 (Arabic), www.iraq-ild.org/LoadLawBook.aspx?SP=REF&SC=281120057260790&Year=1964&PageNum=1, accessed 8 March 2011.

National Revolutionary Command Council Law 1968 (Arabic), www.iraq-ild.org/LoadLawBook.aspx?SP=REF&SC=300120065356659&Year=1968&PageNum=1, accessed 8 March 2011.

Syrian Constitution, www.mideastinfo.com/documents/Syria_Constitution.htm and www.law.yale.edu/rcw/rcw/jurisdictions/asw/syrianarabrep/syria_Constitution.htm, accessed 11 April 2012.

Syrian Constitution 2012, www.albab.com/arab/docs/syria/syria_draft_Constitution_2012.htm, accessed 11 April 2012.

Transitional Administration Law of 2004, www.gjpi.org/wp-content/uploads/2009/01/transition_admin_law.pdf, accessed 8 March 2011.

United Nations, *Iraqi Constitution*, http://uniraq.org/documents/iraqi_constitution.pdf, accessed 3 November 2010.

United Nations, Libyan Constitution 1969, http://unpan1.un.org/intradoc/groups/public/documents/cafrad/unpan004643.pdf, accessed 11 April 2012.

US Constitution (Bill of Rights), www.archives.gov/exhibits/charters/bill_of_rights_transcript.html, accessed 3 April 2012.

Venezuelan Constitution 1999, http://venezuelanalysis.com/constitution or http://venezuela-us.org/live/wp-content/uploads/2009/08/constitucioningles.pdf, accessed 20 July 2014.

Cases

Anglo-Iranian Oil Company v Jaffrate and Others [The Rose Mary] [1953] 1 W.L.R. 246.

Arbitration Award in the Matter of the Libyan American Oil Company (LIAMCO) v The Government of the Libyan Arab Republic, 20 April 1977, 20 ILM 1, 1–87 (1981).

ICSID Case No. ARB/07/27.

Ministry of Oil for the Republic of Iraq v Kurdistan Region of Iraq, US CA 5th, Case: 15-40062/USDC No. 3:14-CV-249.

Contracts

Basra Gas Development Agreement, Exclusive: the Shell gas deal contract' (Initialed Draft 12 July 2011), *Iraq Oil Report* (29 September 2011), www.iraqoilreport.com/energy/natural-gas/exclusive-the-shell-gas-deal-contract-6267/, accessed 15 November 2011.

Entreprise de Recherches et d'Activités Petrolières, contract dated 3 February 1968 – Ratified under Law 5/1968 and published in the Iraqi Gazette Vol. 7. 1968.

Iraq-USSR Oil Agreement, International Legal Materials, Vol. 7, No. 2 (March 1968).

Iraq Oil Ministry, Development and Production Service Contract, www.oil.gov.iq/moo/file_art/Development_and_Production_Service_Contract.pdf, accessed 23 November 2010.

Iraq Oil Ministry, Model Technical Service Contract, www.oil.gov.iq/moo/file_art/Technical_Service_Contract.pdf, accessed 23 November 2010.

KRG Website, Production Sharing Agreements, www.krg.org/pages/page.asp?lngnr=12&rnr=296&PageNr=1, accessed 18 December 2011.

Conferences

Faleh. Jabar, Speakers at Post-American Iraq Conference, Chatham House, 24 March 2010.

Official sources

Abu Dhabi Department of Economic Development (2009), *Sustainability Report 2009.* Available at: http://ded.abudhabi.ae/DED%20Publications/DED_Sustainability%20Report%202009_English.pdf, accessed 17 October 2010.

Abu Dhabi National Oil Company, www.adnoc.ae, accessed 17 October 2010.

Alaska Department of Revenue Permanent Fund Division, http://pfd.alaska.gov, accessed 16 April 2015.

Alaska Oil & Gas Association, 'State Revenue', www.aoga.org/facts-and-figures/state-revenue, accessed 18 April 2015.

Alaska Permanent Fund Corporation, 'About the Alaska Permanent Fund Corporation', www.apfc.org/home/Content/aboutAPFC/aboutAPFC.cfm, accessed 16 April 2015.

Alaska Permanent Fund Corporation, 'Annual Dividend Payout', www.apfc.org/home/Content/dividend/dividendamounts.cfm, accessed 18 April 2015.

Alaskan Permanent Fund Corporation, 'Landmarks in Permanent Fund History', www.apfc.org/home/Content/aboutFund/fundHistory.cfm, accessed 16 April 2015.

Alaska Permanent Fund Corporation, 'The Permanent Fund Dividend', www.apfc.org/home/Content/dividend/dividend.cfm, accessed 18 April 2015.

ANP, 'Oil & Gas Royalties' (November 2009), www.anp.gov.br%2F%3Fdw%3D39991&ei=IHz9VNSGEIK8aaGygbAG&usg=AFQjCNEdF1Wxi5EgLPZGe18wiXmYftHEkg&bvm=bv.87611401,d.d2s, accessed 12 February 2015.

BP Archives, Announcement dated 29.7.69, 'Iraqi-Soviet Oil Cooperation Agreement', 164307 D, ME.3139/E/1.

BP Statistical Review of World Energy (2013), www.bp.com/content/dam/bp-country/fr_fr/Documents/Rapportsetpublications/statistical_review_of_world_energy_2013.pdf, accessed 1 July 2013.

BP Statistical Review of World Energy (2014), www.bp.com/content/dam/bp-country/de_de/PDFs/brochures/BP-statistical-review-of-world-energy-2014-full-report.pdf, accessed 2 July 2014.

BP Statistical Review of World Energy (2015), June 2015, www.bp.com/content/dam/bp/pdf/energy-economics/statistical-review-2015/bp-statistical-review-of-world-energy-2015-full-report.pdf, accessed 24 July 2015.

BP Statistical Review of World Energy (2016), June 2016, www.bp.com/content/dam/bp/pdf/energy-economics/statistical-review-2016/bp-statistical-review-of-world-energy-2016-full-report.pdf, accessed 6 July 2016.

Brazilian Constitution 1988, www.constituteproject.org/constitution/Brazil_2014.pdf, accessed 16 May 2019.

Brazilian Government, www.brasil-rounds.gov.br/arquivos/Seminarios_P1/Apresentacoes/partilha1_tecnico_ambiental_ingles.pdf, accessed 13 January 2016.

British Ministry of Defence Document Provided to the Iraq Inquiry, www.iraqinquiry.org.uk/media/38010/mod-no-fly-zone-r1.pdf, accessed 18 June 2012.

Canada National Energy Board Website, *Energy Reports* (2010), www.neb.gc.ca/clf-nsi/rnrgynfmtn/nrgyrprt/nrgyrprt-eng.html, accessed 17 October 2010.

Canada National Energy Board Website, *Regulatory Documents* (2010), www.neb.gc.ca/clf-nsi/rthnb/rgltrydcmnt/rgltrydcmnt-eng.html, accessed 17 October 2010.

Chevron Website, www.chevron.com/chevron/pressreleases/article/07192012_chevronacquiresinterestinkurdistanconcessions.news, accessed 7 November 2015.

CIA World Factbook, Country Comparison: Population, Estimated 2014, www.cia.gov/library/publications/the-world-factbook/rankorder/2119rank.html#mx, accessed 29 April 2015.

Department of Labor and Workforce Development, *Research and Analysis*, http://labor.state.ak.us/research/pop/popest.htm, accessed 18 April 2015.

Energy Information Administration (EIA), EIA Website (September 2010), *Country Analysis Brief – Iraq*, www.eia.doe.gov/emeu/cabs/Iraq/Background.html, accessed 15 October 2010.

EIA, *Country Analysis Brief 2010*, www.eia.doe.gov/cabs/iraq/oil.html, accessed 14 December 2010.

EIA Website (2010), *International Statistical Reports*, http://tonto.eia.doe.gov/country/country_energy_data.cfm?fips=IZ, accessed 15 October 2010.

EIA Website (2010), *Iraq Energy Profile*, www.eia.gov/beta/international/country.cfm?iso=IRQ, accessed 15 October 2010.

Eni, 'Eni Awarded the Licence for the Zubair Giant Field in Iraq', 13 October 2009, www.eni.com/en_IT/media/press-releases/2009/10/2009-10-13-zubair-field.shtml, accessed 22 October 2015.

ExxonMobil, http://corporate.exxonmobil.com/en/company/worldwide-operations/locations/iraq/about/overview, accessed 7 November 2015.

General Information about Oil and Gas in the Kurdistan Region, http://daccessddsny.un.org/doc/UNDOC/GEN/N93/295/64/IMG/N9329564.pdf?OpenElement, accessed 5 October 2010.

INPEX, Press Release, 8 November 2012, 'INPEX Signed a Service Contract for Onshore Exploration Block 10, Iraq', www.inpex.co.jp/english/news/pdf/2012/e20121108.pdf, accessed 2 November 2015.

International Advisory and Monitoring Board for Iraq, Terms of Reference, www.iamb.info, accessed 12 August 2014.

International Legal Materials (1966), 442–461.

Iraq Gazette (1970), Vol. 49.

Iraq Gazette (1971), Vol. 37.

Iraq Ministry of Oil, *Crude Oil Exports,* www.oil.gov.iq/index.php?name=Pages&op=page&pid=100, accessed 9 January 2016.

Iraqi Council of Representatives (COR) Website (2010), www.parliament.iq/english/, accessed 15 October 2010.

Iraqi Council of Representatives (COR) Website (2010), List of Committees with Contact details, www.parliament.iq/english/Iraqi_Council_of_Representatives.php?name=singal9asdasdas9dasda8w9wervw8vw854wvw5w0v98457475v38937456033t64tg34t64gi4dow7wnf4w4y4t386b5w6576i75page&pa=showpage&pid=4, accessed 15 October 2010.

Iraqi Council of Representatives (COR) Website (2010), *Regions & Governorate (Members)*, www.parliament.iq/english/Iraqi_Council_of_Representatives.php?name=singal9asdasdas9dasda8w9wervw8vw854wvw5w0v98457475v38937456033t64tg34t64gi4dow7wnf4w4y4t386b5w6576i75page&pa=showpage&pid=15, accessed 15 October 2010.

Iraqi Council of Representatives (COR) website (undated), *Rules of Procedure*, www.parliament.iq/manshurat/nizamen.pdf, accessed 15 October 2010.

Iraqi Council of Representatives (COR) (2010), *Resolutions*, www.parliament.iq/english/Iraqi_Council_of_Representatives.php?name=listtopics_gdsgfstter8s4t86683c3487v53b6sr8e7sv7vse85s45h5vlwaw78wv54gy38y538723g872wrelwaaar687wa837&file=listoftitles&topicid=3&gid=3, accessed 15 October 2010.

Iraqi Oil Ministry (2010), *Iraq Crude Oil Exports – August 2010*, www.oil.gov.iq/EXPORT%20CAPACITIES.php, accessed 15 October 2010.

Iraqi Oil Ministry (date unknown), *Tender Results*, www.oil.gov.iq/tender.php, accessed 14 December 2010.

Iraqi Oil Ministry Website (2010), General Information and News Updates, www.oil.gov.iq/, accessed 15 October 2010.

Iraqi Oil Ministry Website, *Ministry of Oil: Illegal Contracts are Prohibited* (undated), www.oil.gov.iq/5551.php, accessed 15 October 2010.

Kingdom of Saudi Arabia Ministry of Petroleum and Mineral Resources Website (2009), *Saudi Arabia's Petroleum Policy and Its Economy*, www.mopm.gov.sa/mopm/detail.do?content=sp_policy, accessed 17 October 2010.

KRG, Ministry of Natural Resources Production Sharing Contracts, http://cabinet.gov.krd/p/p.aspx?l=12&r=296&p=1, accessed 7 November 2015.

KRG Website (2007), *Government – Legal Documents*, www.krg.org/articles/?lngnr=12&rnr=107&smap=04030000, accessed 15 October 2010.

Kurdish Regional Government (KRG) Website (2007), *Kurdistan Oil and Gas Law*, www.krg.org/uploads/documents/Draft%20Iraq%20Oil%20and%20Gas%20Law%20English__2007_03_10_h23m31s47.pdf, accessed 15 October 2010.

KRG Website (2007), *Kurdistan Oil and Gas Law Approved by Kurdistan Parliament*, www.krg.org/uploads/documents/Kurdistan%20Oil%20and%20Gas%20Law%20English__2007_09_06_h14m0s42.pdf, accessed 15 October 2010.

KRG Website, *Natural Resources* (2009), www.krg.org/articles/?lngnr=12&rnr=148&smap=03011100, accessed 15 October 2010.

KRG Website (2007), *Statement by PM Barzani: Kurdistan Region Oil and Gas Law*, www.krg.org/articles/detail.asp?smap=02010100&lngnr=12&rnr=223&anr=19508, accessed 15 October 2010.

Kurdish Regional Government (KRG) Website (2010), *Latest Updated Model PSC*, www.krg.org/articles/detail.asp?rnr=107&lngnr=12&smap=04030000&anr=20267, accessed 9 November 2010.

Library of Congress 'Online Catalog', http://catalog.loc.gov/, accessed 19 December 2010.

Library of Congress 'Iraq Liberation Act 1998', http://thomas.loc.gov/cgi-bin/query/z?c105:H.R.4655.ENR, accessed 1 November 2011.

'Libya: Petroleum Law Amendment (Revision of Existing Concession Agreements)', Vol. 5, No. 3.

Libya Petroleum Law No. 25 of 1955, www.jstor.org/stable/20690064, accessed 2 June 2011.

Mexican Government Website, *Reforms in Action*, http://reformas.gob.mx/en/reforms, accessed 10 May 2015.

Ministry of Oil PCLD, Baghdad, *Final Tender Protocol for the Award of Service Contracts: Iraq's First Petroleum Licensing Round*, 23 April 2009.

Model JV 2015, Latest Version of Form 610, www.landman.org/docs/default-source/forms/2015-joa-(final).pdf, accessed 25 January 2015.

M.O. Ameh, 'The Shift from Joint Operating Agreements to Production Sharing Contracts in the Nigerian Oil Industry: Any Benefits for the Players?' (undated), www.dundee.ac.uk/cepmlp/car/html/CAR10_ARTICLE32.PDF, accessed 4 January 2012.

National Development Fund of the Islamic Republic of Iran (2014), *NDFI Monthly Review*, October 2014, Vol. 2, 22.

National Development Fund of the Islamic Republic of Iran, Fund History, http://en.ndfi.ir/About-Us/History, accessed 15 April 2015.

National Development Fund of the Islamic Republic of Iran, *News, NDFI's AUM Exceeds $62 Billion*, 28 June 2014, http://en.ndfi.ir/News/News/articleType/ArticleView/articleId/634/NDFIs-AUM-exceeds-62-billion, accessed 15 April 2015.

National Iranian Oil Company, Our History, www.nioc.ir/Portal/Home/Default.aspx?CategoryID=f398bd54-e170-44e9-a841-710c6c92b3a0&TabNo=8#a5, accessed 12 April 2015.

National Iranian Oil Company Website, *Factbook*, http://en.nioc.ir/Portal/Home/Default.aspx?CategoryID=1749ab39-6590-49b0-a616-930afcbc8233&TabNo=6, accessed 11 January 2012.

National Oil Corporation, 'The Unified Policy for Contracting at the Oil Companies Affiliated to the National Oil Corporation', http://en.noclibya.com.ly/index.php?option=com_docman&task=doc_view&gid=106, accessed 10 November 2011.

Norges Bank Investment Management, 'Market Value', www.nbim.no/en/the-fund/market-value/, accessed 2 April 2015.

Norges Bank Investment Management 'Investments', www.nbim.no/en/investments/, accessed 15 April 2015.

Norges Bank Investment Management, 'The Fund: Governance Model', www.nbim.no/en/the-fund/governance-model/, accessed 15 April 2015.

Norges Bank Investment Management, 'Transparency', www.nbim.no/en/the-fund/about-the-fund/, accessed 15 April 2015.

Norwegian Government Website, *Norway's Oil History in 5 minutes*, www.regjeringen.no/en/topics/energy/oil-and-gas/norways-oil-history-in-5-minutes/id440538/, accessed 12 April 2015.

Norwegian Ministry of Petroleum and Energy Website (2007), *Norway's Oil and Gas Resources*, www.regjeringen.no/en/dep/oed/Subject/Oil-and-Gas/Norways-oil-and-gas-resources.html?id=443528, accessed 17 October 2010.

Norwegian Ministry of Petroleum and Energy Website (2010), *Oil and Gas*, www.regjeringen.no/en/topics/energy.html?id=212, accessed 17 October 2010.

Norwegian Ministry of Petroleum and Energy website (2007), *The Oil Market and Norway*, www.regjeringen.no/en/dep/oed/Subject/Oil-and-Gas/The-oil-market-and-Norway.html?id=461038, accessed 17 October 2010.

OAPEC, About Us, OAPEC Website, www.oapecorg.org/Home/About-Us/History, accessed 1 January 2016.

Oil Statistics (2001–2008), 2009, www.mopm.gov.sa/mopm/detail.do?content=oil_stats_2001, accessed 17 October 2010.

OPEC Annual Statistical Bulletin (2014), 14.

OPEC 'Conversion Factors', www.opec.org/library/Annual%20Statistical%20Bulletin/interactive/current/FileZ/cfpage.htm, accessed 10 November 2015.

OPEC Website, OPEC Share of World Crude Oil Reserves (2014), www.opec.org/opec_web/en/data_graphs/330.htm, accessed 22 October 2015.

OPEC World Oil Outlook (2015), 56–57, www.opec.org/opec_web/static_files_project/media/downloads/publications/WOO%202015.pdf, accessed 24 December 2015.

Organization of the Petroleum Exporting Countries: Resolution on Libyan Petroleum Law, Vol. 5 No. 3 *International Legal Materials* (1966), 532–533.

Overview of Commercial Law in Iraq (9 December 2003), www.aschq.army.mil/gc/files/Iraqi_Comm_Law.pdf, accessed 2 November 2010.

PDVSA, *A Favorable End for the Republic in the Long Legal Battle of ExxonMobil against the Country*, 9 October 2014, www.pdvsa.com/index.php?tpl=interface.en/design/salaprensa/readnew.tpl.html&newsid_obj_id=12398&newsid_temas=1, accessed 23 February 2015.

Petoro, 'About Petoro', www.petoro.no/about-petoro, accessed 16 April 2015.

Remaining Process Timeline, Ministry of Oil PCLD, Baghdad, *Final Tender Protocol for the Award of Service Contracts: Iraq's First Petroleum Licensing Round*, 23 April 2009, https://openoil.net/wp/wp-content/uploads/2012/03/FinalTenderProtocol_Round1.pdf, accessed 4 June 2011.

State of Alaska Division of Oil and Gas Website (2010), www.dog.dnr.state.ak.us/oil/links/links.htm, accessed 17 October 2010.

Statoil, Our History, www.statoil.com/en/about/history/pages/default3.aspx, accessed 16 April 2015.

Steinar Njå, The Norwegian Licensing Round, Norwegian Petroleum Directorate, www.fni.no/russcasp/SF2-Nja.pdf, accessed 19 January 2013.

UK Government Website, 'Oil and Gas: Petroleum Licensing Guidance', www.gov.uk/guidance/oil-and-gas-petroleum-licensing-guidance, accessed 23 November 2015.

UNCTAD Investment Policy Hub, http://investmentpolicyhub.unctad.org/IIA/CountryBits/27#iiaInnerMenu, accessed 4 March 2015.

United Nations, *Security Council Press Statement on Iraq* SC/10003 IK/625, www.un.org/News/Press/docs/2010/sc10003.doc.htm, accessed 15 October 2010.

United Nations Development Programme (UNDP) Website (undated, only available in Arabic), 'Iraqi Legal Database', www.iraq-ild.org, accessed 15 October 2010.

United Nations General Assembly Resolution 1803 (XVII) (1962), http://daccess-dds-ny.un.org/doc/RESOLUTION/GEN/NR0/193/11/PDF/NR019311.pdf?OpenElement, accessed 26 February 2011.

United Nations General Assembly Resolution 2158 (XXI) (1966), http://daccess-dds-ny.un.org/doc/RESOLUTION/GEN/NR0/004/61/IMG/NR000461.pdf?OpenElement, accessed 26 February 2011.

United Nations General Assembly Resolution 3281 (XXIX) (1974), http://daccess-dds-ny.un.org/doc/RESOLUTION/GEN/NR0/738/83/IMG/NR073883.pdf?OpenElement, accessed 26 February 2011.

United Nations News Centre, *News Focus: Iraq* (2010), www.un.org/apps/news/infocusRel.asp?infocusID=50&Body=Iraq&Body1=, accessed 15 October 2010.

United Nations Office for the Iraq Programme Website (2010), *Oil for Food Programme*, www.un.org/Depts/oip/, accessed 16 October 2010.

United Nations Website, Demarcation of the International Boundary between the Republic of Iraq and the State of Kuwait by the United Nations Iraq-Kuwait Boundary Demarcation Commission, 20 May 1993 (Document S/25811 and S/25811/Add.1).

United Nations Website, *Law No. 71 of 1958 Delimiting the Iraqi Territorial Waters*, www.un.org/Depts/los/LEGISLATIONANDTREATIES/PDFFILES/IRQ_1958_Law.pdf, accessed 15 October 2010.

United Nations Website (undated), *Official Proclamation of 23 November 1957*, www.un.org/Depts/los/LEGISLATIONANDTREATIES/PDFFILES/IRQ_1957_Proclamation.pdf, accessed 15 October 2010.

USAID (2010), *Assistance For Iraq*, www.usaid.gov/iraq/, accessed 15 October 2010.

US Department of State, 'Agreement between the United States of America and the United Mexican States Concerning Transboundary Hydrocarbon Reservoirs in the Gulf of Mexico', 20 February 2012, www.state.gov/p/wha/rls/2012/185259.htm, accessed 30 April 2015.

US Department of State, Bureau of Economic and Business Affairs, '2013 Investment Climate Statement – Venezuela', March 2013, www.state.gov/e/eb/rls/othr/ics/2013/204759.htm, accessed 23 May 2015.

US Department of State, *Iraq Status Report*, 6 October 2010, www.state.gov/documents/organization/149403.pdf, accessed 10 October 2010.

US Department of State, *Iraq Status Reports* (2010), www.state.gov/p/nea/rls/rpt/c34687.htm, accessed 21 December 2010.

US Department of State, *Reports on Near Eastern Affairs* (2009–2010), www.state.gov/p/nea/rls/rpt/c34687.htm, accessed 15 October 2010.

US Department of State Archive for 2001–2009, http://2001-2009.state.gov/p/nea/rls/rpt/, accessed 12 December 2010.

US Department of State Office of the Historian 'The 1928 Red Line Agreement', https://history.state.gov/milestones/1921-1936/red-line, accessed 1 January 2016.

US State Department (17 February 2011), *Iraq Status Report*, www.state.gov/documents/organization/156992.pdf, accessed 23 February 2011.

Books

A. Khalik Salman, *A Macroeconomics Model and Stabilisation Policies for the OPEC Countries: With Special Reference to the Iraqi Economy* (Aldershot, Ashgate, 1999).

Abbas Alnasrawi, *Iraq's Burdens: Oil, Sanctions, and Underdevelopment* (Westport, CT, Greenwood Press, 2002).

Abbas Alnasrawi, *The Economy of Iraq: Oil, Wars, Destruction of Development and Prospects, 1950–2010* (Westport, CT, Greenwood Press, 1994).

Adil Ḥusayn, *Iraq, the Eternal Fire: 1972 Iraqi Oil Nationalization in Perspective* (London, Third World Centre for Research and Publishing, 1981).

Ahmed Yamani, 'Islamic Law and Contemporary Issues', Charles Malik Ed., *God and Man in Contemporary Islamic Thought* (Syracuse University Press, 1972).

Aileen Keating, *Mirage: Power, Politics, and the Hidden History of Arabian Oil* (New York, Prometheus Books, 2005).

Aileen McHarg et al., *Property and the Law in Energy and Natural Resources* (Oxford, Oxford University Press, 2010).

Andrew Arato, *Constitution Making under Occupation: The Politics of Imposed Revolution in Iraq* (New York, Cambridge University Press, 2009).

Ann Rees and Peter Odell, *The International Oil Industry: An Interdisciplinary Perspective* (Oxford, Oxford University Press, 1987).

Anthony Jennings, *Oil and Gas Exploration Contracts* (2nd Ed., London, Sweet and Maxwell, 2008).

Anthony Sampson, *The Seven Sisters* (Kent, Hodder & Stoughton, 1993).

Arab Comparative & Commercial Law: The International Approach: Proceedings International Bar Association First Arab Regional Conference, Cairo 15–19 February 1987, Vol. 1 (Kent, Chippenham, Graham & Trotman and the International Bar Association, 1987).

Charles Hooper, *Laws of Palestine and Transjordan*, Vol. 1 (London, Sweet & Maxwell, 1938).

Charles Tripp, *A History of Iraq* (Cambridge, Cambridge University Press, 2007).

Clark Lombardi, *State Law as Islamic Law in Modern Egypt* (Leiden, Brill, 2006).

Claude Angeli and S. Mesnier, *Notre Allie Saddam* (Paris, Olivier Orban, 1992).

Clifford Singer, *Energy and International War from Babylon to Baghdad and Beyond Singapore* (Hackensack, NJ, World Scientific Publishing, 2008).

Colonial Office, *Special Report by His Majesty's government in the UK of GB and Northern Ireland to the Council of the League of Nations on the Progress of Iraq During the Period 1920–1931* (London, HMSO, 1931).

Courtney Hunt, *The Greenwood Histories of the Modern Nations: The History of Iraq* (Westport, CT, Greenwood Press, 2005).

Edith Penrose, *Iraq: International Relations and National Development* (London, Ernest Benn Limited, 1978).

Edith Penrose, *Large International Firm in Developing Countries: International Petroleum Industry* (London, Allen & Unwin, 1968).

Eduardo Pereira, *The Encyclopaedia of Oil and Gas Law: Volume One: Upstream: 1* (London, Globe Law & Business, 2014).

Eduardo Pereira and Petra Energia (Eds.), *Brazilian Upstream Oil and Gas: A Practical Guide to the Law and Regulation* (London, Globe Law & Business, 2012).
Emirates Center for Strategic Studies and Research, *Gulf Oil in the Aftermath of the Iraq War: Strategies and Policies* (Abu Dhabi, Emirates Center For Strategic Studies And Research, 2007).
Geoffrey Picton-Turbervill, *Oil and Gas: A Practical Handbook* (London, Globe Law & Business, 2009).
Greg Gordon, John Paterson and Emre Usenmez, *Oil and Gas Law: Current Practice and Emerging Trends* (Dundee, Dundee University Press, 2010).
Gregg Muttit, *Fuel on the Fire: Oil and Politics in Occupied Iraq* (London, The Bodley Head, 2010).
Habibollah Ataradi, *Great Powers, Oil and the Kurds in Mosul 1910–1925* (Lanham, MD, University Press of America, 2003).
Habibollah Ataradi, *Great Powers, Oil and the Kurds in Mosul: (Southern Kurdistan/ Northern Iraq), 1910–1925* (Lanham, MA, University Press of America, 2004).
H.A. Henry Foster, *The Making of Modern Iraq: A Product of World Forces* (London, Williams and Norgate Ltd, 1936).
Henry Cattan, *The Evolution of Oil Concessions in the Middle East and North Africa* (New York, Oceana Publications, 1967).
Hugo Grotius, *Freedom of the Seas*, 29 (MaGoffin trans., 1978)(Online Library of Liberty, https://oll.libertyfund.org/titles/grotius-the-freedom-of-the-seas-latin-and-english-version-magoffin-trans).
James Crawford, *Brownlie's Principles of Public International Law* (Oxford, Oxford University Press, 2012).
Jeff Bridoux, *American Foreign Policy and Postwar Reconstruction: Comparing Japan and Iraq* (Abingdon, Routledge, 2011).
Jim Harris, *Property and Justice* (Oxford, Oxford University Press, 1996).
John Creighton, *Oil on Troubled Waters: Gulf Wars, 1980–91* (London, Echoes, 1992).
John Locke, *Two Treatises on Government*, 307–308 (1690).
John Townsend, *Proconsul to the Middle East: Sir Percy Cox and the End of Empire* (New York, I.B. Tauris & Co Ltd, 2010).
Julio Faundez and Celine Tan, *International Economic Law, Globalization and Developing Countries* (Cheltenham, Edward Elgar, 2010).
Justinian Institutes, Book 2, Part 1, ss25–30.
Kadhim Al-Eyd, *Oil Revenues and Accelerated Growth: Absorptive Capacity in Iraq* (New York, Praeger, 1979).
Kamal Hossain and Subrata Chowdhury, *Permanent Sovereignty over Natural Resources in International Law* (London, Pinter, 1984).
Kamal Mahdi, *Iraq's Economic Predicament* (Reading, PA, Ithaca Press, 2002).
Kamal Mahdi, *State and Agriculture in Iraq: Modern Development, Stagnation and the Impact of Oil* (Reading, PA, Ithaca Press, 2000).
Kamil Al-Mehaidi, *Geographical Distribution of Iraqi Oil Fields and its Relation with the New Constitution* (Revenue Watch Institute, 2006), https://resourcegovernance.org/sites/default/files/052706.pdf.
Kemal Baslar, *The Concept of the Common Heritage of Mankind in International Law* (Netherlands, Brill, 1997).
Kemal Faruki, *Islamic Jurisprudence* (Pakistan Publishing House 2962).
Lawrence Becker, *Property Rights: Philosophical Foundations* (Boston, MA, Routledge & Keegan Paul Ltd, 1977).

Marian Kent, *Oil and Empire: British Policy and Mesopotamian Oil, 1900–1920* (London, Macmillan Press Limited, 1976).

Max Grunstein, E.G. Pereira and K. Talus (Eds.), *Upstream Law and Regulation* (Mexico, Globe Law and Business, 2013).

Max Weber, *Economy and Society* (Cambridge, MA: Harvard UP, 1954).

Max Weber, *Economy and Society: An Outline of Interpretive Sociology* (Berkeley, University of California Press, 1978).

Michael Eppel, *Iraq from Monarchy to Tyranny: From the Hashemites to the Rise of Saddam* (Gainesville, University Press of Florida, 2004).

Mike McConville and Wing Hong Chui, *Research Methods for Law* (Edinburgh, Edinburgh University Press, 2007).

Mohd Ma'sum Billah, *Applied Islamic Law of Trade and Finance: A Selection of Contemporary Practical Issues* (3rd Ed., Malaysia, Sweet & Maxwell, 2007).

Muhammad Mughraby, *Permanent Sovereignty Over Oil Resources: A Study of Middle East Oil Concessions and Legal Change* (Beirut, Middle East Research and Publishing Centre, 1966).

Naval Intelligence Division, *Iraq and the Persian Gulf* (Abingdon, Routledge, 2014).

Nick Richie and Paul Roberts, *The Political Road to War with Iraq: Bush, 9/11 and the Drive to Overthrow Saddam* (Abingdon, Routledge, 2007).

Nico Schrijver, *Sovereignty Over Natural Resources: Balancing Rights and Duties* (Cambridge, 1997).

Patrick Clawson, *How has Saddam Hussein Survived?: Economic Sanctions, 1990–93* (Washington, DC, National Defense University, 1993).

Peter Cameron, *International Energy Investment Law: The Pursuit of Stability* (Oxford, Oxford University Press, 2010).

Peter Cameron, *Petroleum Licencing: A Comparative Study* (London, Financial Times Business Information, 1984).

Peter Muchlinski, *Multinational Enterprises and the Law* (Malden MA, Oxford University Press, 2007).

Pierre-Jean Luizard, *La question irakienne* (Paris, Fayard, 2002).

Pufendorf, *On the Duty of Man and Citizen, Book 2*, www.lonang.com/exlibris/pufendorf/puf-215.htm, accessed 1 May 2012.

P. Jones Luong and E. Weinthal, *Oil is Not a Curse: Ownership Structure and Institutions in Soviet Successor States* (Cambridge, Cambridge University Press, 2010).

P.T. Cain and A.G. Hopkins, *British Imperialism: Innovation and Expansion, 1688–1914* (London, Longman 1993).

Quran, http://quran.com, accessed 8 September 2012.

Rahul Mahajan, *Full Spectrum Dominance: U.S. Power in Iraq and Beyond* (New York: Seven Stories Press; London: Turnaround Publisher Services, 2003).

Reidar Visser and Gareth Stansfield, *An Iraq of Its Regions: Cornerstones of a Federal Democracy?* (London, C Hurst & Co Publishers Ltd 2007).

Republic of Iraq, Ministry of Justice (1977), *Legal System Reform Law*.

Rex Zedalis, *Iraqi Legal Claims against Oil and Gas* (Cambridge, Cambridge University Press, 2010).

Rex Zedalis, *Legal Dimensions of Oil and Gas in Iraq: Current Reality and Future Prospects* (Cambridge, Cambridge University Press, 2009).

Rex Zedalis, *Oil and Gas in the Disputed Kurdish Territories* (Abingdon, Routledge, 2012).

Robert Springborg, *Oil and Democracy in Iraq* (SOAS Middle East Series, London, Saqi, 2007).

Russel Hargrove, *Stabilizing and Rebuilding Iraq* (New York, Nova Science Publishers, 2009).

Ruud van Dijk, *Encyclopedia of Cold War*, Vol. 1 (London, Routledge, 2008).

S.H. Amin, *Commercial Law of Iran* (Edinburgh, Royston Publishers, 1986).

Sami Mahmud, *The Quest for Sultan Abdülhamid's Oil Assets: His Heirs' Legal Battle for their Rights* (Istanbul, Isis Press, 2006).

Sami Shubber, *The Law of Investment in Iraq* (Leiden, Brill, 2009).

Shavarsh Toriguian, *Legal Aspects of Oil Concessions in the Middle East* (Beirut, Hamaskaine Press, 1972).

Stephen Longrigg, *Iraq, 1900 to 1950: A Political, Social, and Economic History* (Oxford, Oxford University Press, 1953).

Stephen Longrigg, *Oil in the Middle East* (Oxford, Oxford University Press, 1968)

Stephen Pelletière, *Iraq and the International Oil System: Why America Went to War in the Gulf* (Westport, CT, Praeger, 2001).

Steve LeVine, *The Oil and the Glory: The Pursuit of Empire and Fortune on the Caspian Sea* (New York, Random House, 2007).

Terrance Daintith and Geoffrey Willoughby, *United Kingdom Oil and Gas Law* (London, Sweet & Maxwell, 1984).

Terrance Daintith, *Finders Keepers? How the Law of Capture Shaped the World Oil Industry* (Routledge, 2010).

Tim Niblock, *Iraq, the Contemporary State* (New York, St. Martin's Press, 1983).

V. Necla Geyikdagi, *Foreign Investment in the Ottoman Empire International Trade and Relations 1854–1914* (London, I.B. Tauris Publishers, 2011).

William Clark, *Petrodollar Warfare: Oil, Iraq and the Future of the Dollar* (Gabriola, BC, New Society Publishers, 2005).

William Stivers, *Supremacy and Oil: Iraq, Turkey, and the Anglo-American World Order, 1918–1930* (London, Cornell University Press, 1982).

Yelena Kalyuzhnova, *Economics of the Caspian Oil and Gas Wealth: Companies, Governments, Policies* (New York, Palgrave Macmillan, 2008).

Articles and papers

A. Barrera, 'UPDATE 3-Mexico Gets Stronger Demand in Second Oil Auction, Eni among Winners', *Reuters* (30 September 2015), http://uk.reuters.com/article/mexico-oil-idUKL1N1201UZ20151001, accessed 2 December 2015.

A. Critchlow, 'Opec Refuses to Cut Oil Production, Prices Slump to Five-year Low', *The Telegraph* (27 November 2014), www.telegraph.co.uk/finance/newsbysector/energy/oilandgas/11258509/Opec-refuses-to-cut-oil-production-prices-slump-to-five-year-low.html, accessed 27 November 2014.

A. Nwokolo, 'Is There a Legal and Functional Value for the Stabilisation Clause in International Petroleum Agreements?', 8 *CMPMLP Annual Review*, 2003, www.dundee.ac.uk/cepmlp/car/html/car8_article27.pdf, accessed 27 February 2011.

A. Ulmer and C. Pons, 'Venezuela Ordered to Pay Exxon $1.6 Billion for Nationalization', *Reuters* (9 October 2013), www.reuters.com/article/2014/10/09/us-venezuela-exxon-idUSKCN0HY20720141009, accessed 10 October 2014.

Abascal, Segovia & Asociados 'Litigation, Arbitration and Alternative Dispute Resolution' (May 2013), http://abascalsegovia.com/Notas%20practicas/Litigation_Arbitration%20_and_ADR%20(F).pdf, accessed 10 May 2015.

Abbas Ghandi and Cynthia Lin, 'An Analysis of the Economic Efficiency of Iraq's Oil Service Contracts', www.des.ucdavis.edu/faculty/Lin/Iraq_TSC_paper.pdf, accessed 3 September 2014.

Ahmed Jiyad, 'IEITI 4th Annual Report 2012 – Pros and Cons' (5 January 2015), www.iraq-businessnews.com/2015/01/06/ieiti-4th-annual-report-pros-and-cons/, accessed 8 July 2015.

Alavi & Associates, 'Iran Petroleum Act', www.alaviandassociates.com/documents/petroleum.pdf, accessed 8 July 2014.

A.F.M. Maniruzzaman, 'Damages for Breach of Stabilisation Clauses in International Investment Law: Where Do We Stand Today?', (11 & 12) *International Energy Law and Taxation Review*, 2007, 246. *SSRN*, https://ssrn.com/abstract=1342277.

A.M. Jaffe, 'Iraq's Oil Sector: Past, Present and Future' (2007). James A. Baker III Institute for Public Policy of Rice University, www.rice.edu/energy/publications/docs/NOCs/Papers/NOC_Iraq_Jaffe.pdf, accessed 23 November 2010.

A.M. Jiyad, 'The Legality of Iraqi Oil Contracts Remains Questionable', 53 (2) *Middle East Economic Survey*, 2010.

A.M. Jiyad 'Assessment of the Oil and Gas Contracts in Iraq'. *Iraq oil Report,* 25 June 2009, www.iraqoilreport.com/news/op-ed-assessment-of-the-oil-and-gas-contracts-in-iraq-1841/.

A.M. Jiyad 'Benchmarking The Remuneration Fees For Iraqi Oil Fields', 52 (44) *Middle East Economic Survey*, November 2009, www.mees.com.

A.M. Jiyad, 'Federal Oil and Gas Council: Basic Issues for Consideration' (2009) *Iraq Energy Institute*, www.iraqenergy.org/.

A.M. Jiyad, 'Federal Petroleum Policy in Iraq: Feasibility and Challenges', Paper presented before the International Association of Contemporary Iraqi Studies (IACIS), Third Conference, SOAS, University of London, UK, 16–17 July 2008, www.iraqistudies.org/English/conferences/2008/papers/Jiyad.pdf.

A.M. Jiyad, 'Gas Fields Bid Round in Iraq: Success with Risk'. 53 *Middle East Economic Survey* 45, 8 November 2010.

A.M. Jiyad, 'Geopolitical Determinants of Iraq's Oil Capacities' (August 2010) 1 *Energy & Geopolitical Risk*, 7 (MEES publication), www.mees.com/cms/energy-geopolitical-risk/, accessed 6 February 2011.

A.M. Jiyad, 'INOC Law: Shaky Premises and Doubtful Prospect' (15 May 2011) *Middle East Economic Survey*, www.mees.com/en/articles/1328-inoc-law-shaky-premises-and-doubtful-prospect, accessed 15 May 2011.

A.M. Jiyad, 'Iraq and the Security of Energy Supplies for Europe', 53 *Middle East Economic Survey*, 29 November 2010, www.iraq-businessnews.com/2010/12/03/iraq-and-the-security-of-energy-supplies-for-europe/, accessed 6 February 2011.

A.M. Jiyad, 'Iraqi Federal Oil and Gas Law Revisited', 2 (1) *Energy & Geopolitical Risk*, 2011, www.mees.com/system/assets/000/000/733/original_Geopolitical_JAN2011-3.pdf, accessed 3 February 2011.

A.M. Jiyad, 'Iraqi Oil Fields Development: Profiles of Production, Depletion and Revenue', 53 *Middle East Economic Survey*, 30, 26 July 2010.

A.M. Jiyad, 'Iraqi-Shell Gas Deal: Who Occupies the Driver's Seat?', Posted on *Energy Intelligence*, www.energyintel.com/PubHome.asp?publication_ID=112, 2008.

A.M. Jiyad, 'Key Questions Over the Oil and Gas Law in Iraq', 2 (1) *International Journal of Contemporary Iraqi Studies (IJCIS)* 7–30. doi: 10.1386/ ijcis.2.1.7/1. 2008 (Intellect Books, UK).

A.M. Jiyad, 'Oil in Iraq: Basic Issues, Development and Discourse', 4 (1&2) 155–195, *International Journal of Contemporary Iraqi Studies*, July 2010 (Intellect Books, UK).

A.M. Jiyad, 'Rumaila Economics and Its Implications', 53 (25) *Middle East Economic Survey*, June 2010.

A.M. Jiyad, 'The Feasibility of Fast-tempo Big-push Strategy in Iraq Petroleum Sector', 5 (1) 11–46, *International Journal of Contemporary Iraqi Studies (IJCIS)*, 2011 (Intellect Books, UK).

A.M. Jiyad, 'The Fiscal Regime of the Iraqi Oil Model Contracts', 1 (5) *Energy & Geopolitical Risk*, May/June 2010 (MEES publication), www.mees.com/cms/energy-geopolitical-risk.

A.M. Jiyad, 'The Legality of Iraqi Oil Contracts Remains Questionable', 53 (2) *Middle East Economic Survey*, January 2010, www.mees.com.

A.M. Jiyad, 'The Need to Activate TTSF Promptly and Effectively', *Iraq Oil Report*, www.iraqoilreport.com/oil/production-exports/training-needed-quickly-for-oil-output-increase-5103/, accessed 4 November 2010.

A.M. Jiyad, 'Transparency and Accountability are Needed and Circumventing the Parliament is against National Interests', *Energy Intelligence*, November 2008, www.energyintel.com/n/portal/do-the-bidding-parameters-and-criteria-ensure-fair-competition-in-the-petroleum-licensing-round.aspx.

Andres Schipani, 'Venezuela: Between a Rock and a Hard Place', *Financial Times* (London, 16 January 2015), http://blogs.ft.com/beyond-brics/2015/01/16/venezuela-between-a-rock-and-a-hard-place/, accessed 21 January 2015.

Andrew Arato, 'Post-Sovereign Constitution-Making and Its Pathology in Iraq', 51 *New York Law School Law Review*, 535, 2006–2007.

Ashley Deeks and Matthew Burton, 'Iraq's Constitution: A Drafting History', 40 *Cornell International Law Journal*, 1, 2007, http://unpan1.un.org/intradoc/groups/public/documents/cafrad/unpan004643.pdf, accessed 11 April 2012.

A.V. Dicey, Federal Government, 1 L.Q. Rev 80 (1885).

A. Yee, 'Iraq Oil Hopes Slide on Legal Limbo', *The National*, www.thenational.ae/business/iraq-oil-hopes-slide-on-legal-limbo-1.409840, 20 June 2012.

Ben Lando, 'Erbil, Baghdad Still at Odds Over Oil', *Iraq Oil Report*, 3 December 2010, www.iraqoilreport.com/politics/oil-policy/erbil-baghdad-still-at-odds-over-oil-5192/, accessed 3 December 2010.

Bruce Kramer and Owen Anderson, 'The Rule of Capture – An Oil and Gas Perspective', 35 *Environmental Law*, 899, 2005, http://repository.law.ttu.edu/bitstream/handle/10601/582/Kramer%2035%20Envtl.pdf?sequenc, accessed 8 September 2011.

C. Johnson, 'Iraq: Legal History and Traditions', *The Law Library of Congress* LL File No. 2004-208, www.loc.gov/law/help/iraq-history.php, accessed 4 September 2011.

C. Wolf, 'Does Ownership Matter? The Performance and Efficiency of State Oil vs. Private Oil (1987–2006)', 37 (7) *Energy Policy*, 2642–2652, 2009.

Carlos Bellorin, 'Venezuela's Petroleum Fiscal and Contractual Regime Flexibility Provisions', 3 *International Association for Energy Economics*, 41–45, 2011.

Carlos Navarro, 'State-Run Oil Company PEMEX Awards First Exploration Contracts to British, Mexican Companies', NotiEn: An Analytical Digest About Energy Issues Latin American Energy Policy, (30 August 2011), https://digitalrepository.unm.edu/cgi/viewcontent.cgi?article=1059&context=la_energy_notien.

Clare Seelke et al., 'Mexico's Oil and Gas Sector: Background, Reform Efforts, and Implications for the United States', *Congressional Research Service* (28 September 2015), www.fas.org/sgp/crs/row/R43313.pdf, accessed 30 September 2015.

C.M. Blanchard (March 2010). 'Iraq: Oil and Gas Sector, Revenue Sharing and US Policy', *Congressional Research Service*, http://opencrs.com/document/RL34064/2010-03-03/, accessed 19 December 2010.

Coskun, Eyup (2007). *From Oil Wells to Institution Building: An Approach for Fair Oil Distribution in Iraq.* Masters thesis, Ft. Belvoir, Defense Technical Information Center, http://handle.dtic.mil/100.2/ADA475827, accessed 6 October 2011.

D. Behn, 'Sharing Iraq's Oil: Analyzing Production-Sharing Contracts under the Final Draft Petroleum Law' *SSRN* (17 September 2007), http://papers.ssrn.com/sol3/papers.cfm?abstract_id=976407, accessed 23 August 2010.

D. Malone and J. Cockayne, 'The UN Security Council: 10 Lessons from Iraq on Regulations and Accountability', 2 (2) *Journal of International Law & International Relations*, 1–24, 2006, http://papers.ssrn.com/sol3/ papers.cfm?abstract_id=1008281, accessed 21 January 2010.

D. Wick, 'The Counter-Productivity of ICSID Denunciation and Proposals for Change' (2012) *The Journal of International Business Law* Yale 239, www.law.yale.edu/documents/pdf/11JIntlBusL239.pdf, accessed 2 January 2013.

Dr. Behrooz Akhlaghi & Associates, 'Iran Petroleum Contract (IPC)', *Bi-Weekly News & Analysis of the International Law Office* (7 April 2014), http://akhlaghi.net/wp-content/uploads/2014/06/Iran-Petroleum-Contract-IPC-1st-Bi-Weekly-N-A-April-07-2014.pdf, accessed 5 May 2015.

Dr. F. Jabar speaker at Post-American Iraq Conference, Chatham House, 24 March 2010.

E. Duruigbo, 'Permanent Sovereignty and the Peoples' Ownership of Natural Resources in International Law', 38 *The George Washington International Law Review*, 33–100, 2006.

E. Sherwin, 'Demystifying Legal Reasoning: Part II' (2006) *Cornell Legal Studies Research Paper No. 06-002*, http://ssrn.com/abstract=875637, accessed 29 November 2010.

E.M. Salzberger, 'The Economic Analysis of Law – The Dominant Methodology for Legal Research' (2007), *University of Haifa Faculty of Law Legal Studies Research Paper No. 1044382*, http://papers.ssrn.com/sol3/papers.cfm?abstract_id=1044382, accessed 3 October 2010.

EGEE 120, 'Oil: International Evolution, Opening the Door on the Middle East: The Turkish Petroleum Company', www.e-education.psu.edu/egee120/node/248, accessed 1 January 2016.

EI Sourcebook, '5.1 Policy Context', www.eisourcebook.org/646_51PolicyContext.html, accessed 22 April 2013.

EIA, 'Country Analysis Brief: Iraq' (2 April 2013), www.eia.gov/countries/analysis briefs/Iraq/iraq.pdf, accessed 20 July 2013. See also IMF, 'Iraq Selected Issues', 26 April 2013, 3.

EIA, 'Country Analysis Brief: Mexico' (24 April 2014), www.eia.gov/countries/analysis briefs/Mexico/mexico.pdf, accessed 25 January 2015.

EIA, 'Country Analysis Brief, Brazil' (29 December 2014), www.eia.gov/beta/international/analysis.cfm?iso=BRA, accessed 4 January 2015.

EIA, 'Technically Recoverable Shale Oil and Shale Gas Resources: An Assessment of 137 Shale Formations in 41 Countries Outside the United States' (Washington, DC, June 10, 2013), www.eia.gov/analysis/studies/worldshalegas/, accessed 17 June 2014

EIA, 'Country Analysis Brief: Venezuela' (20 June 2014), www.eia.gov/beta/international/analysis.cfm?iso=VEN, accessed 12 January 2015.

El-Walied and El-Malik 'Mineral Investment under Shari'a law' 8 *Arab Law Quarterly,* 106, 1993.

Elkins and Ginsberg, 'The Iraqi Draft Constitution in Comparative Perspective' (Center for the Study of Democratic Governance, University of Illinois, 2005), http://comparative constitutionsproject.org/reports-and-other-publications/, accessed 17 January 2015.

Eric Davis, 'The Puzzle of Federalism in Iraq', 247, *Middle East Report*, 42, 2008, http://faspolisci.rutgers.edu/davis/ARTICLES/DavisPuzzleIraqFederalismMER.608.pdf, accessed 15 January 2013.

Fiches Thématiques International, Decembre 2007.

Frederico Machado, 'Allocation of Mineral and Oil Tax Rents in Brazil: An Analysis of the Most Recent Changes in Brazilian Legislation from the Perspective of Theoretical Literature', *CEMLP*, 13–14.

F. William Engdahl, 'Iraq and the Problem of Peak Oil', 1 *Centre for Research on Globalisation, Current Concerns*, 2004, http://globalresearch.ca/articles/ENG408A.html, accessed 25 February 2011.

F.N. Semyenov 'The History of the Oil Industry', www.sjvgeology.org/history/index.html, accessed 20 December 2011.

F.W. Engdahl, 'Iraq and the Problem of Peak Oil, Centre for Research on Globalisation', 1 *Current Concerns*, (2004), http://globalresearch.ca/articles/ENG408A.html, accessed 25 February 2011.

G. Muttitt, 'Crude Designs – The Rip-off of Iraq's Oil Wealth' (2005), www.carbonweb.org/documents/crude_designs_large.pdf, accessed 27 February 2011.

G. Muttit, *The Oil and Gas Law – Signing Away Iraq's Future?* (26 February 2007), www.carbonweb.org/documents/oil_law_briefing.pdf, accessed 6 February 2011.

G. Muttitt, 'Nationalizing Risk, Privatizing Reward: The Prospects for Oil Production Contracts in Iraq', 1 (2) *International Journal of Contemporary Iraqi Studies*, 2007, www.intellectbooks.co.uk/journalissues.php?issn=17512867&v=1&i=2, accessed 25 February 2011.

G.M. Vianna, 'Royalties Due for Oil and Natural Gas Produced During Formation Tests' (10 November 2014), *International Law Office*, www.internationallawoffice.com/newsletters/detail.aspx?g=e0d26286-f04c-4790-ba61-c6a3cc5ee32b, accessed 8 March 2015.

Garrett Hering, 'Energy Reform: Will Mexico's Newest Revolution Boost Renewables – Or Just Fossil Fuels?' (2 June 2015), *The Guardian*, www.theguardian.com/sustainable-business/2015/jun/02/mexico-oil-companies-reforms-gas-hydrocarbon, accessed 3 June 2015.

Gina Chon, 'Iraq Awards West Qurna-1 Oil Field to Exxon, Shell' (5 November 2009), *Wall Street Journal*, www.wsj.com/articles/SB125741092983330293, accessed 22 June 2012.

Global Justice Project: Iraq, http://gjpi.org/library/primary/iraqi-constitution/, accessed 24 March 2011.

Global Security, 'Military', www.globalsecurity.org/military/world/iraq/party.htm, accessed 12 March 2011.

Godofredo Vianna and Jose Castro, 'Royalties Due for Oil and Natural Gas Produced During Formation Tests', *International Law Office,* www.internationallawoffice.com/Newsletters/Energy-Natural-Resources/Brazil/Kincaid-Mendes-Vianna-Advogados/Royalties-due-for-oil-and-natural-gas-produced-during-formation-tests, accessed 3 February 2015.

Gregg Muttit, 'The Oil and Gas Law – Signing Away Iraq's Future?', *Carbon Web*, www.carbonweb.org/documents/oil_law_briefing.pdf, accessed 2 February 2013.

H.A. Hamoudi, 'Money Laundering Amidst Mortars: Legislative Process and State Authority in Post-Invasion Iraq', 16 (2) *Transnational Law & Contemporary Problems*, 2007, http://papers.ssrn.com/sol3/papers.cfm?abstract_id=935130, accessed 24 April 2010.

Hooman Farnejad, *How Competitive is the Iranian Buy-Back Contracts in Comparison to Contractual Production Sharing Fiscal Systems*, University of Dundee, 5, www.dundee.ac.uk/cepmlp/gateway/?news=28066, accessed 12 April 2015.

IEITI, 2013, *Iraqi Oil Revenues 2012: Oil Export, Local Consumption and Field Development*, http://ieiti.org.iq/ArticleShow.aspx?ID=96, accessed 26 December 2014.

IMF, 'IMF Executive Board Approves US$436.3 Million in Emergency Post-Conflict Assistance to Iraq' (29 September 2004) Press Release No. 04/206, www.imf.org/external/np/sec/pr/2004/pr04206.htm, accessed 3 August 2012.

International Energy Agency Website, 'Beyond the OECD – Iraq' (2010), http://omrpublic.iea.org/countryresults.asp?country=Iraq&Submit2=Submit, accessed 15 October 2010.

International Energy Agency Website, 'Oil Market Report – Iraq' (2010), www.iea.org/country/n_country.asp?COUNTRY_CODE=IQ, accessed 15 October 2010.

International Energy Agency, 'FAQs', www.iea.org/aboutus/faqs/oil/, accessed 17 January 2013.

International Energy Agency, 'Iraq Energy Outlook' (9 October 2012), www.worldenergyoutlook.org/iraq/, accessed 15 October 2012.

International Law Office Website, 'Principles of Contract under Iraqi Law' (2004), www.internationallawoffice.com/Newsletters/detail.aspx?g=c172c5bc-cac0-456f-9229-8cf9ed044306, accessed 3 November 2010.

'Irak: Réouverture de l'exploitation pétrolière aux compagnies étrangères' (1er juillet 2009) *Risques internationaux* 123, http://doc.sciencespolyon.fr/Signal/index.php?r=numero/view&id=9709, accessed 7 March 2011.

'Irak-Pétrole: Le jeu 'gagnant' de Bagdad' (15 novembre 2009) *Risques internationaux*, 131, http://doc.sciencespolyon.fr/Signal/index.php?r=article%2FsearchSimple&SearchArticleSimple%5Btitre%5D=irak+petrole&yt0=Rechercher, accessed 6 March 2011.

Iraq Oil Forum, 1st Licencing Round Factbox – Bidding1, www.iraqoilforum.com/?cat=802, accessed 23 January 2012.

Iraq Oil Forum, 1st Licencing Round Factbox – Consortia1, www.iraqoilforum.com/?cat=802, accessed 24 January 2012.

Iraq Oil Forum, Oil Ministry Document 'Bid Round Four – The Process', www.iraqoilforum.com/?cat=1316, accessed 5 July 2012.

Iraq Oil Forum, '*Pre-qualification*', www.iraqoilforum.com, accessed 25 July 2012.

Iraq Oil Ministry, 'Crude Oil Exports', www.oil.gov.iq/, accessed 24 July 2013.

Iraq Oil Report, '2010 Year-end special edition', received by e-mail 23 December 2010.

Iraq Oil Report Website, 'News and Information on the Oil Industry in Iraq' (2010), www.iraqoilreport.com/, accessed 15 October 2010.

J. Alexander, 'Iraq: Justice and Withdrawal – Iraq Needs a Better Constitution on Its Own Terms and Timescale' (2005–2006), http://l-r-c.org.uk/files/IRAQ_Alexander.pdf, accessed 8 January 2010.

J. Dargin, 'Securing the Peace: The Battle Over Ethnicity and Energy in Modern Iraq', 7 (1) *Oil, Gas & Law Intelligence*, 2009, http://belfercenter.ksg.harvard.edu/files/Dargin_-_Working_Paper_-_FINAL.pdf, accessed 6 October 2011.

J. Ismael and T. Ismael 'Iraqi Oil, the International System and Chimera of Democracy', 1 (3) *International Journal of Contemporary Iraqi Studies*, 287–291, 2007.

J. Fallows, 'Success Without Victory' (January/February 2005) *The Atlantic*, www.theatlantic.com/magazine/print/2005/01/success-without-victory/3660/, accessed 21 March 2011.

J. Goodman, 'Brazil Population Tops 200 Million as Middle Class Lives Longer' (29 August 2013) *Bloomberg*, www.bloomberg.com/news/print/2013-08-29/brazil-population-tops-200-million-as-middle-class-lives-longer.html, accessed 16 February 2014.

J. Leahy and V. Rodrigues, 'Brazil Hit by Petrobras Downgrade' (25 February 2015) *Financial Times*, www.ft.com/cms/s/0/e8da11d2-bd0f-11e4-b523-00144feab7de.html?siteedition=uk#axzz3TAMhCp3z, accessed 25 February 2015.

J.C. Garcia, 'Rebalancing Oil Contracts in Venezuela' 33 (2) *Houston Journal of International Law*, 243, 2011.

J.C. Garcia, 'Venezuela', *Upstream Law and Regulation*, 299–320.

Jack Chang, 'Developing Countries to the Rescue at G-20' (20 June 2012) *Associated Press News*, http://m.apnews.mobi/ap/db_36972/contentdetail.htm?contentguid=uavwc1fa, accessed 20 June 2012.

H.D. Jafar, 'Key Principles for An Effective Iraqi Petroleum Policy and Regulatory Framework', XLIX *Middle East Economic Survey*, 9 July 2007.

James Crawford, 'The Authority of the Kurdistan Regional Government Over Oil and Gas Under the Constitution of Iraq', 3 *OGEL*, 2008.

James Crawford, 'Legal Opinion Provided to the KRG', KRG Website, http://cabinet.gov.krd/uploads/documents/James_R_Crawford_Kurdistan_Oil_Legal_Opinion_English__2008_07_09_h11m23s26.pdf, accessed 22 February 2012.

James Penner, The 'Bundle of Rights' Picture of Property, 43 UCLA Law Review, 711–820, 1995–1996.

Jeremy Sharp, 'Iraq: A Compilation of Legislation Enacted and Resolutions Adopted by Congress' (27 March 2003) *CRS Report for Congress*, http://fpc.state.gov/documents/organization/17330.pdf, accessed 2 May 2011

Jeremy Waldron, 'What is Private Property?', 5 *Oxford Journal of Legal Studies* 313–318, 1985.

Jonathan Kaiman, 'China Agrees to Invest $20bn in Venezuela to Help Offset Effects of Oil Price Slump' (8 January 2015) *The Guardian*, www.theguardian.com/world/2015/jan/08/china-venezuela-20bn-loans-financing-nicolas-maduro-beijing, accessed 23 February 2015.

J. Mariano and E. Rovere, 'Oil and Gas Exploration and Production Activities in Brazil: The Consideration of Environmental Issues in the Bidding Rounds Promoted by the National Petroleum Agency', 35 *Energy Policy*, 2899–2911, 2007.

J.E. Vinuales, 'The Resource Curse' – A legal perspective' (4 June 2010) *Global Governance. SSRN*, http://ssrn.com/abstract1652739, accessed 4 April 2011.

Jonathan Morrow, 'Iraq's Constitutional Process II: An Opportunity Lost' (November 2005) United States Institute of Peace Special Report.

Jonathan Morrow, 'Weak Viability, The Iraqi Federal State and the Constitutional Amendment Process' (July 2006) United States Institute of Peace Special Report.

Joost Hiltermann, Sean Kane and Raad Alkadiri, 'Iraq's Federalism Quandry', 9 *The National Interest*, www.crisisgroup.org/en/regions/middle-east-north-africa/iraq-iran-gulf/iraq/op-eds/hiltermann-iraqs-federalism-quandary.aspx, accessed 4 April 2012.

K. Vyas, 'Venezuela Asks for Revision of Exxon Arbitration Award' (27 October 2014), *Wall Street Journal*, www.wsj.com/articles/venezuela-asks-for-revision-of-exxon-arbitration-award-1414443586, accessed 4 May 2015.

Kadhim Ajrash and Nayla Razzouk, 'Iraq Revises Its Reserves to 150 Billion Barrels' (10 April 2013) *Bloomberg*, www.bloomberg.com/news/2013-04-10/iraq-revises-its-oil-reserves-to-150-billion-barrels.html, accessed 20 July 2013.

Sean Kane et al., 'Iraq's Federalism Quandry' (28 March 2012) *The National Interest*, 9, http://nationalinterest.org/article/iraqs-federalism-quandary-6512?page=1, accessed 4 March 2012.

Kenneth Katzman, 'Iraq: Elections and New Government' (11 May 2005) *CRS Report to Congress*, http://fpc.state.gov/documents/organization/48386.pdf, accessed 4 July 2011.

Kevin Baxter, '10 Events in Oil's History that Shook the World', *Arabian Oil & Gas*, 2007, www.arabianoilandgas.com/article-5817-10_events_in_oils_history_that_shook_the_world/, accessed 23 July 2012.

Kincaid, 'ANP Prepares a New Bid Round for Exploration of Oil and Natural Gas' (26 January 2015), www.kincaid.com.br/b_newsletter.php?id_noticia=1460&utm_source=Mondaq&utm_medium=syndication&utm_campaign=View-Original, accessed 10 March 2015.

L. Lemos and D. Campello, 'The Non-Ratification of Bilateral Investment Treaties in Brazil: A Story of Conflict in a Land of Cooperation', *SSRN*, 2013, http://ssrn.com/abstract=2243120 or doi: 10.2139/ssrn.2243120, accessed 8 August 2015.

L.P. Almada and V. Parente, 'Oil & Gas Industry in Brazil: A Brief History and Legal Framework', 1 (1) *Panorama of Brazilian Law*, 223–252, 2013.

Law Library of Congress, Global Legal Research Centre, 'Crude Oil Royalty Rates in Selected Countries' (January 2015), www.loc.gov/law/help/crude-oil-royalty-rates/crude-oil-royalty-rates.pdf, accessed 8 March 2015.

Liam Anderson and Gareth Stansfield, 'The Implications of Elections for Federalism in Iraq: Toward a Five-Region Model', 35 (3) *Publius*, 359–382, 2005.

Luis Cuervo, 'The Uncertain Fate of Venezuela's Black Pearl: The Petrostate and Its Ambiguous Oil and Gas Legislation', 32 *Houston Journal of International Law*, 637, 2009–2010.

M. Jalili, '*Claims against Iraq: The Current Status*', 7 *Arab LQ*, 64, 1992–1993.

M. Khadduri, 'Nature and Sources of Islamic Law', 22 *The George Washington Law Review*, 3–23, 1953–1954.

M.G. Salameh, 'The Oil "Price Rise" Factor in the Iraq War: A Macroeconomic Assessment' (June 2008), *The United States Association for Energy Economics Working Paper 08-008*, http://papers.ssrn.com/sol3/papers.cfm? abstract_id=1140333, accessed 21 January 2010.

M.J. Kelly, 'The Kurdish Regional Constitution within the Framework of the Iraqi Federal Constitution: A Struggle for Sovereignty, Oil, Ethnic Identity, and the Prospects for a Reverse Supremacy Clause', 114 (3), *Penn State Law Review*, 707–808, 2010, http://ssrn.com/abstract=1608334, accessed 4 March 2011.

M.J. Sundahl, 'Iraq, Secured Transactions & The Promise of Islamic Law' (March 2007) *Cleveland-Marshall College of Law, Research Paper 07-138*, http://papers.ssrn.com/sol3/papers.cfm?abstract_id=967740, accessed 21 January 2010.

MERIP, Iraq and Kurdish Autonomy, MERIP Reports, No. 27 (April 1974). Published by: Middle East Research and Information Project (MERIP), www.jstor.org/stable/3011338, accessed 19 June 2013.

Michael Gunter, 'Economic Opportunities in Iraqi Kurdistan', XVIII (2) *Middle East Policy Council*, 2011, www.mepc.org/journal/middle-east-policy-archives/economic-opportunities-iraqi-kurdistan?print, accessed 20 December 2011.

Michael Kelly, 'The Kurdish Regional Constitution within the Framework of the Iraqi Federal Constitution: A Struggle for Sovereignty, Oil, Ethnic Identity, and the Prospects for a Reverse Supremacy Clause', *Penn State Law Review*, 707, http://ssrn.com/abstract=1608334, accessed 3 September 2012.

Middle East Economic Survey 53 (41), 2010, www.mees.com.
M. Zborowski, 'Three Blocks Awarded in Mexico's Round One Second Tender', *Oil & Gas Journal,* 2015, www.ogj.com/articles/2015/09/three-blocks-awarded-in-mexicos-round-1-second-tender.html, accessed 8 July 2017.
N. Bozorgmehr, 'Iran Budget not Hit by Fall in Oil Price, Says Hassan Rouhani' (7 November 2014) *Financial Times*, www.ft.com/content/b3259ea6-7df6-11e4-87d9-00144feabdc0.
N. Bozogmehr, 'Iran Offers Flexible Oil Contracts to Attract Foreign Investors' (28 November 2015) *Financial Times*, www.ft.com/cms/s/0/b2f6bf58-95b2-11e5-95c7-d47aa298f769.html, accessed 7 December 2015.
N. Haysom and S. Kane, 'Briefing Paper October 2009 Negotiating Natural Resources for Peace: Ownership, Control and Wealth-sharing' *Centre for Humanitarian Dialogue*, 2009, www.constitutionmaking.org/files/resources_peace.pdf, accessed 3 March 2011.
N. Karam see the Iraqi Civil Code at 3.4-xvii et seq., http://gjpi.org/library/primary/statutes/, accessed 23 December 2011.
Nabeel Saleh, 'Civil Codes of Arab Countries: The Sanhuri Codes', 8 (2) *Arab Law Quarterly*, 161–167, 1993.
Nathan Brown, 'Iraq's Constitutional Process Plunges Ahead' (July 2005) Carnegie Endowment for International Peace, Policy Outlook, Democracy and the Rule of Law, http://carnegieendowment.org/files/PO19Brown.pdf, accessed 10 January 2015.
OECD, 'Basic Elements of a Law on Concession Agreements' (2002) Multilateral Centre for Private Sector Development, www.oecd.org/dataoecd/41/20/33959802.pdf, accessed 27 February 2011.
Oil & Gas Journal editors, 'Iraq KRG Awards Qara Dagh Block to Chevron', *Oil & Gas Journal*, www.ogj.com/articles/2013/02/iraq--krg-awards-qara-dagh-block-to-chevron.html, accessed 7 November 2015.
Oil & Gas Journal editors, 'Mexican Round Nets Two Successful Bids', *Oil & Gas Journal*, 16 July 2015, www.ogj.com/articles/2015/07/mexican-round-nets-two-successful-bids.html, accessed 7 July 2017.
OPEC Website, 'International Developments in the Oil and Natural Gas Markets and their Impact on Arab Countries' (2010), www.opec.org/opec_web/en/1756.htm, accessed 17 October 2010.
OPEC Website, 'Market Indicators as at End August 2010' (2010), www.opec.org/opec_web/static_files_project/media/downloads/data_graphs/MI082010.pdf, accessed 17 October 2010.
OPEC Website, 'Member Countries' Crude Oil Production Allocations' (2007), www.opec.org/opec_web/static_files_project/media/downloads/data_graphs/Production Levels.pdf, accessed 17 October 2010.
OPEC Website, 'Monthly Oil Report' (October 2010), www.opec.org/opec_web/static_files_project/media/downloads/publications/MOMR_October_2010.pdf, accessed 17 October 2010.
OPEC Website, 'OPEC Share of World Crude Oil Reserves 2009', www.opec.org/opec_web/en/data_graphs/330.htm, accessed 17 October 2010.
OPEC Website, 'OPEC Statement on Iraq', www.opec.org/opec_web/en/press_room/1068.htm, accessed 17 October 2010.
OPEC Website, 'Short- and Long-term Oil Price Trends in the Aftermath of the Events in Iraq' (2003), www.opec.org/opec_web/en/press_room/916.htm, accessed 17 October 2010.
OPEC, 'Market Indicators as at End: January 2011', www.opec.org/opec_web/static_files_project/media/downloads/data_graphs/MI012011.pdf, accessed 25 February 2011.

OPEC Website, 'Iraq Facts and Figures' (2009), www.opec.org/opec_web/en/about_us/164.htm, accessed 17 October 2010.

P. Jackson (2009), *Oil and Paper Ownership, Economic Development, and Iraq's 2007 Draft Oil and Gas Law*. Thesis (M.A.), Duquesne University, http://digital.library.duq.edu/u?/etd,98583, accessed 23 August 2013.

C. Dietrich, 'Iraq and the Oil Cold War: A Superpower Struggle and the End of the Iraq Petroleum Company' in Elisabetta Bini, Giuliano Garavini, Federico Romero (Eds.) (2016) *Oil shock: the 1973 crisis and its economic legacy*, London: I.B. Tauris, 2016.

P. Westerman, 'Open or Autonomous? The Debate on Legal Methodology as a Reflection of the Debate on Law' (30 October 2009) *SSRN*, http://ssrn.com/paper=1609575, accessed 11 December 2010.

Peter Cameron and Abba Kolo, 'What is Energy Investment Law and Why Does It Matter? A Working Paper' (2012), www.eisourcebook.org/cms/March_2013/Peter%20&%20Abba%20-%20Energy%20Investment%20Law.pdf, accessed 8 November 2013.

Peter Cameron, 'Managing the Politics of Oil Reforms: Lessons from Iraq: Keynote Address at the Oil and Gas in Federal Systems Conference, March 4, 2010, Washington DC'. International Energy Law and Policy Research Paper Series No. 2010/07 CEPMLP 15.

P.D. Cameron, 'Stabilisation in Investment Contracts and Changes of Rules in Host Countries: Tools for Oil & Gas Investors, Final Report, 5 July 2006', *Association of International Petroleum Negotiators*, http://lba.legis.state.ak.us/sga/doc_log/2006-07-05_aipn_stabilization-cameron_final.pdf, accessed 4 January 2012.

P.J. Baker, 'The doctrine of legal equality of states', 4 *BYIL* 1923/1924

P.M. Muchlinski, 'Law and the Analysis of the International Oil Industry', in Rees J. and Odell P. (Eds.), *The International Oil Industry: An Interdisciplinary Perspective*, 1987, 142–157, Palgrave Macmillan New York.

Press Release No. 05/307, December 23, 2005, IMF Executive Board Approves First Ever Stand-By Arrangement for Iraq, www.imf.org/external/np/sec/pr/2005/pr05307.htm, accessed 3 May 2013.

R. Dallen, 'Venezuela Shortages Spark Fears', *FT Video* (22 January 2015), http://blogs.ft.com/beyond-brics/category/latin-america/venezuela/, accessed 22 January 2015.

Resource Governance Index (2013), www.resourcegovernance.org/sites/default/files/country_pdfs/iraqRGI2013.pdf, accessed 2 January 2014.

Reuters, 'Iraq's Oil Power Grows, but Firms Eye Election', *Iraq Directory* (16 October 2009), www.iraqdirectory.com/DisplayNews.aspx?id=10634, accessed 14 December 2010

Revenue Watch, 'Extractive Industries', www.revenuewatch.org/our-work/countries/iraq/extractive-industries, accessed 24 March 2011.

Revenue Watch International, 'The 2013 Resource Governance Index: Norway', www.resourcegovernance.org/countries/europe/norway/overview, accessed 14 April 2015.

Revenue Watch International, 'The 2013 Resource Governance Index: Mexico', www.resourcegovernance.org/countries/latin-america/mexico/overview, accessed 12 January 2015.

Robert E. Hardwicke, '*The Rule of Capture and Its Implications as Applied to Oil and Gas*', 13 *Texas Law Review* 391, 393 (1935).

Robert Mayhew, 'Aristotle on Property', 46 (4) *The Review of Metaphysics*, 803–831, 1993.

Ronald Watts, 'Models of Federal Power-Sharing', 53 (167) *International Social Science Journal*, 23–32, 2001.

S. Abdullah, 'How Much Foreign Investment Should Iraq Allow in Its Oil Sector?' *CEMLP*, Undated, www.dundee.ac.uk/cepmlp/gateway/files.php?file=CAR-12_16...pdf, accessed 5 January 2011.

S. Behdad, 'Property Rights in Contemporary Islamic Economic Thought: A Critical Perspective', 47 (2) *Review of Social Economy*, 185–211, 1989.

S. Wallensten and K. Kosec, 'The Economic Costs of the War in Iraq', *Working paper 05-19, September 2005*, AEI Brookings Joint Center for Regulatory Studies, http://papers.ssrn.com/sol3/papers.cfm?abstract_id=848408, accessed 21 January 2010.

S.L. Sakmar, 'The Status of the Draft Iraq Oil and Gas Law', 30 (2) *Houston Journal of International Law*, 2008, http://ssrn.com/abstract=1931874, accessed 4 January 2012.

Saad Jawad, 'The Iraqi Constitution: Structural Flaws and Political Implications', *LSE Middle East Centre Paper Series/01*, 2013, www.lse.ac.uk/middleEastCentre/publications/Paper-Series/Iraqi-Constitution.aspx, accessed 4 October 2013.

Samantha Pearson, 'Brazil Inflation Hits Highest in a Decade' (6 March 2015) *Financial Times*, www.ft.com/cms/s/0/c1ec2e0c-c43f-11e4-a949-00144feab7de.html, accessed 9 March 2015.

Sanjeev Gupta, Alex Segura-Ubiergo and E. Flores, 'Direct Distribution of Resource Revenues: Worth Considering?' (June 2014) *IMF* 13, www.imf.org/external/pubs/ft/sdn/2014/sdn1405.pdf, accessed 8 March 2015.

T.A.Q. Al-Emadi, 'Stabilization Clauses in International Joint Venture Agreements', 54–63 *International Energy Law Review, IELR*, 2010.

Talabani. Interview with Al-Jazeera dated 15 April 2012, www.aljazeera.com/indepth/features/2012/04/2012415183347330127.html, accessed 11 July 2012.

UK Department of Energy and Climate Change, 'Press Release: Mexican Energy Reform Offers Opportunities for UK Oil and Gas Industry' (5 March 2015), www.gov.uk/government/organisations/department-of-energy-climate-change, accessed 3 June 2015.

UNCTAD, 'World Investment Report Investing in a Low Carbon Economy' (2010), www.unctad.org/en/docs/wir2010_en.pdf, accessed 5 June 2011.

UNCTAD, 'World Investment Report Transnational Corporations Extractive Industries and Development' (2007), www.unctad.org/en/docs/wir2007_en.pdf, accessed 5 June 2011.

United Nations Development Programme (UNDP) Website, *Iraqi Legal Database* (only available in Arabic, undated), www.iraq-ild.org, accessed 15 October 2010.

United Nations Office for the Iraq Programme Website, 'Oil for Food Programme' (2010), www.un.org/Depts/oip/, accessed 16 October 2010.

Unknown, 'Iraq, Kurds, Turks and oil A tortuous triangle', *The Economist* (22 December 2012), www.economist.com/news/middle-east-and-africa/21568760-governments-turkey-iraq-and-iraqi-kurdistan-play-dangerous-game, accessed 5 May 2013.

Unknown, 'Irak: objectif de 6 Millions de barils/j de pétrole d'ici 10 ans' *Le Blog Finance*, www.leblogfinance.com/2007/09/irak-objectif-d.html, accessed 7 March 2011.

Unknown, 'Shell Expected to Reduce Capex for the Year', *Reuters* (19 July 2015), www.reuters.com/article/us-shell-spending-idUSKCN0PT0RF20150719, accessed 19 July 2015.

Unknown, 'UPDATE 2-Baghdad, Kurdish Oil Clash Deepens Rift', *Reuters* (2 April 2012), www.reuters.com/article/iraq-kurdistan-oil-idUSL6E8F22DW20120402, accessed 6 May 2012.

Unknown, 'Iraqi Kurdistan Threatens to Declare Independence', *Press TV* (21 March 2012), http://ekurd.net/mismas/articles/misc2012/3/state6017.htm, accessed 22 March 2012.

US Senate, 'The International Petroleum Cartel', *Staff Report to the Federal Trade Commission*, released through Subcommittee on Monopoly of Select Committee on Small Business, U.S. Senate, 83rd Congress, 2nd session (Washington, DC, 1952), Chapter 4, 'Joint Control Through Common Ownership–The Iraq Petroleum Co., Ltd.,' 47–112, www.mtholyoke.edu/acad/intrel/Petroleum/ftc5.htm, accessed 21 February 2011.

Vivienne Walt, 'Why Iraq's Oil Law Remains Deadlocked Three Years On', *Time Magazine* (10 October 2009), http://content.time.com/time/world/article/0,8599,1929201,00.html, accessed 23 October 2012.

W.A. Razzak, 'Iraq: Private Ownership of Oil and the Quest for Democracy', *Arab Planning Institute*, Kuwait, 2006, www.iraqoilshares.org/articles/Iraq%20private%20ownership%20of%20oil_%20revised.pdf, accessed 23 November 2010.

W.G. Dunlop, 'Irak: la production pétrolière au plus haut en 20 ans' *La Presse Affaires*, http://lapresseaffaires.cyberpresse.ca/economie/energie-et-ressources/201012/27/01-4355652-irak-la-production-petroliere-au-plus-haut-en-20-ans.php, accessed 6 March 2011.

Will Connors, 'Brazil's Petrobras Is Hit by Oil-Price Drop, Corruption Probe', *Wall Street Journal*, 14 January 2015, www.wsj.com/articles/brazils-petrobras-is-hit-by-oil-price-drop-corruption-1421251707, accessed 4 March 2015.

William S. Livingston, 'A Note on the Nature of Federalism', LXVII (1) *Political Science Quarterly*, 81–95, 1952.

World Bank, 'Development Report 2011 Conflict, Security and Development', http://wdr2011.worldbank.org/sites/default/files/pdfs/WDR2011_Full_Text.pdf, accessed 23 May 2011.

World Bank, 'Doing Business 2015 Going Beyond Efficiency Economy Profile 2015 Venezuela', www.doingbusiness.org/data/exploreeconomies/venezuela/, accessed 3 March 2015.

World Bank, 'Doing Business 2015: Going Beyond Efficiency: Economy Profile 2015: Mexico', Ed. 12, www.doingbusiness.org/data/exploreeconomies/mexico, accessed 15 January 2015.

World Bank, 'ICSID', https://icsid.worldbank.org/apps/ICSIDWEB/about/Pages/Database-of-Member-States.bak.aspx?tab=FtoJ&rdo=BOTH, accessed 8 December 2015.

World Bank, 'Iran Overview' (1 March 2015), www.worldbank.org/en/country/iran/overview, accessed 4 August 2015.

World Bank, 'Iraq: Operation Procurement Review' (June 2005), http://siteresources.worldbank.org/IRFFI/Resources/IraqOPRJune2005final.pdf, accessed 3 March 2013.

World Bank Report, 'Iraq Chapter 5', http://siteresources.worldbank.org/IRFFI/Resources/Iraqch5-final.pdf.

World Population Statistics, 'Population of Mexico 2014', www.worldpopulationstatistics.com/population-of-mexico-2014/, accessed 23 April 2015.

WTO Website, Accession to WTO by Iraq (2008), www.wto.org/english/thewto_e/acc_e/a1_iraq_e.htm, accessed 15 October 2010.

WTO Website, 'Trade Statistics for Iraq by WTO' (March 2010), http://stat.wto.org/CountryProfile/WSDBCountryPFView.aspx?Language=E&Country=IQ, accessed 15 October 2010.

Y-K. Fan, *Ownership and Optimal Extraction of Oil Reserves* (1967), http://sunzi.lib.hku.hk/hkjo/view/12/1200056.pdf, accessed 4 February 2011.

Zaid Al-Ali, 'Constitutional Legitimacy in Iraq What Role Local Context', 635–664 in Rainer Grote and Tilmann Roder (Eds.), *Constitutionalism in Islamic Countries: Between Upheaval and Continuity*, Oxford, Oxford University Press, 2012.

Zuhair E. Jwaideh, 'The New Civil Code of Iraq', 22 *The George Washington Law Review*, 176–186, 1953–1954.

Index

Note: Page numbers followed by "n" denote endnotes.